Study Guide for Modern
REAL ESTATE
Practice

EIGHTEENTH EDITION

Fillmore W. Galaty

Wellington J. Allaway

Robert C. Kyle

Dearborn
Real Estate Education

President: Dr. Andrew Temte
Chief Learning Officer: Dr. Tim Smaby
Vice President, Real Estate Education: Asha Alsobrooks
Development Editors: Julia Marti and Christopher Kugler

STUDY GUIDE FOR MODERN REAL ESTATE PRACTICE EIGHTEENTH EDITION
© 2010 by Kaplan, Inc.
Published by DF Institute, Inc., d/b/a Dearborn Real Estate Education
332 Front St. S., Suite 501
La Crosse, WI 54601
www.dearbornRE.com

Printed in the United States of America
First revision, March 2013
ISBN: 978-1-4277-8945-7 / 1-4277-8945-2
PPN: 1510-0218

Contents

Preface

Most students find their real estate principles class to be a challenging, rewarding, and traumatic experience, all at the same time. For some, mastering the jargon of the real estate industry can be as demanding as learning a foreign language. Students who have not attended classes or studied for exams for several years may find it difficult to get back into the habit—particularly when there are other demands on their time, and homework becomes another responsibility, among many. Because we are aware of the particular challenges facing today's real estate student, this *Study Guide* was written with your needs in mind.

■ ABOUT THIS BOOK

This *Study Guide* was developed as a companion to *Modern Real Estate Practice 18th Edition*. However, it can also be used in conjunction with the following textbooks (a chapter correlation table is located on the inside front cover):

- *Mastering Real Estate Principles*
- *Real Estate Fundamentals*
- *Modern Real Estate Practice* (state-specific)
- *Practice & Law* (state-specific)

The *Study Guide* is designed to reinforce and elaborate on the basic information provided in your main textbook. Specifically, it is designed to help you master the following three fundamental goals, which are vital to academic success:

1. **Recognize** important terms and concepts
2. **Evaluate** your understanding of basic real estate issues
3. **Apply** learned principles to real-world practice

These goals form the basis of the *Study Guide* learning objectives, which are to

- **define and explain** fundamental concepts and vocabulary terms of the real estate industry;
- **identify and discuss** the characteristics of various legal and financial relationships; and
- **perform and apply** basic financial and property-related calculations.

While the real estate examination is exclusively a multiple-choice format, this *Study Guide* uses several different learning strategies. These styles of self-testing have proven to be effective in helping students move from memorizing factual information, to retaining the material. By working through the components of each chapter, you will reinforce your real estate knowledge, as well as improve your test-taking skills.

■ ACKNOWLEDGMENTS

The following individuals provided professional guidance and real-world expertise in the development of this edition of the *Study Guide*:

- ■ **Catherine Izor** is a consultant and writer with more than thirty years' experience in real estate and financial services. She also has an M.A. in Adult Instructional Management from Loyola University in Chicago. This is the third time she has written materials for the *Modern Real Estate Practice* series.

- ■ **Marie S. Spodek**, DREI, is a nationally recognized real estate educator, speaker, and trainer. A popular real estate columnist and former real estate licensee, she brings an informal, easy-to-read style and a wealth of practical experience to her professional publications. She is the author of *Environmental Issues in Your Real Estate Practice*, consulting editor for *Property Management 8th Edition*, and contributing editor of *Language of Real Estate* products.

How to Use This *Study Guide*

Each chapter consists of three primary sections: chapter-specific learning objectives, a number of questions in varying formats, and an answer key.

■ LEARNING OBJECTIVES

Each chapter begins with a series of learning objectives that are identical to the ones found in *Modern Real Estate Practice 18th Edition*. If you are familiar with the material in the learning objectives, then you are ready to move forward in that chapter of the *Study Guide*.

■ QUESTIONS

Each chapter includes some or all of the following types of questions or problems:

- Matching—match each key term with the appropriate definition.
- True or False—determine whether a statement is correct or incorrect.
- Multiple Choice—select which answer is correct.
- Fill-in-the-Blank—select the word or words that best complete the statements.
- Math Practice—solve each mathematical problem using the provided information.
- Activity—activities take a variety of different forms; follow the instructions for each activity.

■ ANSWER KEY

Each chapter includes an answer key so that you can immediately check your comprehension of that chapter's principles. Many entries in the answer key include rationales, which are brief explanations of the answers. Multiple choice and true or false questions have page references to the source material in *Modern Real Estate Practice 18th Edition*.

Instructions

■ MATCHING

Each chapter lists the key terms found in *Modern Real Estate Practice, 18th Edition.* Test yourself to see how many of the key terms and other important real estate terms you can match to the correct definition. (Note: Not all key terms will be used.)

■ TRUE OR FALSE

You are presented with a series of statements based on material in the main text. It is important to read each statement closely and to clearly understand what you have read. Sometimes, just one word changes the statement from being true to false.

■ MULTIPLE CHOICE

This section prepares you for the format and structure of the licensing exam. It may help to recognize that each multiple-choice question is actually four true or false statements. The questions consist of three false statements (answers) and one true statement.

■ FILL-IN-THE-BLANK

This section format re-emphasizes key terms and concepts. Insert the term that best completes the sentence from the list provided. (Note: Not all key terms will be used.)

■ MATH PROBLEMS

Before starting to work a math problem, carefully read the entire question. Separate the irrelevant facts or numbers from the information needed to perform the calculations. For example, if a question asks you to calculate a broker's commission on a sale, you can disregard information about the asking price or mortgage. You should be able to answer a question based only on the facts given; make sure that you know exactly what you are being asked to do.

■ ACTIVITY

Each activity is different; follow the instructions included with each activity to complete it.

CHAPTER 1

Introduction to the Real Estate Business

Before you answer these questions, you should be able to

- **identify** the various careers available in real estate and the professional organizations that support them;

- **describe** the five categories of real property;

- **explain** the operation of supply and demand in the real estate market;

- **distinguish** the economic, political, and social factors that influence supply and demand; and

- **define** the following *key terms*:

broker	market	supply and demand
licensee	salesperson	

MATCHING   *Write the letter of the matching term on the appropriate line.*

a. *home inspection*

b. *salesperson*

c. *appraisal*

d. *market*

e. *brokerage*

f. *immobility*

g. *REALTOR®*

h. *uniqueness*

i. *broker*

j. *property management*

1. ___ A place where goods are bought and sold and a price for goods established

2. ___ The property of real estate that states even if two parcels may appear identical, they are never exactly alike

3. ___ Person who performs real estate activities while employed by, or associated with, a licensed real estate broker

4. ___ In real estate, a licensed person who acts as a go-between on behalf of others for a fee or commission

5. ___ Maintaining and administering another's property for a fee

6. ___ Process of using established methods and good judgment to estimate the value of a property

7. ___ The bringing together of parties interested in making a real estate transaction

8. ___ The property of real estate that refers to the fact that property cannot be relocated elsewhere

9. ___ Report based on visual survey of property structure, systems, and site conditions

10. ___ Person who adheres to the Code of Ethics of the National Association of REALTORS® (NAR)

TRUE OR FALSE   *Circle the correct answer.*

1. T F The six classes of real estate mentioned in the main textbook are residential, commercial, rental, agricultural, mixed-use, and special purpose.

2. T F The real estate market is generally slow to adjust to the changing forces of supply and demand.

3. T F The supply of labor and the cost of construction generally have a direct effect on the demand for real estate in a market.

4. T F Real estate agents generally tend to specialize in one activity or class of real estate.

5. T F Warehouses, factories, and power plants are examples of commercial property.

6. T F Members of the National Association of Real Estate Brokers are known as REALTORS®.

7. T F In general, the most widely recognized real estate activity is brokerage.

8. T F Finding funds to put together real estate transactions is called *appraising*.

9. T F Market trends in supply and demand can be overturned by a natural disaster, such as a hurricane or earthquake.

10. T F Demand for real estate usually drops when jobs are scarce.

MULTIPLE CHOICE   *Circle the correct answer.*

1. Office buildings and retail space are examples of
   a. commercial real estate.
   b. special-use real estate.
   c. residential property.
   d. industrial property.

2. A person who advises a real estate client who is making a purchase to use or invest in real estate is called a(n)
   a. educator.
   b. mortgage broker.
   c. counselor.
   d. subdivider.

3. All of the following factors will tend to affect demand for real estate *EXCEPT*
   a. transfer taxes.
   b. employment levels.
   c. wage rates.
   d. demographics.

4. When the population of a town suddenly increases, which of the following is *MOST* likely to occur?
   a. Rental rates fall due to increased competition
   b. Demand for housing decreases
   c. New housing starts will decrease
   d. Real estate prices will increase

5. Property management, appraisal, financing, and development are all
   a. specializations directly linked to state and federal government financial policies.
   b. separate professions within the real estate industry.
   c. real estate brokerage professions.
   d. demographic factors that affect demand for real property in a commercial market.

6. The idea that no two parcels of land are exactly alike is called
   a. immobility.
   b. subdivision.
   c. uniqueness.
   d. location.

7. All of the following factors can affect the supply of real estate *EXCEPT*
   a. demographics.
   b. labor force.
   c. construction costs.
   d. government controls.

8. A property owner who does not want to deal with the everyday tasks of managing a rental property can hire a(n)
   a. property manager.
   b. appraiser.
   c. home inspector.
   d. developer.

9. When the supply of a certain commodity decreases while demand remains the same, the price of that commodity will tend to
   a. remain the same.
   b. increase.
   c. decrease by 10 percent.
   d. decrease by 20 percent.

10. All of the following are examples of government policies that can affect the real estate market *EXCEPT*
    a. the Federal Reserve Board's discount rate.
    b. a shortage of skilled labor or building materials.
    c. land-use controls, such as zoning.
    d. federal environmental regulations.

FILL-IN-THE-BLANK   *Select the word or words that best complete the following statements:*

agricultural

appraiser

continuing education

demographic

go down

go up

industrial

licensing

market

remain the same

residential

salesperson

subdivision

valuation

1. A person who conducts activities on behalf of a broker is called a(n) _____.

2. Appraisers must have detailed knowledge of the methods of property _____.

3. Real estate licensees keep their skills and knowledge current by obtaining _____.

4. A single-family home is a type of _____ property.

5. If the supply of single-family homes goes up and a major local employer lays off a large number of workers, the price of real estate tends to _____.

6. The splitting of a single piece of property into smaller parcels is called _____.

7. *Niche marketing* refers to the targeted marketing of specific _____ _____ populations.

8. Farms and timberland are considered to be _____ property.

9. A community implements land-use restrictions so that less vacant land is available for residential development. At the same time, demand for housing increases due to higher population. Prices for real estate will tend to _____.

10. The function of a(n) _____ is to provide a setting in which supply and demand can establish the value of real property.

ANSWER KEY

Matching

1. d **2.** h **3.** b **4.** i **5.** j **6.** c **7.** e **8.** f
9. a **10.** g

True or False

1. **False.** The six classes of real estate mentioned in the text are residential, commercial, mixed-use, industrial, agricultural, and special-purpose. Rental is *not* a class of real estate.

2. **True.** Because of real estate's uniqueness and immobility, the market generally adjust slowly to the forces of supply and demand; development and construction are lengthy processes. p. 8

3. **False.** Supply of labor and the cost of construction generally have a direct effect on the *supply* of real estate in a market.

4. **True.** The real estate industry is complex, much more than brokers bringing together buyers and sellers, landlords and tenants. Other specialties include appraisal, property management, financing, education, and home inspection. p. 4

5. **False.** Warehouses, factories, and power plants are examples of *industrial* property.

6. **False.** Members of the National Association of Real Estate Brokers are known as Realtists. REALTORS® are members of the National Association of REALTORS®.

7. **True.** Although many people think that real estate is comprised of only brokers and salespeople, many other specialties exist, including financing, appraising, education, and property management. p. 4

8. **False.** Finding funds involves *financing*; estimating the value of property is *appraising*.

9. **True.** Even when supply and demand can be forecast with some accuracy, natural disasters, such as hurricanes and earthquakes, can disrupt market trends; the market also can be affected by sudden changes in financial markets or plant relocations. p. 8

10. **True.** When job opportunities are scarce or wage levels are low, demand for real estate usually drops; in fact, the market may be drastically affected by a single major employer moving in or shutting down. p. 10

Multiple Choice

1. **a.** Office buildings and retail space are examples of commercial real estate. Special use includes churches and dormitories; industrial includes warehouses and factories.

2. **c.** A real estate counselor provides clients with competent independent advice based on sound professional judgment. An educator provides education; a mortgage broker searches for financing; and a subdivider splits larger properties into smaller ones. p. 5

3. **a.** Transfer taxes affect the supply; employment levels, wage rates and demographics affect demand. p. 9–10

4. **d.** With a sudden influx of people, rental rates will increase; demand for housing will increase; and more new homes will be started to satisfy demand. p. 9–10

5. **b.** Property management, appraisal, financing, and development are not linked to the government; they are all linked to real estate business. p. 4

6. **c.** No matter how identical they may appear, no two parcels of real estate are ever exactly alike; each occupies its own unique geographic location. p. 8

7. **a.** Demographics affect the *demand* for real estate. The labor force, construction costs, and government controls affect the supply of real estate. p. 7

8. **a.** A property manager handles the day-to-day tasks of managing property for an owner. An appraiser estimates value; a home inspector looks for problems with the property; and the developer improves the property. p. 5

9. **b.** When consumers continue to demand a product for which there is limited supply, the price generally increases.

10. **b.** A shortage of skilled labor will affect the supply of real estate, and this labor shortage is not generally associated with governmental policies.

Fill-in-the-Blank

1. A person who conducts activities on behalf of a broker is called a *salesperson*.

2. Appraisers must have detailed knowledge of the methods of property *valuation*.

3. Real estate licensees keep their skills and knowledge current by obtaining *continuing education*.

4. A single-family home is a type of *residential* property.

5. If the supply of single-family homes goes up and a major local employer lays off a large number of workers, the price of real estate tends to *go down*.

6. The splitting of a single piece of property into smaller parcels is called *subdivision*.

7. Niche marketing refers to the targeted marketing of specific *demographic* populations.

8. Farms and timberland are considered to be *agricultural* property.

9. A community implements land-use restrictions so that less vacant land is available for residential development. At the same time, demand for housing increases due to higher population. Prices for real estate will tend to *go up*.

10. The function of a *market* is to provide a setting in which supply and demand can establish the value of real property.

CHAPTER 2

Real Property and the Law

■ **LEARNING OBJECTIVES** *Before you answer these questions, you should be able to*

■ **identify** the rights that convey with ownership of real property and the characteristics of real estate;

■ **describe** the difference between real and personal property;

■ **explain** the types of laws that affect real estate;

■ **distinguish** between the concepts of land, real estate, and real property; and

■ **define** the following *key terms*:

accession	fixture	severance
air rights	improvement	situs
annexation	land	subsurface rights
appurtenance	manufactured housing	surface rights
area preference	nonhomogeneity	trade fixture
bundle of legal rights	personal property	water rights
chattel	real estate	
emblements	real property	

MATCHING *Write the letter of the matching term on the appropriate line.*

a. *annexation*

b. *bundle of legal rights*

c. *improvement*

d. *surface rights*

e. *emblements*

f. *fixture*

g. *subsurface rights*

h. *real estate*

i. *real property*

j. *severance*

k. *personal property*

l. *water rights*

m. *chattels*

n. *trade fixture*

o. *air rights*

1. ___ An article installed by a tenant under a commercial lease and removable before the lease expires

2. ___ Any property that is not real property

3. ___ Conversion of personal property to real property

4. ___ Ownership of all legal rights to the land: control, possession, exclusion, enjoyment, and disposition

5. ___ The interests, benefits, and rights automatically included in the ownership of land and real estate

6. ___ The right to use the open space above the surface of a property

7. ___ A portion of the earth's surface extending down to the center and up into space, including all natural and artificial attachments

8. ___ Ownership rights in the water, minerals, gas, and oil that lie beneath a parcel of land

9. ___ Personal property that is converted to real property by being permanently attached to the real estate

10. ___ Any structure or modification erected or imposed on a site

11. ___ Changing an item of real estate to personal property by detaching it from the land

12. ___ Ownership rights excluding air or mineral rights

13. ___ Common law right of owners of land next to rivers, lakes, or oceans

14. ___ Another name for personal property

15. ___ Growing crops, such as corn or soybeans, that remain personal property

TRUE OR FALSE   *Circle the correct answer.*

1. T F The terms *land*, *real estate*, and *real property* are interchangeable and refer to the same thing.

2. T F *Real property* is defined as the earth's surface extending downward to the center of the earth and upward to infinity, including permanent natural objects, such as trees and water.

3. T F The term *real property* includes land, rights, and real estate.

4. T F The transfer of the right to use the surface of the earth always includes the right to the natural resources that lie beneath the surface of the earth.

5. T F Trees, perennial shrubbery, and grasses that do not require annual cultivation are considered personal property.

6. T F The process by which personal property becomes real property is called *annexation*.

7. T F A *trade fixture* is an article owned by a tenant and attached to a rented space or building used in conducting a business.

8. T F The economic characteristics of real estate are scarcity, improvements, permanence of investment, and uniqueness.

9. T F Immobility, indestructibility, and scarcity are physical characteristics of real property.

10. T F The image of a bundle of sticks is the traditional illustration of the set of legal rights of ownership.

11. T F When determining if an item is a fixture, decide whether the item is actually being used as real or personal property.

12. T F The economic characteristic of *permanence of investment* refers to the concept that the total supply of land is limited.

13. T F One of the rights of real property ownership is the right of enjoyment, or the right to use the property in any legal way.

14. T F A property's air rights extend upward into outer space.

15. T F Trade fixtures are typically excluded from a mortgage.

MULTIPLE CHOICE   *Circle the correct answer.*

1. Land, mineral, and air rights in the land are included in the definition of
    a. attachments.
    c. subsurface rights.
    b. real property.
    d. improvements.

2. Which of the following is an example of an economic characteristic of land?
    a. Immobility
    c. Uniqueness
    b. Indestructibility
    d. Scarcity

3. Another word for *uniqueness* is
    a. scarcity.
    c. fructus industrials.
    b. nonhomogeneity.
    d. immobility.

4. All of the following are included in the bundle of rights *EXCEPT*
    a. possession.
    c. exclusion.
    b. control.
    d. expansion.

5. The right to dispose of real property by will or deed is contained in the
    a. bundle of rights.
    b. deed.
    c. statutory law of the federal government.
    d. statutory law of the state.

6. Growing trees, fences, and buildings would all be considered
    a. chattels.
    c. fixtures.
    b. land.
    d. real estate.

7. The most important economic characteristic of land is
    a. permanence.
    c. uniqueness.
    b. location.
    d. possession.

8. A tenant farmer built a chicken coop and a tool shed. These buildings belong to the
    a. tenant.
    b. owner of real estate.
    c. owner, but the owner must reimburse the tenant.
    d. tenant, but the tenant must pay additional rent for them.

9. The developer added sewer lines and utilities and built two streets. What are these items called?
    a. Fixtures
    b. Additions
    c. Improvements
    d. Permanence of investment

10. The new owner received the land, a garage, and the right to drive on his neighbor's driveway. This right is an example of a(n)
    a. improvement.
    c. appurtenance.
    b. fixture.
    d. chattel.

11. Method of annexation, adaptation, and agreement are the legal tests for determining whether an item is
    a. a chattel or an emblement.
    b. real property or personal property.
    c. land or real estate.
    d. fructus naturales or fructus industriales.

12. After suffering through a tornado and then flooding from the river, the buildings were gone. The land was still there. This is an example of
    a. uniqueness.
    b. scarcity.
    c. location.
    d. indestructibility.

13. The seller asked the real estate agent to draw up several documents relating to seller financing. Under these circumstances, the agent should
    a. ask the broker for assistance.
    b. draw up the documents.
    c. ignore the instructions.
    d. refer the seller to an attorney.

MULTIPLE CHOICE　*(Continued)*

14. A man particularly liked the ornate brass lighting fixtures in a woman's house and immediately made an offer, which the woman accepted. On moving day, the man discovered that the woman had replaced all the ornate brass fixtures with plain steel ones. Which of the following is MOST likely a correct assumption?

    a. Woman: "As long as I replaced them with something of comparable value, I can take them with me."

    b. Man: "Lighting fixtures are normally considered to be real property."

    c. Woman: "The lighting fixtures were personal property when I bought them at the store, so they're personal property forever."

    d. Woman: "The lighting fixtures belong to me because I installed them."

15. A farmer has posted a number of "No Trespassing" and "No Hunting" signs on his property. Which *stick* in the bundle of rights gives the farmer this authority?

    a. Exclusion　　c. Control

    b. Enjoyment　　d. Disposition

16. A right or privilege tied to real property, although not necessarily part of the property, is called a(n)

    a. emblement.　　c. appurtenance.

    b. trade fixture.　d. deed.

17. An important characteristic of personal property is that it is

    a. small enough to be carried by a person.

    b. movable.

    c. alive.

    d. less than 100 years old.

18. *Mobile home*, rather than *manufactured housing*, is the term used for a factory-built home that was built before

    a. 1976.　　c. 1987.

    b. 1980.　　d. 1990.

19. To determine whether an item is a fixture, the MOST important test is whether the

    a. effort needed to remove the item is significant.

    b. item must be dismantled for removal.

    c. value of the item is high.

    d. person who installed it intended for it to be permanent.

20. A woman planted a rose bush on her property and plans to dig it up and take it with her when her house is sold. The sales contract explicitly excludes the rose bush from the sale. This provision is necessary because the rose bush is considered to be

    a. a trade fixture.　c. an emblement.

    b. personal property.　d. real estate.

ACTIVITY: Real Property or Personal Property?

Enter check marks in the appropriate columns to indicate whether each item is real or personal property, and whether it is a fixture or a trade fixture (if applicable).

Property Description	Type of Property		Fixture	Trade Fixture
	Real	Personal		
1. Sidewalks and sewers in a subdivision				
2. Bushes surrounding a residence				
3. Wheat or corn crops on a farm				
4. Kitchen sink installed in a home				
5. Booths in a restaurant installed by tenant				
6. Curtains installed by a tenant				
7. Pumps installed by a gas station tenant				
8. Water well pump installed by the landowner				
9. Crystal chandelier hung from the ceiling				
10. An 80-gallon water heater with fiberglass insulating jacket				

ANSWER KEY

Matching

1. n   **2.** k   **3.** a   **4.** b   **5.** i   **6.** o   **7.** h   **8.** g
9. f   **10.** c   **11.** j   **12.** d   **13.** l   **14.** m   **15.** e

True or False

1. **False.** The terms *land, real estate*, and *real property* are not interchangeable. They refer to different aspects of ownership rights. p. 16

2. **False.** *Land* is defined as the earth's surface extending downward to the center of the earth and upward to infinity, including permanent natural objects, such as trees and water. *Real property* is defined as the interests, benefits, and rights that are considered part of the ownership of land and real estate. p. 17

3. **True.** The term real property is the broadest of all; it includes both land and real estate, as well as the interests, benefits, and rights that are automatically included in the ownership of land and real estate. p. 17

4. **False.** The transfer of the surface does not necessarily include the rights to the subsurface rights, which are the natural resources that lie beneath the surface. An owner may transfer surface rights without transferring subsurface rights p. 18

5. **False.** Trees, perennial shrubbery, and grasses that do not require annual cultivation are considered *real estate*. p. 20

6. **True.** It is possible to change personal property into real property through the process known as annexation, such as mixing cement, stones, sand, and water (personal property). p. 20

7. **True.** An article owned by a tenant and attached to a rented space and used in conducting a business is a trade fixture; it may be removed prior to the termination of the lease. p. 22

8. **False.** Economic characteristics of land include scarcity, improvements, permanence of investment, and *area preference*. p. 23

9. **False.** Physical characteristics of land include immobility, indestructibility, and *uniqueness*. p. 23

10. **True.** Because the rights of ownership (like sticks in a bundle) can be separated and individually transferred, the sticks become symbolic of those rights. p. 17

11. **True.** During the course of time, the same materials may be both real and personal property, depending on their use and location. For example, a refrigerator, usually considered personal property, but when installed so as to become part of the kitchen cabinetry, it then becomes real property. p. 21

12. **False.** *Permanence of investment* refers to the concept that the return on investment in real estate tends to be long-term and relatively stable. *Scarcity* refers to the concept that the total supply of land is limited. p. 23

13. **True.** Traditionally, ownership rights of real property include the right of possession, control, enjoyment, exclusion, and disposition. p. 17

14. **False.** Property air rights began to be limited when air travel became common. Now, light and solar rights may limit air rights in certain areas. p. 19

15. **True.** Because trade fixtures are considered personal property, they are not included in the sale, mortgage, or real estate, except by special agreement. p. 22

Multiple Choice

1. **b.** Subsurface rights and improvements are included in the definition of real estate. Real property also includes rights and privileges. p. 18

2. **d.** Immobility, indestructibility, and uniqueness are physical characteristics, while scarcity is an economic characteristic. p. 23

3. **b.** Uniqueness, or nonhomogeneity, indicates that no two parcels of land are alike. p. 23

4. **d.** The bundle of rights includes possession, control, exclusion, enjoyment, and disposition. There is no right to expansion, except by acquiring another parcel. p. 17

5. **a.** *Real property* is described as a bundle of legal rights that contains the right of disposition. p. 17

6. **d.** The definition of *real estate* includes fences, buildings, and growing trees. *Chattels* are personal property. The definition of *land* would not include fences and buildings. p. 20

7. **b.** Location is sometimes referred to as *area preference* or *situs*. p. 23

8. **a.** The coop and tool shed would be considered trade fixtures, and the tenant has the right to remove them up to the end of the lease. p. 22

9. **c.** Human-made permanent attachments are called *improvements*. p. 22–23

10. **c.** An *Appurtenance* is a right or privilege associated with the property, although not necessarily a part of it; typical appurtenances include parking spaces in multiunit buildings, easements, water rights, and other improvements. p. 18

11. **b.** Whether an item is a fixture or personal property may be determined by method of annexation, adaptation to real estate, or agreement of the parties. p. 21

12. **d.** Land cannot be destroyed, although the improvements might be removed, as they are in this case. p. 23

13. **d.** Real estate licensees should be careful not to *practice* law unless they are, in fact, licensed attorneys. p. 24

14. **b.** While the woman might say the other things, the man is correct in assuming that lighting fixtures are normally part of the real property. If the woman had wanted to remove the fixtures, she should have done so before she put the house on the market, or she should have written her intention to remove them into the agreement of sale. p. 21

15. **a.** A real estate owner has the inherent right to exclude others from the property, although this right is not absolute. An adjacent property owner may have an easement right to use the property. p. 17

16. **c.** An appurtenance is a right or privilege association with the property, although not necessarily a part of it. An *emblement* or *trade fixture* is a tangible item on the property. The *deed* is a document that transfers title. p. 18

17. **b.** Personal property is all the property than can be owned and that does not fit the definition of real property; the most important distinction between real and personal property is that personal property is moveable. p. 19

18. **a.** The term *mobile home* was phased out with the passage of The National Manufactured Housing Construction and Safety Standards Act of 1976 when manufactured homes became federally regulated. p. 20

19. **d.** The *intent* of the person who installed the item is the most important test of whether the item is a fixture. p. 21

20. **d.** Because the rose bush is a perennial shrub, it is considered real estate p. 21

Activity: Real or Personal Property?

Property Description	Type of Property		Fixture	Trade Fixture
	Real	**Personal**		
1. Sidewalks and sewers in a subdivision	✓			
2. Bushes surrounding a residence	✓			
3. Wheat or corn crops on a farm		✓		
4. Kitchen sink installed in a home	✓		✓	
5. Booths in a restaurant installed by tenant		✓		✓
6. Curtains installed by a tenant		✓		
7. Pumps installed by a gas station tenant		✓		✓
8. Water well pump installed by the landowner	✓		✓	
9. Crystal chandelier hung from the ceiling	✓		✓	
10. An 80-gallon water heater with fiberglass insulating jacket	✓		✓	

CHAPTER 3

Concepts of Home Ownership

■ **LEARNING OBJECTIVES**   *Before you answer these questions, you should be able to*

- ■ **identify** the various types of housing choices available to homebuyers;

- ■ **describe** the issues involved in making a home ownership decision;

- ■ **explain** the tax benefits of home ownership;

- ■ **distinguish** the various types of homeowners insurance policy coverage; and

- ■ **define** the following *key terms*:

coinsurance clause	liability coverage	replacement cost
homeowners insurance policy	PITI (principal, interest, taxes, and insurance)	

MATCHING   *Write the letter of the matching term on the appropriate line.*

a.   *apartment complex*

b.   *actual cash value*

c.   *coinsurance*

d.   *planned unit development*

e.   *cooperative*

f.   *mixed-use development*

g.   *condominium*

h.   *manufactured housing*

i.   *replacement cost*

j.   *homeowners' insurance*

1. ____ A group of low-rise or highrise rental residences that may include parking, security, etc.

2. ____ A multiunit residential building owned by a corporation and operated on behalf of stockholder-tenants who hold proprietary leases

3. ____ A package insurance policy against loss due to fire, theft, and liability

4. ____ Cost of repairing damaged property without deduction for depreciation or annual wear and tear

5. ____ A multiunit development in which owners own their units separately and share ownership of common facilities

6. ____ A merger of diverse land uses into a subdivision or development

7. ____ Type of housing that is also known as a mobile home and has a semi-permanent foundation

8. ____ Clause in an insurance policy that requires the property to be insured for a specified percentage (usually 80 percent) of its replacement cost

9. ____ In insurance, replacement value minus depreciation

10. ____ Highrise development that combines commercial and residential uses in a single structure

TRUE OR FALSE   *Circle the correct answer.*

1. T F One way that some lenders evaluate whether a prospective buyer can afford a home is by setting a limit on PITI of 28 percent of gross monthly income, and on total debt payments of 36 percent of gross monthly income.

2. T F When lenders evaluate whether a prospective buyer can afford a home, expenses such as utilities and routine medical care are excluded from the calculation of debt payments.

3. T F A *cooperative* is a form of residential ownership in which residents share ownership of common areas while owning their own units individually.

4. T F A *planned unit development* is a type of property in which warehouses, factories, office buildings, hotels, and other structures have been converted to residential use.

5. T F Single taxpayers are allowed to exclude $250,000 from capital gains tax for profits on the sale of a principal residence.

6. T F A taxpayer can use the exclusion from capital gains tax for profits on the sale of a principal residence only once in a lifetime.

7. T F First-time homebuyers can withdraw up to $10,000 (for a down payment) from their tax-deferred IRAs without a tax penalty.

8. T F Under most homeowners' insurance policies, the insured is usually required to maintain insurance equal to at least 41 percent of the replacement cost of the dwelling, including the price of the land.

9. T F If a borrower's property is located in a designated flood area, no exemptions are allowed from the flood insurance requirement under the National Flood Insurance Act.

10. T F FEMA's definition of a flood includes mudflows or mudslides on land that is usually dry.

MULTIPLE CHOICE   *Circle the correct answer.*

1. The P in the acronym PITI stands for
   a. primary amount.
   b. prepaid items.
   c. principal.
   d. prorations.

2. Which of the following may be deducted from a homebuyer's gross income for income tax purposes?
   a. Appraisal fee
   b. Mortgage insurance premiums
   c. VA funding fees
   d. Loan discount points

3. A man's homeowners' insurance policy contains a coinsurance provision; the house is insured for replacement cost. If the man's home burns, which of the following statements is *TRUE*?
   a. The man's claim will be settled for the actual cash value of the damage.
   b. The man's claim will be prorated by dividing the percentage of replacement cost by the minimum coverage requirement.
   c. The man may make a claim for the full cost of the repair without deduction for depreciation.
   d. The man may make a claim for the depreciated value of the damage.

4. A couple purchased their home seven years ago for $250,000. Now, they are being transferred to a new city and must sell their home, currently valued at $350,000. They are 52 and 53 years old, respectively, and they are concerned about paying capital gains on their apparent profit of $100,000. Which of the following statements is important to them?
   a. No taxes are due because they have lived there for the required time period and the gain is under the allowed amount.
   b. There is no problem as long as they purchase a new home for $350,000 or more within the next 24 months.
   c. They will have to pay taxes on their gain, because the amount is more than the excluded amount.
   d. They will have to pay taxes on the amount of the gain if they decide to rent rather than buy a new home.

5. A highrise building that includes office space, stores, and residential units is an example of a
   a. loft building.
   b. master-planned community.
   c. planned unit development.
   d. mixed-use development.

6. A single man is 57 years old. He has lived in the same house for the past four years. When the sale of his house closes next week , how will taxes be determined on any gain from the sale of the home?
   a. The gain will be taxed at a lower rate because of his age.
   b. Taxes will need to be paid, because he has lived in the house for less than the required time period.
   c. The gain is excluded from taxation if it is less than $250,000.
   d. The gain is excluded from income taxation up to $125,000 at most because of his age and time-in-residence.

7. All of the following are examples of items that a monthly condominium assessment would cover *EXCEPT*
   a. real estate taxes on individual units.
   b. management fees.
   c. maintenance of building exteriors.
   d. maintenance of common facilities.

8. A woman's house is constructed so that the floor of her home is built several inches above the 100-year flood mark. If the woman applies for a federally related mortgage loan, how will her mortgage lender apply flood insurance rules?
   a. It may exempt the woman's house from the flood insurance requirement.
   b. It must require flood insurance.
   c. It is prohibited by federal law from requiring flood insurance.
   d. It may invoke the National Flood Insurance Act for properties lying inside, or within 500 feet of, a designated flood-prone area.

MULTIPLE CHOICE   *(Continued)*

9. A prospective buyer wants to purchase a house. His gross monthly income is $6,500. He wants to estimate how much he can reasonably afford to pay for a monthly PITI payment. What is the maximum monthly PITI payment that he can afford based on the past *rule* for this calculation?

    a. $1,635   c. $1,820
    b. $1,775   d. $2,340

10. All of the following expenses may be deducted from a homeowner's gross income for income tax purposes *EXCEPT*

    a. loan-prepayment penalties.
    b. loan discount points.
    c. interest paid on overdue real estate taxes.
    d. real estate taxes.

11. A married couple is planning to purchase a house. She earns $45,000, and he earns $37,500 per year. Their college loan payments total $350 per month, and a car payment is $375 per month. Using the old *rules* for calculating maximum monthly debt payment and PITI, what is the maximum amount of PITI they estimate they can afford?

    a. $1,750   c. $2,475
    b. $1,925   d. $2,818

12. Which of the following property coverages is included in both basic form and broad-form homeowners insurance policies?

    a. Collapse of the building
    b. Lightning damage
    c. Damage due to the weight of ice on the roof
    d. Damage from frozen plumbing pipes

13. A broad-form homeowners' insurance policy generally covers all of the following *EXCEPT*

    a. frozen pipes.   c. flooding.
    b. vandalism.   d. theft.

14. The reason that homeowners buy homeowners' insurance is to

    a. be reimbursed for financial losses suffered because of events, such as fire or theft.
    b. pay for replacing the furnace or roof because of age.
    c. be reimbursed for monetary losses due to a defect in the title.
    d. protect the homeowner for accidents on other peoples' property.

15. Which of the following is a characteristic of penalty-free IRA withdrawals for first-time homebuyers?

    a. The limit on the withdrawn amount is $15,000.
    b. The withdrawn amount must be spent entirely within 120 days on a down payment.
    c. The buyer must be no more than 30 years old.
    d. The withdrawn amount is not subject to income tax.

16. People buy homes for all of the following reasons *EXCEPT*

    a. homes can appreciate in value.
    b. they can provide federal income tax deductions.
    c. home ownership gives a sense of belonging to the community.
    d. home ownership usually gives residents more leisure time than renting provides.

17. Retirement communities are often developed as

    a. converted-use properties.
    b. planned unit developments.
    c. time-shares.
    d. industrial complexes.

18. In addition to examining the financial ability of applicants to handle loan payments, lenders also assign a key role in the loan decision to

    a. credit scores.
    b. the age of the home.
    c. whether the borrower is under age 55.
    d. the size of the property.

MULTIPLE CHOICE   *(Continued)*

19. The decision to rent or buy a home is affected by all of the following factors *EXCEPT*

    a. mortgage interest rates.
    b. tax consequences.
    c. how long the person wants to live in a certain area.
    d. convenience of shopping.

20. A characteristic of both planned unit developments and condominiums is

    a. title to the units is held by a corporation.
    b. an association that collects fees from owners and maintains common areas.
    c. small lot sizes and street areas.
    d. conversion of a property from a prior use, such as a factory or warehouse, to residential use.

21. To insure against losses due to visitor injuries within the owner's unit, condominium owners typically obtain a policy that includes

    a. a basic form type of homeowners' insurance.
    b. a broad form type of homeowners' insurance.
    c. liability insurance.
    d. errors and omissions insurance.

22. A database of consumer claim history that makes it possible for insurance companies to access prior claim information is called the

    a. National and Fiduciary Insurance Program (NFIP).
    b. Comprehensive Loss Underwriting Exchange (CLUE).
    c. Database of Prior Insurance Claims (DBPI).
    d. Fannie Mae Databank (FMD).

23. Why should agents note whether a property for sale is located on a flood plain?

    a. Buyers have lower expenses for insurance.
    b. Higher transfer fees are required to transfer title to the property.
    c. The federal government may require a house to be removed from the property.
    d. Property value is negatively affected.

24. A large tree on a man's property died and slowly rotted. Eventually, a large branch fell off from its own weight and damaged the back porch roof. What type of homeowners' insurance policy would cover this damage?

    a. Liability insurance
    b. Basic-form policy
    c. Broad-form policy
    d. Emblements insurance

25. How is flood insurance coverage determined?

    a. It covers either the property value or mortgage loan amount (up to a limit).
    b. It is calculated as 80 percent of the property value.
    c. It is based on a table of standard values for properties in the flood-prone area.
    d. It depends on the income level of the property owners.

ACTIVITY: Check the Ads

On the numbered lines below, write the type of housing indicated by each ad.

Good view, quiet, roof new, garage, and security, furniture for sale. Easily refinanced if you wish. $286,000.

Call 773-555-5873

1 HERE'S A TIP—BUY STOCK IN YOUR HOME

Select units are now available in Gleason Tower: Lavish 4 & 5-bedroom apartments with all the extras! Approved buyers become stockholders in Gleason Tower Corp. From $260,000.

Call 312-555-9887

OPEN HOUSE 1-3
6033 OAK HILLS DR

Executive 2 story townhouse. 3 bed, 4 bath, 2 car, appliances free! Other features include: rec room with wetbar, open kitchen with appliances, great room with fireplace, walk out to heated swimming pool, convenient to I-80. $280's. R.E.G. 815-555-2600, Pennie Long, 815-555-0123. Do not miss out, come by TODAY!

OPEN SUN 1-4
10728 BERRY PLAZA

By owner. Applewood Town-homes. Huge beautiful town-ome, 1504

pool. Near park, tennis court, schools location in the west.

2 CLOCK TOWER LOFTS

The old Mennsen-Hart Watch Factory is now 20 fabulous luxury lofts above the exclusive Watchmaker Mall! Studios, 1&2 BR; security. From $1,900/mo.

773-555-5678

WILLOW WOOD CONDO
12889 Burdette Circle Wonderful condition, 2 bedrooms, 2 baths, 2 car garage. Sits on cul-de-sac. Only $189,900.

Hurry—708-555-3241

6 1275 OAKVIEW TERRACE

3 bedroom, 2 bath unit; dining room, pool, 24-hour doorman. Great downtown location close to subway and bus routes. $275,000 Monthly assessment only $880.

312-555-7890

Cabin Rental by day or week. Near Fort Robinson, Wisconsin, along the Scenic Fox River. Fishing and hiking. No Pets. Call 608-555-3826

LOOKING FOR A QUALITY TOWN HOME?

both only 3 minutes from train station and mall. Call Jeff 630-555-2837

Love where you work:

LOGAN VILLAGE **3**

This quiet, tree-lined new community features lots of open space. Shops, schools and recreation: Logan village has it all! Townhomes start in the mid-180s; residences from $235,000.

773-555-0372

Elkhorn North   212
21586 Arabian Rd. By owner 3 bed, 2 bath, 2 car garage Elkhorn School District. See for yourself, (No Brokers please). 312-555-7864 leave message.

HICKORY HILLS
VILLAGE

2 bedroom, 2 bath unit with balcony. Utilities included. No pets. Pool, tennis, golf and health club. Located on private forest preserve. $1,900 per month; available May 1st. **5**

E-Z access to all amenities, 4BR, 2.5BA, office, full bsmt, all appliances stay, motiv seller, a must see $380,000. 630-555-4736.

3 AURORA FSBO.OAK-HURST OPEN SAT/SUN 1-4 2331 Waterbury Cir. Naper Dist 204 schools. 4BR, w/1st floor den. Gorgeous traditional w/ cherry kit & hwd floors. Brick FP, crown moldings, custom ceilings, finished bsmt. Fully landscaped. Located on quiet circle on oversized lot. 630-555-3456

4 THE SKY IS YOUR LIMIT

Fabulous downtown building offers stunning views super amenities, 5 world-class restaurants, great shopping and lifestyle services under one 85th floor rooftop garden. Residences start on the 62nd floor Priced from mid-900's.

Call 312-555-9275

1. _____

2. _____

3. _____

4. _____

5. _____

6. _____

ANSWER KEY

Matching

1. a **2.** e **3.** j **4.** i **5.** g **6.** d **7.** h **8.** c
9. b **10.** f

True or False

1. **True.** To determine whether a prospective buyer can afford a certain purchase, most lenders require that the monthly housing costs do not exceed 28 percent of gross income, and total debt payments no more than 36 percent of gross monthly income. p. 35

2. **True.** Expenses such as insurance premiums, utilities, and routine medical care are not generally included in the 36 percent figure, but they must be covered by the remaining 64 percent of the buyer's monthly income. p. 35

3. **False.** A *condominium* is a form of residential ownership in which residents share ownership of common areas while owning their own units individually. A coop owner actually purchases shares of stock in the corporation, and not their individual units. p. 32–33

4. **False.** Warehouses, factories, office buildings, hotels, and other structures that have been remodeled for residential use are referred to as *converted use properties*. Planned unit developments (PUDs) merge diverse land uses, such as housing, recreation, and commercial units into one self-contained development. p. 33

5. **True.** Taxpayers who file single are entitle to a $250,000 exclusion of capital gains, while married taxpayers filing jointly may exclude up to $500,000. p. 36

6. **False.** The exemption may be used repeatedly, so long as the homeowners own and occupy the property as their primary residence for at least two of the past five years. p. 36

7. **True.** First-time homebuyers may make penalty-free withdrawals from their tax-deferred individual retirement funds (IRAs) for down payments on their first homes; the withdrawal is still subject to income tax. p. 36

8. **False.** Under most homeowners' insurance policies, the insured is usually required to maintain insurance equal to 80 percent of the replacement cost of the dwelling, excluding the price of the land. p. 37

9. **False.** If a borrower's property is located in a designated flood area, it may be exempt from the National Flood Insurance Act's flood insurance requirement. However, the borrower needs to produce a survey showing that the lowest part of the structure is above the 100-year flood mark. p. 38

10. **True.** FEMA defines a flood as "a general and temporary condition of partial or complete inundation of two or more acres of normally dry land or two or more property from [among other things] mudflows or mudslides on the surface of normally dry land." p. 39

Multiple Choice

1. **c.** PITI stands for principal, interest, taxes, and insurance. These expenses comprise the typical monthly payment to a lender. p. 35

2. **d.** Among the changes to the tax laws that benefit home ownership is the right to deduct loan discount points (whether paid by the buyer or the seller) from gross income. Appraisal fees, mortgage insurance premiums, and VA funding fees are not considered deductible interest, but they can be considered part of the acquisition cost and figured into the cost basis. p. 36

3. **c.** Because the man has insured the property for replacement value and has a coinsurance clause, he may make a claim for the full cost of replacement without deduction for depreciation. p. 37

4. **a.** Because the couple have lived in the home at least two of the past five years and their capital gain is less than $500,000, they will not have to pay any capital gains tax. p. 36

5. **d.** A *planned unit-development* is also referred to as a *master planned community*. A loft building is a less-than-complete answer. A mixed-use development is usually a highrise that offers a mixture of uses. p. 33

6. **c.** The man will not have to pay any tax because he has lived there at least two of the past five years, and the gain is less than $250,000. p. 36

7. **a.** Individual condo owners are responsible for real estate taxes on their individual units. Monthly assessments cover costs that all unit owners share as a group, such as management fees and maintenance of building exteriors and common facilities. p. 32

8. **a.** Because the lowest level is several inches above the 100-year flood mark, the owner may not be required to buy flood insurance. p. 38

9. **c.** The man can afford a PITI payment of $1,820: $6,500 × 28% = $1,820. p. 35

10. **c.** Homeowners may deduct from their gross income mortgage interest payments on first and second home, real estate taxes (but not interest paid on overdue taxes) certain loan origination fees, loan discount points and loan prepayment penalties. p. 36

11. **a.** Five steps: (1) Calculate their total monthly income: $45,000 + $37,500 = $82,500 annual ÷ 12 = $6,875 monthly income. (2) Now, apply the old *rule* for maximum PITI: $6,875 × 28% = $1,925. (3) Then, apply the old *rule* for maximum total debt payments, including PITI: $6,875 × 36% = $2,475. (4) Then, subtract the debt payments to determine the estimated maximum PITI: $2,475 − $350 − $375 = $1,750. Because of the debts, they decide they are more likely to qualify for the lower amount. p. 35

12. **b.** A broad-form homeowners' insurance policy covers a much wider range of potential damage than the basic form. Both forms cover damage from sources, such as fire, lightning, theft, and windstorm.

13. **c.** Most homeowners' insurance policies cover many perils, but not flooding. Flood insurance must always be purchased separately. p. 38

14. **a.** Homeowners' insurance is purchased to protect the property owner from financial losses caused by events, such as fire, theft, or vandalism. It does not pay for routine maintenance, title defects, or accidents on other people's property. p. 37

15. **b.** The limit is $10,000; there is no age restriction, and the withdrawn amount is subject to income tax. p. 36

16. **d.** People buy homes for financial reasons, such as appreciation and federal tax deductions. They also buy them for psychological reasons, such as a sense of belonging to the community. However, home ownership may require more time for management and maintenance than renting. p. 32

17. **b.** Retirement communities are often structured as PUDs. Converted-use properties are unlikely to be easily changed over to meet needs of retired individuals. Time-share ownership is not a long-term type of residential ownership. Industrial complexes are not residential in nature. p. 33

18. **a.** Today, credit scores and the borrower's history of repaying loans play a key role when lending institutions decide whether to lend money. Condition, not age, is an important factor about the home. Lenders need to be concerned about age discrimination in terms of the borrower. p. 35

19. **d.** Mortgage interest rates affect whether a person can afford to buy a home. A short length of residence can negatively affect the tax benefits of home ownership. Shopping convenience is not usually affected by whether residential units are rented or owned. p. 34

20. **b.** Fees to maintain commonly owned property are characteristic of condominiums, cooperatives, PUDs, and mixed use buildings. p. 32–33

21. **c.** Special apartment and condominium policies generally provide liability coverage for injuries or losses sustained with the unit, but not losses or damages to the structure. p. 37

22. **b.** CLUE contains up to five years of personal property claim history. p. 38

23. **d.** Required flood insurance is costly, and if it is required by the National Flood Insurance Program (NFIP), this results in higher expenses for the buyer and also negatively affects property values. p. 39

24. **c.** A *broad-form* policy covers damage from falling objects, such as a tree branch. *Basic-form* and *liability* insurance do not. p. 37

25. **a.** Flood insurance policies may be purchased from a licensed property insurance broker or the National Flood Insurance Program. They are written for the property value or mortgage loan amount, which is subject to the maximum limits available. p. 38

Activity: Check the Ads

1. cooperative

2. converted use

3. planned unit development

4. mixed-use development

5. apartment complex

6. condominium

CHAPTER 4

Agency

MATCHING A   *Write the letter of the matching term on the appropriate line.*

a. nonagent

b. customer

c. fiduciary relationship

d. special agent

e. agent

f. general agent

g. implied agency

h. law of agency

i. puffing

j. principal

1. ___ The basic framework that governs the legal responsibilities of an agent to a principal

2. ___ An agent who is authorized to represent the principal in one specific act or business transaction, under detailed instructions

3. ___ The individual who is authorized and consents to represent the interests of another person

4. ___ The establishment of an agency relationship as the result of the actions of the parties that indicate mutual consent

5. ___ The individual who hires and delegates to the agent the responsibility of representing the individual's interests

6. ___ An affiliation of trust and confidence as between a principal and an agent

7. ___ Nonfraudulent exaggeration of a property's benefits or features

8. ___ An agent authorized to represent the principal in a broad range of matters related to a specific business or activity

9. ___ In a real estate agency relationship, the third party (or nonrepresented consumer) who receives some level of service and who is entitled to honesty and fair dealing

10. ___ An intermediary between a buyer and seller who assists both parties with a transaction, but who represents neither party

MATCHING B   *Write the letter of the matching term on the appropriate line.*

a. disclosed dual agency

b. common law agent duties

c. buyers' agents

d. client

e. undisclosed dual agency

f. latent defect

g. stigmatized property

h. universal agent

i. express agreement

j. errors and omissions insurance

1. ___ An agency relationship in which the agent represents two principals simultaneously, without their knowledge or permission

2. ___ A contract in which the parties formally state their intention to establish an agency relationship

3. ___ Real estate licensees who represent buyers exclusively

4. ___ Type of insurance that covers liability for mistakes and negligence in the usual activities of a real estate office

5. ___ A property that has been branded as undesirable because of the events that occurred in or near it

6. ___ The principal in a real estate agency relationship

7. ___ An agency relationship in which the agent represents two principals simultaneously, with their knowledge or permission

8. ___ The responsibilities of care, obedience, accounting, loyalty, and disclosure

9. ___ A person who is empowered to do anything the principal could do personally; this person has unlimited authority

10. ___ A hidden structural problem that would not be discovered by ordinary inspection

TRUE OR FALSE   *Circle the correct answer.*

1. T   F   The *fiduciary* is the individual who hires and delegates to the agent the responsibility of representing the fiduciary's other interests.

2. T   F   Examples of nonagents are facilitators, transactional brokers, transactional coordinators, and contract brokers.

3. T   F   An agent works with a client and for the customer.

4. T   F   Under the common law of agency, the agent owes the principal the following six duties: care, obedience, loyalty, disclosure, accounting, and confidentiality. (Use the acronym COLD AC.)

5. T   F   The common law fiduciary duty of *obedience* obligates the agent to obey all the principal's instructions.

6. T   F   The common law duty of *loyalty* requires that an agent avoid disclosing material facts about the condition of the property.

7. T   F   The source of compensation is the key determining factor in whether an agency relationship exists.

8. T   F   A buyer's agent is responsible to the buyers to help them prepare the strongest offer.

9. T   F   A real estate broker is usually the general agent of a buyer or seller.

10. T   F   Real estate licensees can sell property in which they have a personal interest, but only if the licensee informs the buyer of that interest.

11. T   F   In a *dual agency* relationship, the agent represents two principals in the same transaction.

12. T   F   A dual agency relationship is legal if either the buyer or the seller consents to the dual representation.

13. T   F   An agent owes a customer the duties of reasonable care and skill, honest and fair dealing, and disclosure of known facts.

14. T   F   A negligent misrepresentation occurs when the broker makes a statement, such as "This is the prettiest house I've ever seen."

15. T   F   When a property has a hidden structural defect that could not be discovered by ordinary inspection, it is referred to as a *stigmatized property*.

MULTIPLE CHOICE   *Circle the correct answer.*

1. An individual who is authorized and consents to represent the interests of another person is a(n)

   a. customer.
   b. principal.
   c. agent.
   d. facilitator.

2. A broker represents a woman but is currently working with a man to find a home. Assuming that no statute has replaced the traditional common law, which of the following correctly identifies the parties in this relationship?

   a. The broker is the man's agent; the woman is the broker's client.
   b. The man is the broker's client; the woman is the broker's principal.
   c. The woman is the broker's customer; the man is the broker's client.
   d. The broker is the woman's agent; the man is the broker's customer.

3. The agent's obligation to use skill and expertise on behalf of the principal arises under which of the following common-law duties?

   a. Care
   b. Obedience
   c. Loyalty
   d. Disclosure

4. An agent representing the seller has a duty to disclose to the principal all of the following EXCEPT

   a. the offers that are ridiculously low.
   b. the buyer's financial ability to offer a higher price.
   c. the agent's advertising budget.
   d. the buyer's intention to resell the property for a profit.

5. A broker has an agency agreement to represent a seller in the sale of a house. The agreement's expiration date is June 10. On May 5, the house is struck by lightning and burns. The seller, overwhelmed by grief, dies. Based on these facts, which of the following is TRUE?

   a. The agency agreement was terminated by the fire, although the seller's death also would have done so.
   b. The agency agreement was not terminated until the seller's death on June 11.
   c. If the house had not been destroyed by the fire, the seller's death would not have terminated the agreement; the broker would become the broker for the seller's estate.
   d. Only the mutual agreement of the parties can terminate a valid agency agreement before its expiration date.

6. A person who is designated by the principal in a broad range of matters related to a particular transaction or activity is a

   a. facilitator.
   b. special agent.
   c. designated agent.
   d. general agent.

7. A real estate broker signed an agency agreement with a seller. The asking price for the seller's house was $499,000. A few days later, the broker met a prospective buyer who was interested in buying a home in the $480,000 to $510,000 price range. The broker agreed to help the buyer locate such a property and to represent him in negotiating a favorable purchase price. Based on these facts, which of the following statements is TRUE?

   a. The broker's relationships and the buyer and seller are separate issues, and no dual agency question arises.
   b. The seller is the broker's client, and the buyer is the broker's customer; there is no dual agency problem.
   c. The broker has created a potential undisclosed dual agency problem and should disclose the relationships to both parties before showing the seller's home to the buyer.
   d. The broker has created a dual agency problem and should immediately terminate the agreement with either the buyer or seller.

MULTIPLE CHOICE   *(Continued)*

8. A broker is showing a house to a prospective buyer. He points out the rustic charm of the sagging front porch and refers to a weed-choked backyard as a delightful garden. The broker is engaging in which of the following?

   a. Intentional misrepresentation
   b. Negligent misrepresentations
   c. Puffing
   d. Fraud

9. A house built over a ditch covered with decaying timber, or a house with ceilings that are improperly attached to the support beams are examples of

   a. stigmatized properties.
   b. environmental hazards.
   c. latent defects.
   d. conditions that need not be disclosed.

10. The seller's agent has certain duties to the client-principal. All of the following are duties of the principal *EXCEPT*

    a. cooperating with the agent.
    b. compensating the agent.
    c. suggesting marketing strategies to the agent.
    d. dealing with the agent in good faith.

11. Every state has mandatory agency disclosure laws that stipulate

    a. how an implied agency may occur.
    b. when, how, and to whom licensees must reveal for whom they provide client-based services.
    c. restrictions on disclosure of confidential information.
    d. how a customer is differentiated from a client.

12. Who is the agent's principal?

    a. Seller
    b. Buyer
    c. Person who pays the commission
    d. Whoever hired the agent

13. The broker was hired to represent the seller, to market the property, and to solicit offers to purchase. The broker is called a

    a. general agent.   c. facilitator.
    b. special agent.   d nonagent.

14. A house was the scene of a drug arrest and a violent murder last year. When it was listed on the market, many people considered it to be a

    a. latent property.
    b. stigmatized property.
    c. damaged property.
    d. property with a material defect.

15. All of the following will terminate an agency relationship *EXCEPT*

    a. the death of either party.
    b. the destruction of the property.
    c. an offer made on the property.
    d. an expiration of the agreement.

16. What is a seller's agent required to disclose to prospective buyers about material defects in the property?

    a. Only information about material defects the seller has provided the agent.
    b. Only information about material defects that the agent has personally observed.
    c. Both information the seller has provided the agent, and material defects that the agent has personally observed.
    d. All information about material defects that the agent knows or should know.

17. Which of the following statements could be negligent misrepresentation?

    a. "The uneven floors just mean that the building dates to colonial times."
    b. "I think these low doorways are a charming part of the Cape Cod style."
    c. "The simple design is uncluttered and can give you many possibilities for decor."
    d. "The size of the bedrooms makes them wonderfully cozy and perfect for your children."

18. The seller's agent is aware of, but does not disclose to a buyer that a new landfill has been approved for development on the adjacent property. This could be an example of

    a. negligent misrepresentation.
    b. a latent defect.
    c. fraudulent misrepresentation.
    d. unnecessary disclosure.

MULTIPLE CHOICE   *(Continued)*

19. A key element of an agent's fiduciary responsibility of loyalty is to
    a. report the status of all funds received from, or on behalf of, the principal.
    b. avoid conflicts of interest.
    c. obey the principal's instructions in accordance with the contract.
    d. reveal relevant information or material facts.

20. When a broker places trust funds of others into the company's operating account and then withdraws funds for the firm's use, what illegal practice has taken place?
    a. Escrowing
    b. DBA accounting
    c. Conversion
    d. Asset-liability management

FILL-IN-THE-BLANK   *Select the word or words that best complete the following statements:*

accounting

buyer's agent

designated agent

fraud

implied agreement

listing agreement

confidentiality

negligent
   misrepresentation

obedience

operation of law

seller disclaimer

stigmatized property

1. The written employment contract that establishes the agency relationship between the seller and the broker is called a(n) _____.

2. The requirement that brokers promptly deposit funds entrusted to the broker in a special trust account is an example of how brokers fulfill the fiduciary duty of _____.

3. Even when a property is sold *as is* or with a(n) _____, the seller must still disclose known problems with the property if they will affect the health and well-being of the occupants.

4. Although not available in all states, when a person is authorized by the broker to act as the agent of a specific principal-seller (in an in-house sale by two agents), this agent is called a(n) _____.

5. The intentional misrepresentation of a material fact in such a way as to harm or take advantage of another person is called _____.

6. Discovery of a methamphetamine lab on a property can result in the property being regarded as a(n) _____.

7. A man tells a real estate broker that he has been thinking about selling his condominium. The broker contacts several buyers that she knows are looking for a condominium, and one makes an offer for the property. The broker presents the offer to the man, who accepts it. Although no documents were signed by the man, an agency may have been created by _____.

8. If a buyer's agent reveals to the seller that the buyer must move within one month, this action would violate the agent's fiduciary duty of _____ to the buyer.

9. An agent who has a buyer as principal and the seller as a customer is called a(n) _____.

10. An agency is terminated by _____ when a principal declares bankruptcy and property title transfers to a court-appointed receiver.

ANSWER KEY

Key Term Matching (A)

1. h **2.** d **3.** e **4.** g **5.** j **6.** c **7.** i **8.** f
9. b **10.** a

Key Term Matching (B)

1. e **2.** i **3.** c **4.** j **5.** g **6.** d **7.** a **8.** b
9. h **10.** f

True or False

1. **False.** The *principal* is the individual who hires and delegates to the agent the responsibility of representing the principal's other interests. p. 46

2. **True.** A nonagent (facilitator, transactional broker, transactional coordinator, and contract broker) is a middleman between a buyer and a seller (or a landlord and a tenant), who assists one or both parties with the transaction without representing either party's interest. p. 46

3. **False.** An agent works *for* the client and *with* the customer. The client is the principal. p. 45–46

4. **True.** The six common-law fiduciary duties are care, obedience of lawful instructions, loyalty, disclosure of material facts, accounting, and confidentiality. p. 50

5. **False.** The common law fiduciary duty of *obedience* obligates the agent to obey all of the principal's *lawful and ethical* instructions. p. 50

6. **False.** The common law duty of *loyalty* requires that an agent place the principal's interests above all others. However, the law of most states requires that the agent disclose material facts about the condition of the property. p. 50–51

7. **False.** The source of compensation is not the key determining factor in whether an agency relationship exists. An agent's commission may be paid, in whole or in part, by someone other than the agent's client-principal. Moreover, an agency can exist even when no fee is involved. p. 47

8. **True.** A buyer's agent represents the buyer in the transaction and is strictly accountable to the buyer; a buyer agency relationship is established in the same way as any other agency relationship: by contract or agreement. p. 54

9. **False.** A real estate broker is usually the *special agent* of a buyer or seller, with limited responsibilities; for instance, the real estate broker may not bind the principal to any contract. p. 52

10. **True.** The duty of loyalty requires that the agent place the principal's interests above those of all others, including the agent's own self-interest. Neither real estate brokers nor real estate salespeople may sell property in which they have a personal interest without disclosing information about their interests to the purchaser. p. 50

11. **True.** In a dual agency, the agent represents two principals in the same transaction, thus requiring equal loyalty to two different principals at the same time. While practical methods of ensuring fairness and equal representation may exist, it should be noted that a dual agent can never fully represent either party's full interests.

12. **False.** The states that permit dual agency require that the both the seller and the buyer consent to the dual representation. p. 55

13. **True.** Even though an agent's primary responsibility is to the principal, the agent also has duties to third parties; such duties include reasonable care and skill in performance, honest and fair dealing, and disclosure of all facts that materially affect the value or desirability of the property. p. 58

14. **False.** *Puffing* occurs when the broker engages in exaggeration of a property's benefits or features. Brokers need to be careful about statements of fact or opinion. In this case, the broker is expressing what is clearly an opinion and is not concealing any defects. Beauty is in the eye of the beholder. p. 59

15. **False.** When a property has a hidden structural defect that could not be discovered by ordinary inspection, it is referred to as having a *latent defect*. A stigmatized property is one that society has found undesirable because of events that occurred there. p. 60

Multiple Choice

1. **c.** The agent is hired by the principal. The customer or facilitator is a third party. p. 45–46

2. **d.** Watch the terminology: The broker is working *for* (representing) the woman and is working *with* the man (a customer) to find a home. p. 46

3. **a.** *Care* requires skill and expertise; *obedience* requires following lawful instructions; *loyalty* is putting the client's interests above the agent's; and *disclosure* refers to material defects of the property. p. 49

4. **c.** The seller's (special) agent must present all offers and any facts about the buyers that would assist the seller in making a decision, including the fact that the buyer intends to resell the property. There is no requirement that the agent disclose an advertising budget. p. 51

5. **a.** An agency agreement may be terminated by either destruction of the property or death of either party. In this case, destruction of the property occurred first. p. 52

6. **d.** A *special agent* is given limited authority for a limited time. A *general agent* is given broad authority in a specific circumstance; a property manager is typically a general agent for the owner as are most real estate salespeople representing their broker. p. 52

7. **c.** The broker is representing the seller and now is at least implying that she will represent the buyer in locating a property; hence, there are two clients. If the broker intends to show the seller's property, she must disclose her relationship with both clients, gain their agreement to a dual agency, and only then proceed. p. 54–55

8. **c.** Because any prudent buyer can see the sagging porch and weed-choked garden, these are *puffing* statements. Agents must take care that they do not make statements in such a way as to harm the buyer or take advantage of the buyer's ignorance, which would constitute *fraud*. p. 59

9. **c.** A latent defect is a hidden structural defect that would not be discovered by ordinary inspection. p. 60

10. **c.** Marketing is the agent's responsibility. The principal who hired the agent is responsible for cooperating with the agent, disclosing material defects, and compensating the agent. p. 46

11. **b.** Mandatory agency disclosure laws now exist in every state. In addition, state laws may require a particular type of written form be used and may require that all agency alternatives be explained. p. 56

12. **d.** The most complete answer is *whoever hired the agent*. That could be either the buyer or the seller, but who pays the compensation is not the determining factor. p. 46

13. **b.** A *special agent* is one who is hired for a limited time and given limited authority. A broker taking a listing is generally a special agent. p. 52

14. **b.** Presuming that the property is physically intact, the drug arrest and violent murder may create psychological reactions to the property, rendering it *stigmatized*. p. 60

15. **c.** An offer on the property does not terminate the agency relationship; however, the death of either party, destruction of the property, or expiration of the term will terminate the relationship. p. 52

16. **d.** Agents are responsible for disclosing information they are told or that they discover on their own, plus information they should have known. p. 50

17. **a.** Presenting an opinion is acceptable as long as it is not presented as a fact. Uneven floors could mean a latent defect, such as rotten supports. p. 59

18. **c.** This is an example of misleading a party by withholding a material fact. It is deliberate misrepresentation by silence. The proposed landfill adjacent to the property is not a latent defect, because it does not threaten structural soundness or personal safety. p. 51, 59–60

19. **b.** Reporting the status of funds is an accounting responsibility. Obeying the principal's instructions relates to obedience. Revealing relevant information relates to the responsibility of disclosure. p. 50

20. **c.** Both commingling the funds and the practice of conversion are illegal. p. 51

Fill-in-the-Blank

1. The written employment contract that establishes the agency relationship between the seller and the broker is called a *listing agreement*.

2. The requirement that brokers promptly deposit funds entrusted to the broker in a special trust account is an example of how brokers fulfill the fiduciary duty of *accounting*.

3. Even when a property is sold *as is* or with a *seller disclaimer*, agents should still disclose known problems with the property if they could affect the health and well-being of the occupants.

4. Although not available in all states, when a person is authorized by the broker to act as the agent of a specific principal-seller (in an in-house sale by two agents), this agent is called a *designated agent*.

5. The intentional misrepresentation of a material fact in such a way as to harm or take advantage of another person is called *fraud*.

6. Discovery of a methamphetamine lab on a property can result in the property being regarded as a *stigmatized property*.

7. A man tells a real estate broker that he has been thinking about selling his condominium. The broker contacts several buyers that she knows are looking for a condominium, and one makes an offer for the property. The broker presents the offer to the man, who accepts it. Although no documents were signed by the man, an agency may have been created by *implied agreement*.

8. If a buyer's agent reveals to the seller that the buyer must move within one month, this action would violate the agent's fiduciary duty of *confidentiality* to the buyer.

9. An agent who has a buyer as principal and the seller as a customer is called a *buyer's agent*.

10. An agency is terminated by *operation of law* when a principal declares bankruptcy and property title transfers to a court-appointed receiver.

CHAPTER 5

Real Estate Brokerage

■ **LEARNING OBJECTIVES** *Before you answer these questions, you should be able to*

■ **identify** the roles of technology, personnel, and license laws in the operation of a real estate business;

■ **describe** the various types of antitrust violations common in the real estate industry and the penalties involved with each;

■ **explain** how a broker's compensation is usually determined;

■ **distinguish** employees from independent contractors and explain why the distinction is important; and

■ **define** the following *key terms*:

antitrust laws	employee	procuring cause
brokerage	independent contractor	ready, willing, and able
commission	Internet advertising	buyer
disclaimers	Internet Listing Display	Uniform Electronic
electronic contracting	Policy	Transactions Act
Electronic Signatures in	minimum level of services	(UETA)
Global and National	National Do Not Call	
Commerce Act (E-sign)	Registry	

MATCHING   *Write the letter of the matching term on the appropriate line.*

a. *allocation of markets*

b. *antitrust laws*

c. *caveat emptor*

d. *commission*

e. *salesperson*

f. *brokerage*

g. *independent contractor*

h. *rules and regulations*

i. *employee*

j. *ready, willing, and able buyer*

k. *real estate broker*

l. *procuring cause*

m. *group boycotting*

n. *real estate license laws*

o. *sole proprietorship*

1. ___ The common law doctrine of *let the buyer beware*

2. ___ Statutes enacted by state legislatures to protect the public and ensure a standard of competence in the real estate industry

3. ___ The device by which a state licensing authority defines and enforces the statutory law

4. ___ The business of bringing parties together

5. ___ An individual who is licensed to buy, sell, exchange, or lease property for others, and to charge a fee for those services

6. ___ Company held by a single owner

7. ___ A person who is licensed only to perform real estate activities on behalf of a broker

8. ___ A salesperson whose activities are closely controlled, and who is entitled to benefits, unemployment compensation, and income tax withholding

9. ___ Licensees who work under the terms of a written contract and receive more than 90 percent of their income from sales production rather than hours worked

10. ___ A form of compensation computed as a percentage of the total sales price of a property

11. ___ The broker who starts an uninterrupted chain of events that results in the sale of a property

12. ___ A person who is prepared to buy on the seller's terms

13. ___ A conspiracy by two or more businesses against another

14. ___ An illegal division of territories to avoid competition

15. ___ Law that prohibits price fixing and tie-in agreements

TRUE OR FALSE   *Circle the correct answer.*

1. T F Only a few states regulate the activities of real estate brokers and salespeople.

2. T F The real estate license laws set up a disciplinary system to enforce the acceptable standards of conduct and practice for licensees.

3. T F A real estate salesperson is licensed to buy, sell, exchange, or lease real property for others, and to charge a fee for those services.

4. T F The Internal Revenue Service has established criteria for determining whether a real estate licensee is classified as an employee or an independent contractor for income tax purposes.

5. T F The amount of a broker's compensation is always negotiable.

6. T F A real estate salesperson is an individual who is licensed to perform real estate activities on behalf of a licensed broker.

7. T F If present at the time the transaction closes, a broker is considered to be the procuring cause of a sale.

8. T F Price-fixing, group boycotting, and allocation of markets are three examples of antitrust violations.

9. T F The practice of illegally setting standard prices for products or services is referred to as a *tie-in agreement.*

10. T F Under the Sherman Antitrust Act, people who fix prices or allocate markets may be subject to a maximum $1 million fine and ten years in prison.

MULTIPLE CHOICE   *Circle the correct answer.*

1. Why have real estate license laws been put into effect?

   a. To protect licensees from lawsuits
   b. To protect the public and establish standards of professionalism
   c. To prevent licensees from engaging in profit-making activities
   d. To establish maximum levels of competency and a moral marketplace

2. In real estate, a salesperson is always a(n)

   a. independent contractor.
   b. employee of a licensed broker.
   c. licensee who performs real estate activities on behalf of a broker.
   d. combination office manager, marketer, and organizer with a fundamental understanding of the real estate industry, who may or may not be licensed.

3. All of the following are requirements for independent contractor status used by the Internal Revenue Service *EXCEPT*

   a. a current real estate license.
   b. specific hours stated in a written agreement.
   c. a written agreement that specifies that the individual will not be treated as an employee for tax purposes.
   d. 90 percent or more of the individual's income is based on sales production rather than hours worked.

4. The broker who owns a realty agency does not permit his salespeople to charge less than an 8 percent commission in any transaction. After reading a newspaper article about this realty agency's policies, the broker of another realty agency decides to adopt the 8 percent minimum, too. Based on these facts, which of the following statements is *TRUE*?

   a. The realty agency's policy is price-fixing and violates the antitrust law.
   b. Although the realty agency's original policy was legal, the second realty agency's adoption of the minimum commission may constitute an antitrust violation if both brokers are in the same real estate market.
   c. Both brokers engaged in illegal price-fixing.
   d. Neither broker has committed an antitrust violation.

5. A real estate broker had a listing agreement with a seller that specified a 6 percent commission. The broker showed the home to a prospective buyer. The next day, the buyer called the seller directly and offered to buy the house for 5 percent less than the asking price. The seller agreed to the price and informed the broker in writing that no further brokerage services would be required. The sale went to closing six weeks later. Based on these facts, which of the following statements is *TRUE*?

   a. While the broker was the procuring cause of the sale, the seller properly canceled the contract; without a valid employment agreement in force at the time of closing, the broker is not entitled to a commission.
   b. The broker is entitled to a partial commission, and the buyer is obligated to pay it.
   c. Under the facts as stated, the broker is not the procuring cause of this sale but is still entitled to a commission.
   d. The broker was the procuring cause of the sale and is entitled to the full 6 percent commission.

6. A qualified buyer makes a written offer on a property on March 6 by filling out and signing a sales agreement. Later that day, the seller accepts and signs the agreement, keeping one copy. The broker gives a copy of the signed agreement to the buyer on March 8. The seller's deed is delivered on May 1. The deed is recorded on May 7, and the buyer takes possession on May 15. When is the broker's commission payable if this is a *usual* transaction?

   a. March 8   c. May 7
   b. May 1   d. May 15

7. All of the following are violations of the federal antitrust laws *EXCEPT*

   a. group boycotting.
   b. allocation of customers.
   c. commission splitting.
   d. tie-in agreements.

MULTIPLE CHOICE *(Continued)*

8. All of the following are ways for a broker to charge for services *EXCEPT*
    a. standard community rate.
    b. flat fees.
    c. hourly rate.
    d. commission based on a percentage of the selling price.

9. What is the main value of a multiple-listing service (MLS) for sellers?
    a. Agents do not have to work as hard to secure property listings.
    b. It simplifies closing procedures.
    c. An MLS reduces cooperation among brokers.
    d. It exposes the property to a greater number of prospective buyers.

10. After license laws are enacted by the legislature, who is responsible for adopting rules and regulations?
    a. A sub-committee that reports to the legislature
    b. Local REALTOR® association
    c. Licensing authority (division, commission, etc.)
    d. Brokers and salespeople appointed by the governor

11. When communicating with clients or consumers via e-mail, all of the following are examples of professional e-mail etiquette *EXCEPT*
    a. using spell check.
    b. providing useful information in the subject line.
    c. avoiding sending large attachments.
    d. responding to e-mails within one week.

12. Although state laws vary regarding Internet advertising, which of the following is a typical element of state policy or law?
    a. E-mail sent by a licensee needs to include the licensee's name, phone number, and real estate license number.
    b. Ads must avoid misleading the potential client or customer.
    c. On a Web site containing their ads, real estate professionals only need to identify themselves as a broker or salesperson on the site's home page.
    d. It is acceptable for only the salesperson's name (without the broker's name) to be shown in an ad.

13. The broker may still be entitled to a commission in which of the following situations where a pending property sale did *NOT* close?
    a. The buyer wanted to add the kitchen appliances to the sale, but the seller refused.
    b. The buyer decided not to buy the property.
    c. The seller decided not to sell.
    d. Financing fell through for the buyer.

14. An arrangement to sell one product only if the buyer purchases another product as well is called a(n)
    a. tie-in agreement.
    b. fee-for-services.
    c. buydown provision.
    d. allocation of customers.

15. An agreement that a listing broker offers no services other than placing a listing in the MLS is called a(n)
    a. exclusive-brokerage agreement.
    b. full-service listing agreement.
    c. limited-service listing agreement.
    d. dual agency.

16. Even if a consumer has requested placement on the National Do Not Call Registry, a real estate professional may call the consumer up to how many months after the consumer's last purchase?
    a. 3   c. 12
    b. 6   d. 18

MULTIPLE CHOICE *(Continued)*

17. The name for the current policy of the National Association of REALTORS® that allows all MLS members equal rights to display MLS data is the
    a. virtual office Web site.
    b. Internet Listing Display Policy.
    c. Internet Data Exchange.
    d. Open Listing Data Service.

18. An important purpose of the "E-Sign" Act is to
    a. give contracts formed using e-mail the same legal standing as those on paper.
    b. require stringent security measures for e-mail communication.
    c. prevent notarization of electronically transmitted agreements.
    d. require all parties to use electronic contracting if the seller prefers it.

19. What is the compensation plan called if a salesperson's commission split increases depending on whether the salesperson achieves higher production goals?
    a. Procuring cause commission
    b. Cooperating broker commission
    c. Graduated commission split
    d. 100 percent commission plan

20. What is the practice called when a consumer selects specific services to use and only pays the licensee for those services?
    a. Unbundling services
    b. Tie-in agreement
    c. Discounted services
    d. Allocation of markets

MATH PRACTICE   *Circle the correct answer.*

1. A seller listed and sold her property for $325,000. She agreed to pay the listing broker a 7 percent commission. The listing broker offered a listing 40/60 selling split to any cooperating broker who sold the property. How much did the seller have to pay in commission fees?
    a. $9,100
    b. $13,650
    c. $11,375
    d. $22,750

2. The salesperson's agreement with the broker was a 40/60 split with the broker keeping 40 percent of the commission. The seller was charged 5.5 percent. How much did the salesperson receive if she listed and sold a house for $279,500?
    a. $6,149.00
    b. $7,686.25
    c. $9,223.50
    d. $15,372.50

3. A broker listed a seller's home for $425,000 with a 4 percent commission, plus $3,000 for advertising costs. The buyer offered $380,000, and after several counteroffers, finally agreed to $400,000. What was the total cost to the seller?
    a. $16,000
    b. $18,000
    c. $19,000
    d. $20,000

4. Salespeople in a realty agency are compensated based on the following formula: 35 percent of the commission earned on any sale, less a $200 per-transaction desk rental. Salespeople are responsible for paying 75 percent of all marketing and sales expenses for any property they list, and a $75 per-transaction fee to cover the monthly expenses of advertising and marketing the agency's services. If a salesperson sold a house for $500,000, with a 6 percent commission, how much would the salesperson be paid if the sale incurred $800 in marketing and advertising costs?
    a. $9,625
    b. $9,700
    c. $10,225
    d. $10,500

5. At a realty agency, salespeople pay a monthly desk rent of 15 percent of their monthly income. In May, one salesperson receives 5 percent on a $560,000 sale; 6 percent on a $348,000 sale; and 6.75 percent on an $89,500 sale. The only other salesperson at the agency who received a commission in May got 6 percent on a $410,000 sale. How much did the agency receive in May?
    a. $11,928.19
    b. $7,095.97
    c. $12,251.53
    d. $14,945.00

ACTIVITY: Who's Who?

Based on their statements below, place each speaker's name in the appropriate box of Open Door Realty's organizational chart.

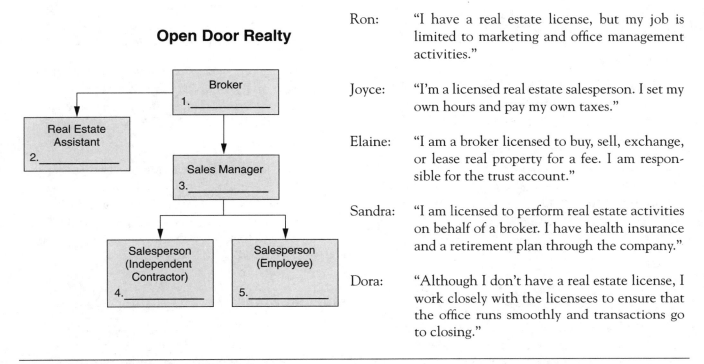

Open Door Realty

Broker
1._____

Real Estate
Assistant
2._____

Sales Manager
3._____

Salesperson
(Independent
Contractor)
4._____

Salesperson
(Employee)
5._____

Ron: "I have a real estate license, but my job is limited to marketing and office management activities."

Joyce: "I'm a licensed real estate salesperson. I set my own hours and pay my own taxes."

Elaine: "I am a broker licensed to buy, sell, exchange, or lease real property for a fee. I am responsible for the trust account."

Sandra: "I am licensed to perform real estate activities on behalf of a broker. I have health insurance and a retirement plan through the company."

Dora: "Although I don't have a real estate license, I work closely with the licensees to ensure that the office runs smoothly and transactions go to closing."

ACTIVITY: State License Requirements

Fill in the license requirements in the following table based on your state's license laws, rules, and regulations.

Requirements	Sales License	Broker License
Age		
Education		
Experience		
Bond		
Credit Report		
Recommendations		
Photograph		
Fingerprints		
Continuing Education		
Licensure Period		
Expiration Date		

ANSWER KEY

Matching

1. c **2.** n **3.** h **4.** f **5.** k **6.** o **7.** e **8.** i
9. g **10.** d **11.** l **12.** j **13.** m **14.** a **15.** b

True or False

1. **False.** All 50 states, the District of Columbia, and all Canadian provinces license and regulate the activities of real estate brokers and licensees. p. 68.

2. **True.** The real estate license laws not only set standards for conduct and practice, but they also enforce those standards. p. 69

3. **False.** A real estate *broker* is licensed to buy, sell, exchange, or lease real property for others, and to charge a fee for those services. p. 70

4. **True.** The Internal Revenue Service (IRS) has established three requirements needed to establish an independent contractor state (1) must have a current real estate license, (2) a written contract with the broker specifying that the licensee will not be treated as an employee for federal tax purposes, and (3) at least 90 percent of the individual's income as a licensee must be based on sales production and not on the number of hours worked. p. 75

5. **True.** Because the real estate industry is subject to antitrust laws, the amount of a broker's compensation is always negotiable and may not be set or determined by a multiple listing association or any professional organization. p. 76

6. **True.** A real estate salesperson is any person licensed to perform real estate activities on behalf of a licensed real estate broker; the broker is fully responsible for the actions performed in the course of the real estate business performed on behalf of the broker. p. 70

7. **False.** A broker is considered the *procuring* cause of a sale if the broker started an uninterrupted chain of events that resulted in the sale. p. 71

8. **True.** Antitrust laws prohibit monopolies and any contracts, combinations, and conspiracies that unreasonably restrain trade, such as price-fixing, group boycotting, allocation of customers or markets, and tie-in agreements. p. 76

9. **False.** *Price-fixing* is the practice of competitors setting prices for products or services. A *tie-in agreement* is an agreement to sell one product only if the buyer purchases another product, as well. p. 76

10. **True.** The penalties for violating antitrust laws are severe, and people who fix prices or allocate markets may be subject to a maximum $1 million fine and up to ten years in prison; the penalty may be as high as $100 million for corporations. p. 77

Multiple Choice

1. **b.** Real estate license laws protect the public by ensuring a standard of competence and professionalism in the real estate industry. p. 69

2. **c.** While the salesperson may be treated as an independent contractor for income tax purposes, the salesperson must still work directly under the broker's name. p. 70

3. **b.** The real estate broker may require an employee to follow rules, such as working a certain number of hours. However, the broker may not do so if treating the affiliated licensee as an independent contractor. p. 75

4. **d.** Brokers must independently determine commission rates or fees for their own firms. Because the second agency's broker learned about the realty agency's policies from a public source; that is, the newspaper, and without discussing the policy with the realty agency, neither broker has committed an antitrust violation. p. 76

5. **d.** Because the broker introduced a ready, willing, and able buyer to the seller prior to the seller's cancellation of the listing agreement, the broker is entitled to the commission. p. 71

6. **b.** Although the commission was earned when the buyer was notified of the seller's acceptance (March 8), the commission is typically paid at the time the deed is delivered. p. 71

7. **c.** Brokers may legally share and split commissions. Price fixing, allocation of customers, and group boycotting are illegal under the antitrust laws. p. 76

8. **a.** Under antitrust laws, brokers may not collaborate and agree to charge the same rates to customers. Brokers may charge for services using a flat fee, an hourly rate, or a commission based on a percentage of the selling price. p. 76

9. **d.** The MLS exposes the property to many different agents, encouraging cooperation among brokers and expediting sales. p. 68

10. **c.** Rules and regulations are written and adopted by the licensing authorities in each state. They have the same force as the law, but they are easier to change because they do not require legislative approval. p. 69

11. **d.** Examples of e-mail etiquette include using the subject line in a useful and helpful manner; avoiding spelling errors; responding promptly to all e-mail messages; and being specific, to the point, and brief. Do not send unsolicited e-mails. p. 77

12. **b.** A phone number and license number are not usually required in an e-mail. Status as a broker or agent should be disclosed on every page of a Web site with ads. Both the salesperson's name and the broker's name should be shown in the ads. p. 78

13. **c.** If the sale is not completed due to the seller's default (deciding not to sell), then the broker is generally due a commission. Courts may prevent a real estate broker from receiving a commission if the broker knew that the buyer was unable to perform. p. 71

14. **a.** A tie-in arrangement is an agreement to sell one product only if the buyer purchases another product; the sale of the first desired product is tied to the purchase of a second, less-desirable product. *Fee-for-services* refers to splitting apart the collection of services that a broker offers. A *buydown provision* is a financing option. *Allocation of customers* refers to dividing a market and refraining from competing. p. 76

15. **c.** A limited service listing agreement stipulates that a listing real estate broker offers no services other than listing the property in the MLS. An exclusive-brokerage agreement specifies a minimum level of services that a consumer should expect from a licensee. p. 74

16. **d.** Real estate licensees may call consumers with whom they have an established business relationship for up to 18 months after the consumer's last purchase, delivery, or payment, even if the consumer is listed on the National do Not Call Registry. However, if the consumer specifically asks the company not to call, then the company must stop calling. p. 79

17. **b.** The Internet Listing Display Policy replaces the Virtual Office Web site (BOW) and the Internet Data Exchange (IDX) policies. p. 77

18. **a.** The "E-Sign" Act diminishes legal barriers in electronic contracting, but it does not specify required security measures. Notarization is allowed. Parties are not required to use electronic contracting. p. 78

19. **c.** A graduated commission split is based on a salesperson's achieving specified production goals. A 100 percent commission plan provides for a salesperson to pay a monthly service charge to the broker so that the salesperson can keep 100 percent of the commissions earned. p. 72

20. **a.** Unbundling services means offering services as the consumer desires them. With discounted services, the consumer receives the full package of services but pays a discounted price. Allocation of markets involves an agreement between brokers to divide their markets and stop competition. p. 73

Math Practice

1. **d.** What the brokers agree to regarding splitting the commission is not relevant to the total cost to the seller. The seller paid $22,750 in commission fees: $325,000 × 7% = $22,750.

2. **c.** The salesperson received $9,223.50: $279,500 × 5.5% × 60% = $9,223.50.

3. **c.** The seller's total cost is $19,000: $400,000 × 4% + $3,000 = $19,000.

4. **a.** The salesperson is paid $9,625:

   $500,000 × 6% = $30,000

   $30,000 × 35% = $10,500

   $10,500 − $200 − $75 − $600 ($800 × 75%) = $9,625.

5. **a.** In May, the realty agency received $11,928.19:

   $560,000 × 5% = $28,000

   $348,000 × 6% = $20,880

   $89,500 × 6.75% = $6,041.25

   $410,000 × 6% = $24,600

   $28,000 + $20,880 + $6,041.25 + $24,600 = $79,521.25

   $79,521.25 × 15% = $11,928.19

Activity: Who's Who

1. Broker   Elaine

2. Real Estate Assistant   Dora

3. Sales Manager   Ron

4. Salesperson (Independent Contractor) Joyce

5. Salesperson (Employee)   Sandra

Activity: State License Requirements

Each state will have different answers. Students should work together, when possible.

CHAPTER 6

Listing Agreements and Buyer Representation

■ **LEARNING OBJECTIVES**   *Before you answer these questions, you should be able to*

■ **identify** the different types of listing and buyer representation agreements and their terms;

■ **describe** the ways in which a listing may be terminated;

■ **explain** the listing process and the parts of the listing agreement;

■ **distinguish** between the characteristics of the various types of listing and buyer representation agreements; and

■ **define** the following *key terms*:

buyer agency agreement	exclusive-right-to-sell listing	net listing
exclusive-agency listing	multiple listing service (MLS)	open listing

MATCHING   *Write the letter of the matching term on the appropriate line.*

a. *buyer agency agreement*

b. *broker protection clause*

c. *exclusive-agency listing*

d. *home warranty program*

e. *exclusive-right-to-sell listing*

f. *listing agreement*

g. *MLS*

h. *net listing*

i. *hold harmless wording*

j. *open listing*

1. ____ An employment contract for a broker's services for a property seller

2. ____ A listing agreement under which the seller must pay the broker a commission regardless of who sells the property

3. ____ A listing agreement with a single broker, under which the seller retains the right to sell the property independently without being obligated to pay a commission

4. ____ A listing agreement in which the seller may employ multiple brokers, retains the right to market the property independently, and is obligated to compensate only the broker who produces a buyer, if any

5. ____ A marketing organization whose broker members make their own exclusive listings available to other brokers

6. ____ A listing agreement in which the seller receives a specific dollar amount from the sales price, and the selling broker retains the balance as compensation

7. ____ An employment contract where the broker is employed as a purchaser's agent to find a suitable property

8. ____ An item in a listing agreement that states the broker and seller agree not to sue one another for any incorrect information supplied by one to the other

9. ____ An optional item in the listing contract that protects the buyer against the expense of certain types of repairs (such as plumbing, electrical, and heating systems) after the sale is completed

10. ____ A part of a listing agreement that stipulates that the property owner will pay the listing broker a commission if the broker was the procuring cause of a sale that is completed after the listing expired

TRUE OR FALSE   *Circle the correct answer.*

1. T F Under a typical net listing, the broker's commission is based on a percentage of the seller's net from the transaction.

2. T F A *listing agreement* is a contract for the sale of real estate.

3. T F The parties to a listing agreement are a broker and a seller.

4. T F A listing agreement in which the seller retains the right to employ any number of brokers as agents is referred to as a *multiple listing*.

5. T F In an exclusive-agency listing, one broker is authorized to act as the exclusive agent of the principal, who retains the right to sell the property without obligation to the broker.

6. T F In buyer agency, the source of compensation is the major factor that determines the relationship.

7. T F In an exclusive-right-to-sell listing, the seller must pay the broker's commission even if the seller finds a buyer without the broker's assistance.

8. T F Because a listing agreement is a personal service contract between a broker and seller, the broker may transfer the listing to another broker with or without the seller's consent.

9. T F Verbal agreement by the seller is adequate for a broker to list the property in a MLS.

10. T F A broker protection clause in a listing contract provides for payment of a commission to the listing broker if the owner sells the property within a certain number of days after the listing expires and to a broker-introduced buyer.

11. T F The seller disclosures of property conditions usually cover structural, mechanical, and other conditions that the buyer needs to know to make an informed decision.

12. T F Many states allow for a home warranty program to be provided in a listing contract or offer to purchase.

MULTIPLE CHOICE   *Circle the correct answer.*

1. In a typical buyer agency agreement, the buyer is the
   a. principal.
   b. customer.
   c. agent.
   d. employee.

2. The owner listed her home for sale with a broker. When the owner sold the home herself, she did not owe anyone a commission. Based on these facts, what type of listing did the broker and the owner most likely sign?
   a. Exclusive-right-to-sell listing
   b. Net listing
   c. Multiple listing
   d. Open listing

3. All of the following information is generally included in a listing agreement *EXCEPT*
   a. lot size.
   b. termination clause.
   c. client's specific requirements for a suitable property to buy.
   d. property condition disclosures.

4. On January 10, a salesperson met with a seller and described the advantages of listing the seller's property with his broker's office. On January 15, the seller agreed to the listing, and the salesperson and the seller signed the agreement. On January 18, the broker signed the listing agreement as required by the office policy. On January 20, the salesperson posted a For Sale sign in front of the house. When did the listing agreement become effective?
   a. January 10
   b. January 15
   c. January 18
   d. January 20

5. What is a listing agreement?
   a. Contract between buyer and seller
   b. Contract to purchase real property
   c. Employment agreement between broker and salesperson
   d. Employment contract between seller and broker

6. Who are the parties to a listing agreement?
   a. Buyer and seller
   b. Seller and broker
   c. Seller and salesperson
   d. Buyer and salesperson

7. There are five different brokerage signs in the front yard. Evidently, the seller has signed a(n)
   a. exclusive-agency listing.
   b. exclusive-right-to-sell listing.
   c. net listing.
   d. open listing.

8. The broker has just explained the value of signing an exclusive-agency listing with a broker who is a member of the multiple-listing service. The broker is trying to overcome the misconceptions of the seller who asked about a(n)
   a. open listing.
   b. option listing.
   c. exclusive-right-to-sell listing.
   d. net listing.

9. What kind of listing agreement is illegal in many states because of the potential for conflict of interest between a broker's fiduciary responsibility to the seller and the broker's profit motive?
   a. Open listing
   b. Net listing
   c. Exclusive-right-to-sell
   d. Exclusive-agency listing

10. Buyer agents may be compensated in any of the following ways *EXCEPT*
    a. flat fee for service.
    b. percentage of selling price.
    c. hourly rate.
    d. percentage of list price.

11. Any of the following will terminate a listing agreement *EXCEPT*
    a. performance.
    b. expiration.
    c. an offer to purchase.
    d. abandonment by broker.

12. A broker is retiring and wants to submit his listings to another broker. How can he do this?
    a. The broker must sign over the listings to the new broker.
    b. The new broker has to sign an acceptance agreement.
    c. Each salesperson must sign over the listings to the new broker.
    d. The sellers must agree to a new listing with the new broker.

MULTIPLE CHOICE   *(Continued)*

13. In which of the following types of listing agreements is the broker appointed as the seller's only agent?

    a. Exclusive-right-to-sell and exclusive-agency listings
    b. Open listing
    c. Net listing
    d. Option listing

14. In most states, a broker's license can be suspended or revoked if the broker

    a. breaches the terms of the listing agreement.
    b. cancels the listing agreement without cause.
    c. takes a listing that does not include a date on which the listing expires.
    d. does not include an automatic extension clause in the listing agreement.

15. All of the following are information needed for the listing agreement *EXCEPT*

    a. the dimensions of the lot.
    b. the possibility of seller financing.
    c. the age of the seller.
    d. the most-recent property taxes.

16. An example of personal property that a seller may leave with the property and, therefore, must be identified on the listing agreement is

    a. a built-in dishwasher.
    b. the door key.
    c. stacked firewood.
    d. a ceiling light fixture.

MATH PRACTICE   *Circle the correct answer.*

1. The brokerage charged the seller $1,000 as an advertising fee and 4 percent of the selling price. The house was listed for $439,500 and sold for $429,350. What was the total amount the seller paid the brokerage?

   a. $15,174
   b. $15,580
   c. $16,580
   d. None of the above

2. The seller agreed to a 5 percent commission on a sale price of $175,000. The brokerage split with salespeople is 30/70, with 30 percent remaining with the company. How much is the salesperson's share if the salesperson both lists and sells the property?

   a. $2,625
   b. $6,125
   c. $8,750
   d. None of the above

3. It is the broker's office policy that salespeople keep 60 percent of the firm's share of any commission earned from any property they list. The salesperson listed a property that was later sold by a cooperating broker for $285,000. If the two brokers agree to split the 6.5 percent commission equally, what will the salesperson receive?

   a. $5,557.50
   b. $6,092.00
   c. $7,235.25
   d. $7,654.00

4. The commission on the sale of a house was $16,500, which was based on a 7.5 percent commission rate. What was the final selling price of the house?

   a. $127,000
   b. $145,000
   c. $199,000
   d. $220,000

5. The broker listed a home for $360,000 under a 90-day exclusive-right-to-sell listing agreement with a 6 percent commission. The next week, the broker began advertising the home in a local paper and showed the property to two prospective buyers. Later that week, the seller announced that he had decided to sell his home to a relative for $340,000. The seller is liable to the broker for

   a. $1,200.
   b. $20,400.
   c. $21,600.
   d. none of the above.

ACTIVITY: Listing Contracts

Label each of the following three diagrams to indicate the type of listing contract it represents.

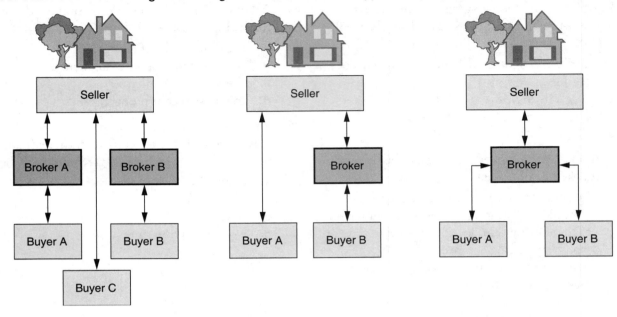

Seller retains any number of brokers; seller does not pay a commission to broker if seller finds the buyer.

1. _____

Broker is the exclusive agent of the buyer; seller does not pay a commission to broker if seller finds the buyer.

2. _____

One broker is the seller's only agent; seller pays broker a commission no matter who sells the property.

3. _____

ACTIVITY: Listing Worksheet

Complete the following practice listing worksheet using the floor plan of John and Martha Rambler's property (128 Winding Way). The scale is 1 inch = 12 feet (approximate dimensions are acceptable). The property is a 20-year-old, stuccoed, ranch-style house with terra cotta roof and no basement. Last year's taxes were $1,875. The original carpeting throughout is quite worn, but the tile baths are in excellent condition. Six years ago, a security system and TV cabling were installed. The kitchen was remodeled three years ago with new dishwasher, range, refrigerator, compactor, disposal, and vinyl floor covering.

Property Address: _____   Lot Size: _____

Owners: _____   Taxes: _____

Style _____ **Utilities:**   Softener _____ Sunroom _____

Sq. Ft. _____ Electric _____   Sewer _____ Pool _____

Bedrooms _____ Heat _____   **Exterior:**   Shed _____

Age _____ A/C _____   Roof _____ Fence _____

Stories _____ Humidifier _____   Siding _____ Landscaping _____

Basement _____ Air Filter _____   Deck _____ Other _____

Garage _____ Water _____   Patio _____ _____

Rooms	Level	Size	Floor Cover	Features	Comments
Living Room		x			
Dining Room		x			
Family Room		x			
Kitchen		x			
Rec. Room		x			
Master BR		x			
Bedroom 1		x			
Bedroom 2		x			
Bedroom 3		x			
Bath (full)		x			
Bath (¾)		x			
Bath (½)		x			
Other (Den)		x			
Utility Room		x			

John and Martha Rambler

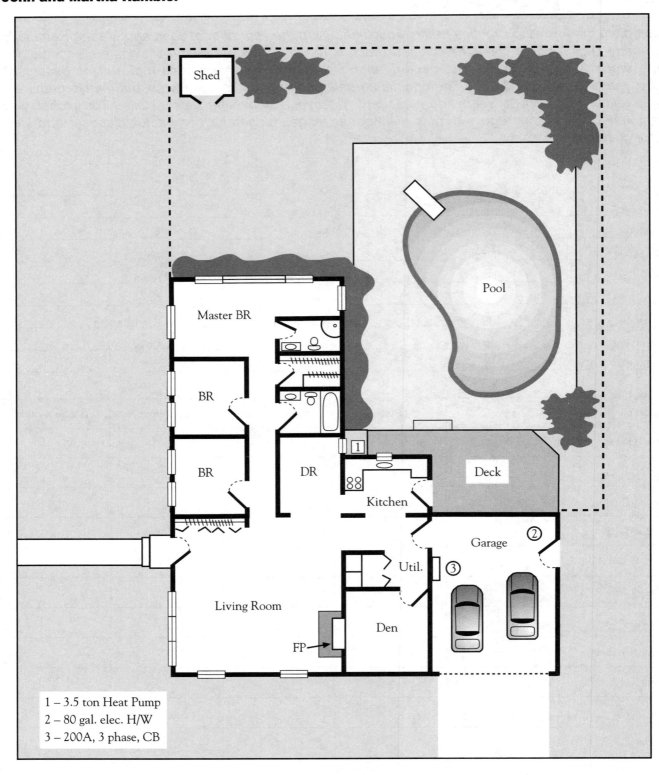

1 – 3.5 ton Heat Pump
2 – 80 gal. elec. H/W
3 – 200A, 3 phase, CB

ANSWER KEY

Matching

1. f **2.** e **3.** c **4.** j **5.** g **6.** h **7.** a **8.** i
9. d **10.** b

True or False

1. **False.** Under a typical *net listing,* the broker's commission is based on the amount by which the sales price exceeds the seller's required net. There is a potential for a conflict of interest between the broker's fiduciary responsibility to the seller and the broker's profit motive. A net listing is illegal in many states and discouraged in others. p. 90

2. **False.** A *listing agreement* is an employment contract, not a contract for the sale of real estate. p.88

3. **True.** A listing agreement is an employment contract between a broker and a seller; it is a contract for the real estate professional services of the broker, not for the transfer of real estate. p. 88

4. **False.** A listing agreement in which the seller retains the right to employ any number of brokers as agent is referred to as an *open listing.* p. 89

5. **True.** Under an exclusive-agency listing, the seller retains the right to sell the property without the obligation to pay the broker. p. 89

6. **False.** In buyer agency, as in any agency relationship, the party who does the hiring determines the relationship. The source of compensation is not the major factor that determines the relationship. p. 100

7. **True.** In an exclusive-right-to-sell listing, one broker is appointed as the seller's agent and is given the exclusive right to market the seller's property; the seller must pay the broker a commission if the property is sold during the term of the listing. p. 88

8. **False.** Because the broker's services are unique, a listing may not be assigned to another broker without the seller's written consent. p. 90

9. **False.** The broker must have the written consent of the seller to include the property in an MLS. p. 90

10. **True.** A broker protection clause provides that the property owner will pay the listing broker a commission if the owner transfers the property to someone the broker originally introduced to the owner, thus protecting the broker who was the procuring cause from losing a commission because the transaction was completed after the listing expired. p. 91

11. **True.** Most states require that the sellers disclose property conditions that could affect the buyer's decision to buy, including structural, mechanical, etc. p. 92

12. **True.** Courts generally discourage the use of automatic extension clauses in exclusive listings. Extension clauses are illegal in many states, and most listing contract forms specifically provide that there can be no automatic extensions of the agreement. p. 91

Multiple Choice

1. **a.** The buyer hires the agent in a buyer agency agreement; therefore, the buyer is the principal-client. p. 100

2. **d.** Under the open listing, the seller is permitted to sell the house and is not be obligated to pay a commission. p. 89

3. **c.** When obtaining the listing, the agent should gather as much information as possible, including the lot size, and property conditions. The listing should also include a termination clause. However, when taking the listing from the seller, the agent is not concerned about the seller's future housing needs. p. 91

4. **c.** Although some brokers delegate the responsibility for signing the listing agreement to the salesperson, this company has a policy of having the broker sign the listing, so it does not become effective until the broker signs it on January 18. p. 100

5. **d.** Although the broker can *subcontract* the work to salespeople, the listing agreement is an employment contract between the seller and the broker. p. 88

6. **b.** The seller and broker are parties to the listing agreement. Listings remain the property of the broker even if the salesperson leaves the company. p. 88

7. **d.** In an open listing, the seller retains the right to sell the property and may employ more than one broker to perform agency duties. p. 89

8. **a.** Sellers are often confused, thinking that the only way to find buyers from a number of brokers is to enter into an open listing. Explaining the advantages of the multiple-listing service can overcome the misconception. p. 88–89

9. **b.** Because a broker is free to offer the property at any price greater than the net amount, net listing can create a conflict of interest between the broker's fiduciary responsibility to the seller and the broker's profit motive. Thus, net listings are illegal in many states and discouraged in others. p. 90

10. **d.** Buyer agents are most likely compensated by sharing the commission by the seller, a flat fee, percentage of selling price, or an hourly rate. Although very uncommon, a few buyer's agents have been compensated by a percentage of the listing price when the buyers feel that this will encourage the buyer's agent to negotiate an even lower sale price. p. 100

11. **c.** Because an offer to purchase may not be accepted, it would not terminate the listing agreement. p. 91

12. **d.** Because the listing agreement is a contract for the personal services of the original broker, the sellers have the right to cancel their listing agreement and not go to the new broker. p. 91

13. **a.** Under an exclusive-right-to-sell and exclusive-agency listing, one broker is appointed as the seller's sole agent. Open and option listings do not specifically exclude other brokers from acting as the seller's agent. p. 88

14. **c.** If the broker breaches the listing contract or cancels it without cause, the broker may be liable for damages; however, it is not usually grounds for suspension or revocation of the license. Courts discourage the use of automatic extension clauses, and these clauses are even illegal in some states. p. 91

15. **c.** Information needed for the listing agreement includes lot size, possibility of seller financing, and the property taxes. The age of the seller is not needed. p. 92

16. **c.** Firewood is not attached to the real property and is therefore considered personal property. All the other items, even the door key, are normally considered to be part of the real property. p. 92

Math Practice

1. **d.** The seller paid the brokerage none of the above: The sales price is $429,350 \times 4\% + \$1,000 = \$18,174$ (none of the above).

2. **b.** The salesperson's share is $6,125: $\$175,000 \times 5\% \times 70\% = \$6,125$.

3. **a.** The salesperson receives $5,557.50: $\$285,000 \times 6.5\% \times 50\% \times 60\% = \$5,557.50$.

4. **d.** The selling price was $220,000: $\$16,500 \div 7.5\% = \$220,000$

5. **b.** The seller is liable to the broker for $20,400: $\$340,000 \times 6\% = \$20,400$. Because the seller had signed an exclusive-right-to-sell listing agreement, the seller is responsible for paying a commission regardless of who finds the buyer.

Activity: Listing Contracts

1. open listing

2. exclusive-agency listing

3. exclusive-right-to-sell listing

Activity: Listing Worksheet

The following answers were derived from the floor plan and information included in the narrative. The room dimensions are approximate and were determined by measuring the floor plan with a digital tape measure. Keep in mind that garages are not considered living space; thus, they are not included in the house square footage. The lot size was measured as 96' × 79' (7,584 sq. ft.) and converted to acres (7,584 ÷ 43,560 = 0.174 acres). The electrical and heating system specifications presume some familiarity with these technical aspects of the floor plan.

Property Address: _____128 Winding Way_____   Lot Size: _____7,584 sq. feet (approximate) or .17 acre_____

Owners: _____John and Martha Rambler_____   Taxes: _____$1,875_____

Style _____Ranch_____   **Utilities:**   Softener ____??____   Sunroom ____none____

Sq. Ft. _____1,356 ±_____   Electric __200 amp. 3 phase cir brkr__   Sewer ____??____   Pool ____yes____

Bedrooms ____3____   Heat ____3.5 ton heat pump____   **Exterior:**   Shed ____yes____

Age ____20____   A/C ____3.5 ton heat pump____   Roof ____terra cotta____   Fence ____yes____

Stories ____1____   Humidifier ____??____   Siding ____stucco____   Landscaping ____yes____

Basement ____none____   Air Filter ____??____   Deck __yes—11 × 16 + 3 × 8__   Other _____

Garage ____2-car attached____   Water ____80 gal. elec. h/w____   Patio ____yes—around pool____   _____

Rooms	Level	Size	Floor Cover	Features	Comments
Living Room	1	20 x 21	carpet	fireplace, closet	carpet worn
Dining Room	1	8 x 10	carpet		
Family Room	–	–	–		
Kitchen	1	7 x10	vinyl	modernized 2002	
Rec. Room	–	–	–		
Master BR	1	10 x 21	carpet	walk-in closet	
Bedroom 1	1	9 x 10	carpet		
Bedroom 2	1	9 x 10	carpet		
Bedroom 3	–	–	–		
Bath (full)	1	6 x 8	tile		
Bath (¾)	1	4 x 8	tile		
Bath (½)	1	–	–		
Other (Den)	1	11 x 10	carpet		
Utility Room	1	4 x 10	??	has washer & dryer	

CHAPTER 7

Interests in Real Estate

■ **identify** the kinds of limitations on ownership rights that are imposed by government action and the form of conveyance of property;

■ **describe** the various estates in land and the rights and limitations they convey;

■ **explain** concepts related to encumbrances and water rights;

■ **distinguish** the various types of governmental powers and how they are exercised; and

■ **define** the following *key terms:*

appurtenant easement	escheat	license
avulsion	estate in land	lien
condemnation	fee simple	life estate
deed restrictions	fee simple absolute	littoral rights
easement	fee simple defeasible	police power
easement by necessity	fee simple determinable	prior appropriation
easement by prescription	fee simple subject to a	pur autre vie
easement in gross	condition subsequent	remainder interest
eminent domain	freehold estate	reversionary interest
encroachment	future interest	riparian rights
encumbrance	homestead	taxation
	legal life estate	

MATCHING A   *Write the letter of the matching term on the appropriate line.*

a. condemnation

b. defeasible fee

c. eminent domain

d. escheat

e. estate in land

f. fee simple absolute

g. freehold estates

h. leasehold estates

i. police power

j. taxation

1. ___   A state's ability to enact legislation to preserve order, protect the public health and safety, and promote the general welfare

2. ___   The right of a government to acquire privately owned real estate for public use

3. ___   The process by which the government exercises its right of eminent domain

4. ___   A charge imposed on real estate to raise funding for government services

5. ___   The automatic transfer of real property to the state when the owner dies without heirs or a will

6. ___   The degree, quantity, nature, and extent of an owner's interest in real property

7. ___   A class of estates in land that lasts for an indeterminable period of time

8. ___   A class of estates in land for which the length of time can be determined

9. ___   The highest interest in real estate recognized by law

10. ___   An estate qualified by some action or activity that must or must not be performed

MATCHING B   *Write the letter of the matching term on the appropriate line.*

a. deed restriction

b. prior appropriation

c. encroachment

d. encumbrance

e. homestead

f. easement

g. life estate
    pur autre vie

h. lien

i. right of re-entry

j. remainderman

1. ___   The owner's right to retake possession of property through legal action if a limiting condition is broken

2. ___   An estate based on the lifetime of a person other than the life tenant

3. ___   The person to whom property passes when a life estate ends

4. ___   A legal life estate in which an individual's primary residence is protected, in whole or in part, against certain creditors

5. ___   Any claim, charge, or liability that attaches to real estate

6. ___   A charge against property that provides security for a debt or obligation of the property owner

7. ___   A private agreement that affects the use of land

8. ___   The right to use another's land for a particular purpose

9. ___   All or part of a structure that extends beyond the land of its owner or beyond legal building lines

10. ___   The doctrine that the right to use any water, with the exception of limited domestic uses, is held and controlled by the state

TRUE OR FALSE   *Circle the correct answer.*

1. T F A state's power to enact legislation that preserves order, protects the public health and safety, and promotes the general welfare is referred to as its *police power*.

2. T F The four governmental powers that affect real estate are taxation, eminent domain, escheat, and police.

3. T F The process by which the government exercises its right to acquire privately owned real estate for public use through either judicial or administrative proceedings is called *condemnation*.

4. T F The purpose of *escheat* is to expand governmental property holdings.

5. T F A *freehold estate* is the highest interest in real estate recognized by law.

6. T F *Riparian rights* are common-law rights granted to owners of land that lie along the course of a river, stream, or similar body of water.

7. T F If the grantor is silent about what happens to property after a life estate ends, the grantor has a *remainder interest* in the property.

8. T F A *homestead* is a legal life estate in real estate occupied as a family home.

9. T F An appurtenant easement is said to run with the land and this benefit transfers with the deed of the servient tenement.

10. T F An easement that arises when an owner sells property that has no access to a street or public way except across the seller's remaining land is an *easement by prescription*.

11. T F The concept of *tacking* provides that successive periods of discontinuous occupation by a different party may be combined to reach the required total number of years necessary to establish a class for an easement in gross.

12. T F A license may be terminated or canceled by the person who granted it, and a license ends on the death of either party or the sale of the affected property by the licensor.

13. T F Dower and curtesy are types of legal life estates.

14. T F Littoral rights allow owners of land bordering an ocean to own the land adjacent to the water up to the average low-water mark.

15. T F To secure water rights in a state in which the doctrine of prior appropriation is in effect, landowners must demonstrate that they plan a beneficial use for the water.

MULTIPLE CHOICE   *Circle the correct answer.*

1. An elderly man left the family home to his second wife with the provision that when she dies, the home goes to a son by his first wife. The second wife owns a bundle of rights; however, she does not own the right to
   a. will the property.
   b. sell the property.
   c. lease the property.
   d. decorate the property.

2. Every workday for the past 20 years, a woman has parked her car in a specific place in the nearby parking garage. Today, she receives a notice that the garage will be replaced by an office building. Can they do this to her after all the years she parked there?
   a. No, because she has been parking there for more than 20 years; she has an easement by prescription.
   b. No, because she paid regularly and on time.
   c. Yes, because she only had a license.
   d. Yes, because she has nothing in writing.

3. A man conveyed a one-acre parcel of land to a preschool. In the deed, the man stated that the property was to be used only as a playground; the man reserved a right of re-entry. What kind of estate has the man granted?
   a. Leasehold
   b. Fee simple subject to a condition subsequent
   c. Fee simple absolute
   d. Curtesy

4. A man owns a farm that lies along the edge of a river, which is too shallow to be navigable. If the man does not live in a jurisdiction that recognizes the doctrine of prior appropriation, how much (if any) of the river does he own?
   a. The man owns the land to the edge of the river; the land under the river is owned by the state.
   b. The man owns the land to the mean high water mark, and a right to apply for a water use permit.
   c. The man owns the land up to the water's edge and the right to use the water.
   d. The man owns the land under the river to the exact center of the waterway, and the right to use the water.

5. Over the past 15 years, a river has been slowly depositing soil along its eastern bank. As a result, the river is some 12 feet narrower than it used to be, and a parcel of property on the east side of the river is now 12 feet larger than it used to be. This scenario is an example of which of the following processes?
   a. Reliction
   b. Erosion
   c. Alluvion
   d. Accretion

6. If the government acquires privately owned real estate through a condemnation suit, it is exercising its power of
   a. escheat.
   b. reverter.
   c. eminent domain.
   d. defeasance.

7. A man owned two acres of land. He sold one acre to a woman and reserved an easement appurtenant for entrance and exit over her acre to reach the public road. The woman's land is
   a. capable of being cleared of the easement if the woman sells to a third party.
   b. called the servient tenement.
   c. called the dominant tenement.
   d. subject to an easement in gross.

8. A man owns a large undeveloped parcel of land on the side of a hill. The property borders a road on the lower edge. The owner sells the lower portion of the property to a woman, and she builds a home on it. Several years later, the owner sells the upper-portion of the property to another man. This man's property does not border any road. For this man to gain access to the road, he must claim by implication of law an easement
   a. by necessity.
   b. in gross.
   c. by prescription.
   d. by restriction.

9. If the dominant estate merges with the servient estate, which of the following is *TRUE*?
   a. The easement remains in effect for the entire parcel.
   b. The easement is suspended but cannot be terminated.
   c. The easement is terminated.
   d. The new owner must bring a suit seeking severance of the easement from the combined properties.

MULTIPLE CHOICE *(Continued)*

10. The homestead exemption in a town is $15,000. Four years ago, a man purchased a home for $58,000 and then experienced hard times. At a court-ordered sale, the man's property is purchased for $60,000. If the man has an outstanding mortgage balance of $35,000 and credit card debts amounting to $24,360, how much is protected by the homestead exemption?
    a. $640
    b. $2,140
    c. $15,000
    d. $16,500

11. In some states, a husband cannot sell his property unless his wife also signs the deed. His wife's interest is called
    a. personal property rights.
    b. homestead rights.
    c. curtesy rights.
    d. dower rights.

12. The state's authority to enact legislation to protect the public is passed through to municipalities and counties through
    a. police power.
    b. enabling acts.
    c. licensing laws.
    d. processing papers.

13. The state requires enough land to build a four-lane highway. For the state to acquire the needed land, the state must do all of the following *EXCEPT*
    a. demonstrate that this is for the public good.
    b. pay a fair and just compensation to the owner.
    c. allow the property owner the right to appeal any decision.
    d. reimburse the property owner for the amount that the property owner paid for the land.

14. A woman died in a nursing home. She had outlived all of her heirs and had not written a will. What happens to her $250,000 estate?
    a. It escheats to the state or county.
    b. The nursing home gets to keep it.
    c. It will be split between the nursing home and the county.
    d. It can be paid over to her church.

15. Which of the following is defined as a claim, charge, or liability that attaches to real estate?
    a. Lien
    b. Easement
    c. Deed restriction
    d. Encumbrance

16. Which of the following must exist for an appurtenant easement to exist?
    a. Two adjacent parcels, different owners
    b. Two adjacent parcels, one owner
    c. Landlocked property that requires passage to the street
    d. Long-time unauthorized usage

17. What are deed restrictions?
    a. Public land restrictions
    b. Illegal land restrictions
    c. Private agreements affecting the use of the land
    d. Informal agreements between neighbors

18. The electric company has the right to extend its wires over 50 parcels of land. What right does the electric company have?
    a. Appurtenant easement
    b. Easement by necessity
    c. Easement by prescription
    d. Easement in gross

19. For as long as anyone can remember, neighbor families have used a foot path to get to the river. Recently, the current owner erected a fence across the path. Which of the following easements might the neighbors claim, which would require him to remove the fence?
    a. Easement by necessity
    b. Easement by prescription
    c. Easement in gross
    d. Appurtenant easement

20. The rights of property owners of land next to large bodies of water, such as the ocean or the Great Lakes, are called
    a. riparian rights.
    b. littoral rights.
    c. prior appropriation.
    d. reversionary rights.

FILL-IN-THE-BLANK   *Select the word or words that best complete the following statements:*

accretion

appurtenant

avulsion

by necessity

by prescription

conventional life estate

freehold estate

future interest

in gross

legal life estate

public use

special limitation

reversionary interest

1. Due to a court decision in 2005, many states are drafting legislation to establish a narrow meaning to the term _____ in eminent domain proceedings to stop condemnations justified solely for economic reasons.

2. A type of life estate established by state law rather than voluntarily by an owner is a(n) _____.

3. A fee simple determinable is qualified by a(n) _____ that ends the estate automatically on the current owner's failure to comply with this element.

4. A life estate is a type of _____ that is limited in duration to the life of the owner or some other specified person or persons.

5. In a fee simple subject to a condition subsequent estate, the right of re-entry may never take effect. Therefore, this right is considered to be a(n) _____.

6. A railroad right of way is an example of an easement _____.

7. If the creator of a life estate does not name a remainderman, the original owner retains a(an) _____ upon the end of the life estate.

8. When a mudslide into the ocean removes several feet of land from a man's property, the process is called _____.

9. When a claimant has used another person's land for a certain period of time and in a manner defined by state law, the claimant can claim an easement _____.

10. When two properties share a party wall that straddles the boundary line between the two lots, each lot owner owns the half of the wall on each lot and has a(n) _____ easement in the other half of the wall.

ACTIVITY: Compound Interests in Spindley Acres

Based on the narrative below, enter the name of each player in the Spindley Acres scenario into the appropriate box. Also label his or her interest in the estate and how it is conveyed from one to another.

Ben conveys a life estate in Spindley Acres to Carol, with a remainder to Bob, "so long as Spindley Acres continues to be a working farm." If it ceases to be a farm, the property will go back to Ben (or his estate).

Meanwhile, Carol conveys a life estate in Spindley Acres to Sally "for as long as my Cousin Tom shall live." When Tome dies, the estate will return to Carol for the remainder of her life.

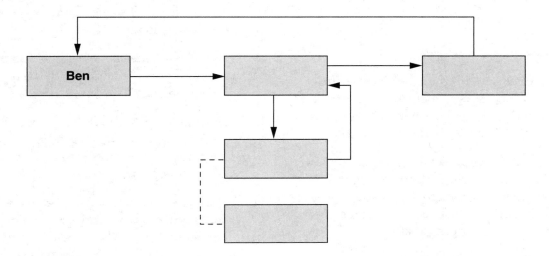

ANSWER KEY

Matching A

1. i   **2.** c   **3.** a   **4.** j   **5.** d   **6.** e   **7.** g   **8.** h
9. f   **10.** b

Matching B

1. i   **2.** g   **3.** j   **4.** e   **5.** d   **6.** h   **7.** a   **8.** f
9. c   **10.** b

True or False

1. **True.** Police power is the state's right to enact legislation to preserve order, protect the public health, and promote the general welfare of its citizens. p. 100

2. **True.** Government powers include police power (building codes), eminent domain (right to acquire private property for public use), taxation (raise funds to meet public needs), and escheat (acquires private property that has become ownerless). p. 100–112

3. **True.** Eminent domain is the right of the government to acquire privately owned real estate for pubic use; condemnation is the process by which the government exercises this right. p. 100

4. **False.** Escheat is a process by which the state acquires privately owned property when it has become ownerless. For example, when an owner dies and leaves no heirs and there is no will. p. 112

5. **False.** A freehold estate lasts for an indeterminable length of time; a *fee simple absolute estate* is the highest interest in real estate recognized by law. p. 112

6. **True.** *Riparian rights* are common-law rights granted to owners of land that lie along the course of a river, stream, or similar body of water. State law governs such rights, but generally, they include the unrestricted right to use the water. p. 119

7. **False.** When the creator of a life estate choose not to name a remainderman, ownership is said to revert to the original owner upon the end of the life estate. p. 114

8. **True.** A legal life estate is a form of life estate established by state law and becomes effective automatically when certain events occur. Homestead is a legal life estate in real estate occupied as the family home. p. 114–115

9. **False.** An *appurtenant easement* is said to run with the land and transfers with the deed of the *dominant* tenement. p. 116

10. **False.** An easement that arises when an owner sells property that has no access to a street or public way except across the seller's remaining land is an *easement by necessity*. p. 118

11. **False.** The concept of *tacking* provides that successive periods of continuous occupation by different parties may be combined to reach the required total number of years necessary to establish a claim for an *easement by prescription*. p. 118

12. **True.** A license is a personal privilege to enter the land of another for a specific purpose; it can be terminated or canceled and ends with the death of either party or with the sale of the land. p. 119

13. **True.** A legal life estate is a form of life estate established by state law and becomes effective automatically when certain events occur. Dower and curtesy provide that the nonowning spouse has a lifetime right to an interest in the real estate, even if the owning spouse wills the estate to others. p. 114

14. **False.** Littoral rights allow owners of land bordering an ocean to own the land adjacent to the water up to the average *high-water mark*. p. 119–120.

15. **True.** Under the doctrine of prior appropriation, the right to use any water, with the exception of limited domestic use, is controlled by the state rather than by the landowner adjacent to the water. To secure water rights, then, the landowner must demonstrate to a state agency that the owner's plans are for beneficial use, such as crop irrigation. p. 120–121

Multiple Choice

1. **a.** The second wife owns a life estate, and she has the entire bundle of rights, except the right to will the property. p. 114

2. **c.** A license is a personal right to enter the property for a specific purpose. There is no *build-up* of rights. p. 119

3. **b.** The man has granted a fee simple subject to a condition subsequent. If, at some point in the future, the land is not used as a playground, the man or his heirs may exercise the right of re-entry by retaking physical possession of the land. p. 113

4. **d.** Unless otherwise stipulated by state rules or a deed, the owner of property along a river has the right to use the water and owns the land under the water to the center of the stream. p. 119

5. **d.** Accretion is the increase in the land resulting from the deposit of soil by the water action. The new deposits may be referred to as alluvion. Reliction is the resulting land when water dries up, and erosion is the slow washing away of land by natural forces. p. 120

6. **c.** The right of the state to acquire private property for public use is *eminent domain*. The court action is called *condemnation*. Property *escheats* back to the state when it becomes ownerless; that is, the owner dies leaving no heirs and no will. p. 100–111

7. **b.** The man's parcel is the dominant tenement and benefits from the easement. The easement runs over the woman's property, the servient tenement. p. 116–117

8. **a.** An *easement by necessity* could be created by court order to permit legal access to the second man's property. p. 116

9. **c.** *Merger,* that is, one owner with two lots, terminates the easement. p. 118

10. **c.** The homestead exemption is $15,000. So, when the property is sold for $60,000, the mortgage of $35,000 is paid, and $15,000 is reserved, leaving $10,000 for the credit card debt. p. 115

11. **d.** A wife's interest in her deceased husband's property is *dower*; a husband's interest is *curtesy*; protection for some part of the family home is referred to as *homestead rights*. p. 114

12. **b.** The state passes police power to local counties and municipalities through enabling acts. Licensing laws are an example of police power. p. 100

13. **d.** To acquire private property through eminent domain, the state must prove that the purchase is for public good, pay a fair price, and allow the property owner full rights to appeal. The price may or may not reflect what the owner had actually paid for the property. p. 100–111

14. **a.** Because the woman died without a will and there are no heirs, essentially, the $250,000 is ownerless. It reverts to the state or county. p. 112

15. **d.** An encumbrance is a claim, charge, or liability that attaches to real estate, such as liens, easements, and deed restrictions. p. 115

16. **a.** An easement appurtenant must have two owners and two parcels of land. A landlocked parcel would require an easement by necessity; long-time unauthorized usage would lead to an easement by prescription. p. 116

17. **c.** *Deed restrictions* are private agreements written into the deed and are privately enforced. Examples of public restrictions include zoning and building codes. p. 116

18. **d.** Commercial easements such as this are called easements in gross. There are only servient tenements, no dominant tenement. p. 117

19. **b.** Long-time unauthorized usage may create legal rights leading to an easement by prescription. An easement in gross is a personal right, often used by utility companies. An easement by necessity could be imposed by court order to provide access to a landlocked property. p. 117–118

20. **b.** Property owners along large bodies of water have littoral rights; riparian rights are those found along rivers and streams. The doctrine of prior appropriation refers to the state controlling the right to water from the river, rather than the adjacent property owner. p. 119

Fill-in-the-Blank

1. Due to a court decision in 2005, many states are drafting legislation to establish a narrow meaning to the term *public use* in eminent domain proceedings to stop condemnations justified solely for economic reasons.

2. A type of life estate established by state law rather than voluntarily by an owner is a *legal life estate*.

3. A fee simple determinable is qualified by a *special limitation* that ends the estate automatically on the current owner's failure to comply with this element.

4. A life estate is a type of *freehold estate* that is limited in duration to the life of the owner or some other specified person or persons.

5. The right of re-entry may never take effect. Therefore, this right is considered to be a *future interest*.

6. A railroad right of way is an example of an *easement in gross*.

7. If the creator of a life estate does not name a remainderman, the original owner retains a *reversionary interest* upon the end of the life estate.

8. When a mudslide into the ocean removes several feet of land from a man's property, the process is called *avulsion*.

9. When a claimant has used another person's land for a certain period of time defined by state law, the claimant can claim an easement *by prescription*.

10. When two properties share a party wall that straddles the boundary line between the two lots, each lot owner owns the half of the wall on each lot and has an *appurtenant* easement in the other half of the wall.

Activity: Compound Interests in Spindley Acres

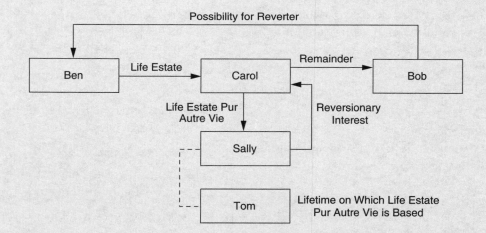

CHAPTER 8

Forms of Real Estate Ownership

■ **LEARNING OBJECTIVES** *Before you answer these questions, you should be able to*

■ **identify** the four basic forms of co-ownership;

■ **describe** the ways in which various business organizations may own property;

■ **explain** how a tenancy in common, joint tenancy, and tenancy by the entirety are created and how they may be terminated;

■ **distinguish** cooperative ownership from condominium ownership; and

■ **define** the following *key terms*:

common elements	limited liability company	severalty
community property	(LLC)	tenancy by the entirety
condominium	limited partnership	tenancy in common
cooperative	partition	time-share
co-ownership	partnership	town house
corporation	PITT	trust
general partnership	right of survivorship	
joint tenancy	separate property	

MATCHING A   *Write the letter of the matching term on the appropriate line.*

a. *tenancy in common*

b. *joint tenancy*

c. *partition*

d. *partnership*

e. *proprietary lease*

f. *severalty*

g. *tenancy by the entirety*

h. *board of directors*

i. *trust*

j. *testamentary trust*

1. ___ The ownership of real estate by one individual

2. ___ A form of property ownership in which owners hold undivided fractional interests that are inheritable by their heirs

3. ___ A form of ownership in which multiple owners hold property with a right of survivorship

4. ___ A legal method for dissolving a co-ownership

5. ___ A special form of co-ownership for married couples

6. ___ A device by which one person transfers ownership of property to someone else to hold or manage for the benefit of a third party

7. ___ A form of trust established by will after the owner's death

8. ___ An association of two or more persons who carry on a business for profit as co-owners

9. ___ The evidence of the right to occupy a unit in a cooperative

10. ___ The governing body of a cooperative

MATCHING B   *Write the letter of the matching term on the appropriate line.*

a. *assessments*

b. *condo fee*

c. *condominium*

d. *corporation*

e. *general partnership*

f. *right of survivorship*

g. *limited liability company*

h. *separate property*

i. *time-share estate*

j. *time-share use*

1. ___ A business organization in which all members participate in the operation and management of the business and share full liability for business losses and obligations

2. ___ A business organization that is a legal entity managed and operated by a board of directors

3. ___ On the death of a joint tenant, the deceased's interest transfers directly to the remaining joint tenants

4. ___ A business organization that combines the tax advantages of limited partnerships and the limited liability of corporations

5. ___ In a community property state, real or personal property that was owned solely by either spouse prior to marriage, or acquired by inheritance or gift during the marriage

6. ___ A form of property ownership in which each owner holds an undivided interest in certain common elements in addition to holding individual property in fee simple

7. ___ Special payments required of condominium unit owners to address specific expenses

8. ___ Recurring fees required of condominium unit owners to cover basic maintenance and operations

MATCHING B   *(Continued)*

9. ___ A fee simple interest in a property that entitles the owner to use the facility for a certain period of time

10. ___ A contract right under which a developer retains ownership of property and the purchaser receives the right to occupy and use the facilities for a certain period

TRUE OR FALSE   *Circle the correct answer.*

1. T F The three basic ways in which a fee simple estate may be held are in severalty, in co-ownership, and in trust.

2. T F The term *severalty* means that there is only one owner of a single property.

3. T F In a tenancy in common, property is owned by two or more owners with the right of survivorship.

4. T F The ownership of an undivided fractional interest in a property is characteristic of a tenancy in common.

5. T F When all of the other owners' interests in a joint tenancy have passed to the one surviving owner, that owner then holds title in entirety.

6. T F When title to a single parcel of real estate is held by two or more individuals, the parties may be referred to as *concurrent owners.*

7. T F The four unities characteristic of a tenancy in common are possession, interest, title, and time.

8. T F When a joint tenant conveys interest in the jointly held property to a new owner, the new owner becomes a joint tenant.

9. T F Co-tenants may terminate their co-ownership by asking a court to partition the property.

10. T F In a tenancy by the entirety, neither spouse can convey a half-interest to a third party, and neither spouse may take court action to partition or divide the property.

11. T F In a *community property* state, community property includes all property, both real and personal, acquired by either party prior to or during the marriage.

12. T F The person who creates a trust is referred to as the *trustor.*

13. T F In a general partnership, the death of one of the partners does not affect the organization's continuity.

14. T F Condominium owners hold their own units in fee simple and the common elements under proprietary leases.

15. T F The management and operation of a cooperative are determined by the bylaws of the corporation that owns the property.

16. T F Ownership of a cooperative interest is personal property.

17. T F A time-share estate includes the right to use the property for a certain specified period of time.

18. T F An owner can transfer or sell a condominium unit to anyone, unless the condominium association provides for a right of first refusal.

19. T F A major advantage of living trusts is that they reduce the time and costs of probate.

20. T F A real estate investment trust is a type of housing connected by common walls.

MULTIPLE CHOICE   *Circle the correct answer.*

1. Which of the following cannot take title as a joint tenant with right of survivorship?

   a. Wife and husband
   b. Two female business partners
   c. Two brothers in partnership
   d. A corporation

2. When two or more individuals decide to buy a property together, it results in a

   a. cooperation.
   b. co-ownership.
   c. community effort.
   d. joint venture.

3. Three brothers bought a farm together, and the deed listed only each of their names. What form of ownership are they presumed to have taken?

   a. Tenancy by the entireties
   b. Joint tenancy with right of survivorship
   c. Tenancy in common
   d. In severalty

4. What form of ownership is employed when one person transfers ownership to someone else to hold and manage for a third person?

   a. Joint venture
   b. Joint tenancy
   c. Trust
   d. Severalty

5. A man with two sons and a woman with two daughters are getting married, and they are buying a house together. They ask the real estate licensee for advice about how to take title. What advice should the licensee offer?

   a. Tenants in common, so that each one-half in interest would go to the appropriate children
   b. Joint tenancy to protect, so that if one dies, the other gets the house
   c. Suggest that they consult with the employing broker
   d. Suggest that they consult with an attorney

6. A will provided that the local banker take care of the deceased person's estate until the children reach age 25. What kind of trust is this?

   a. Testamentary trust
   b. Living trust
   c. Land trust
   d. Trust deed

7. What kind of ownership do the horizontal property acts regulate?

   a. Cooperatives
   b. Condominiums
   c. Time-sharing
   d. Planned unit development

8. Shareholders in a cooperative receive shares of stock that entitle them to a

   a. common element lease.
   b. trust deed.
   c. proprietary lease.
   d. corporate deed.

9. Membership camping is similar to

   a. cooperative ownership.
   b. condominium ownership.
   c. planned use development.
   d. time-share use.

10. In a large highrise condominium, each unit is owned by individual owners. The elevators, parking garage, and swimming pool are referred to as

    a. community property.
    b. separate property.
    c. common elements.
    d. proprietary elements.

11. Two women own an apartment building together as joint tenants. They share equally in the expenses and profits. One day, one of the women decides to end the relationship. If she sells her interest to a man by signing and delivering a deed, which of the following statements is *TRUE*?

    a. The man will become a joint tenant with the remaining woman.
    b. The man and the remaining woman will be tenants in common.
    c. The man will be a tenant in common with the remaining woman and a joint tenant with the leaving woman.
    d. The conveyance will be invalid; the two women will remain joint tenants.

MULTIPLE CHOICE   *(Continued)*

12. In February, a seller conveyed an undivided one-half interest in a parcel of land to a woman. In March, the seller conveyed the remaining one-half interest to a man. The deed to the man included the following statement: "This man is to be a joint tenant with the woman." Both deeds were recorded. Based on these facts, which of the following statements is *TRUE*?

    a. The man and woman hold title to the land as joint tenants under the terms of the two conveyances from the seller.
    b. The man and woman own the land by partition.
    c. The man and woman are tenants in common.
    d. The man owns the land as a joint tenant; the woman owns the land as a tenant in common.

13. Three people own a large parcel of undeveloped land in joint tenancy. One of them wants to build a shopping center on the property, while the other two want to use it as an organic farm. The individual tries to buy the other tenants' interests, but they refuse to sell. Which of the following is her *BEST* option?

    a. File a suit for partition
    b. Begin building a shopping center on one-third of the property
    c. Wait for the other two to die
    d. File a suit to quiet title

14. A man owns and lives year-round in a cottage in a lakefront community. His ownership of the cottage is in fee simple. He also owns an undivided percentage interest in a parking lot, a golf course, and a swimming pool, all located in the development. Based on these facts alone, the man's ownership is probably *BEST* described as a

    a. time-share estate.
    b. time-share use.
    c. condominium.
    d. cooperative.

15. Mike, Rebecca, and Noah agree to purchase and operate a property as a permanent investment. Mike and Rebecca each contribute $50,000. Noah contributes $30,000 and agrees to run the day-to-day operations of the business, which they call "Property Group Partners." Neither Mike nor Rebecca has any right to participate in the operation of the venture. Based on these facts, what type of business organization has Mike, Rebecca, and Noah established?

    a. Joint venture
    b. Limited partnership
    c. General partnership
    d. Limited liability company

16. Based on the facts in the previous question, if the property collapses, resulting in injury and property damage worth $275,000, what will be Mike's liability?

    a. None   c. $91,667
    b. $50,000   d. $100,000

17. All of the following are unities required for a joint tenancy *EXCEPT*

    a. unity of title.   c. unity of time.
    b. unity of ownership.   d. unity of possession.

18. All of the following are characteristics of a tenancy by the entirety *EXCEPT*

    a. title may be conveyed only by a deed signed by both parties.
    b. the surviving spouse automatically becomes sole owner of the property upon the death of the other spouse.
    c. each spouse owns an equal, undivided interest in the property as a single, indivisible unit.
    d. the surviving spouse automatically owns one-half of the property acquired during the marriage.

MULTIPLE CHOICE   *(Continued)*

19. A man creates a trust to pay for a broker's real estate education. The trust is operated by a woman, who makes payments on behalf of the broker directly to the real estate school. Based on these facts, which of the following statements *BEST* characterizes the relationships among these parties?

    a. The woman is the trustor, the broker is the beneficiary, and the man is the trustee.
    b. The man is the trustor, the real estate school is the beneficiary, and the woman is the trustee.
    c. The man is the trustor, the broker is the beneficiary, and the woman is the trustee.
    d. The man is the trustor, the broker is the beneficiary, the woman is the trustee, and the real estate school is the fiduciary.

20. A company is a legal entity, created by charter under the laws of the state. The company is managed and operated by a board and is permitted to buy and sell real estate. When one of its directors dies, the company continues to operate. Because of its structure, the company's income is subject to double taxation. The company is *BEST* described as a

    a. partnership.
    b. condominium trust.
    c. corporation.
    d. limited liability company.

21. When a corporation takes complete ownership of a property, it is considered to be ownership in

    a. joint tenancy.
    b. tenancy in common.
    c. partnership.
    d. severalty.

22. In a tenancy in common, if the fractions of ownership are *NOT* stated in the deed, how are they determined?

    a. The tenants need a judicial decision to determine the fractional shares.
    b. The tenants are presumed to hold equal shares.
    c. The tenants settle the issue through binding arbitration.
    d. The tenants must terminate the tenancy in common through partition.

23. In the case of land trusts, the beneficiary is usually also the

    a. trustor.   c. fiduciary.
    b. trustee.   d. attorney in fact.

ACTIVITY: Types of Ownership

Check the characteristics that apply to ownership for each type of property.

Condominium

☐ corporate ownership
☐ undivided interest in common elements
☐ occupancy and use for limited periods
☐ proprietary lease
☐ fee simple ownership of units

Cooperative

☐ corporate ownership
☐ undivided interest in common elements
☐ occupancy and use for limited periods
☐ proprietary lease
☐ fee simple ownership of units

Time-Share

☐ corporate ownership
☐ undivided interest in common elements
☐ occupancy and use for limited periods
☐ proprietary lease
☐ fee simple ownership of units

ANSWER KEY

Matching A

1. f   **2.** a   **3.** b   **4.** c   **5.** g   **6.** i   **7.** j   **8.** d
9. e   **10.** h

Matching B

1. e   **2.** d   **3.** f   **4.** g   **5.** h   **6.** c   **7.** a   **8.** b
9. i   **10.** j

True of False

1. **True.** Although the forms of ownership available are controlled by state laws, a fee simple estate may be held in three basic ways: in severalty, in co-ownership, and in trust. p. 126

2. **True.** Ownership in severalty occurs when property is owned by one individual or corporation. p. 126

3. **False.** In a *joint tenancy*, property is owned by two or more owners with the right of survivorship. p. 127

4. **True.** In a tenancy in common, each tenant holds an undivided fractional interest in the property; the co-owners have unity of possession, meaning that they are entitled to possession of the whole property. It is the ownership interest not the property that is divided. p. 126

5. **False.** A joint tenancy continues indefinitely, until there is only one remaining owner, who then holds title in *severalty*. p. 127

6. **True.** When title to one parcel of real estate is held by two or more individuals, those parties are called co-owners or concurrent owners. p. 126

7. **False.** The four unities characteristic of a *joint tenancy* are possession, interest, title, and time. p. 127

8. **False.** A joint tenant may freely convey interest in the jointly held property to a new owner; however, doing so will destroy the unities of time and title, and the new owner *cannot* become a joint tenant. p. 127–128

9. **True.** Partition is a legal way to dissolve the relationship when the parties do not voluntarily agree to its termination. p. 128

10. **True.** During their lives, under tenancy by the entirety, a husband and wife can convey title only by a deed signed by both parties. p. 129

11. **False.** In a community property state, *community property* includes all property, both real and personal, acquired by either party only during the marriage, except by gift or inheritance. p. 129–130

12. **True.** A trust is a device by which one person, called the trustor, transfers property to the trustee, who is entrusted to carry out the trustor's instruction regarding the trust. The party who benefits from the trust is called the beneficiary. p. 130

13. **False.** A general partnership must be dissolved and reorganized if one partner dies. p. 132

14. **False.** Condominium owners hold their own units in fee simple and the common elements as *tenants in common*. p. 133

15. **True.** The bylaws of the corporation that owns the property determine the management and operation of a cooperative. p. 135

16. **True.** When buying into a cooperative, the purchaser becomes a shareholder in the corporation by virtue of stock ownership and receives a proprietary lease to the apartment for the life of the corporation. p. 135

17. **True.** Time-share ownership permits multiple purchasers to buy interest in real estate; each purchaser receives the right to use the facilities for a certain period. p. 137

18. **True.** Under condominium ownership, each unit becomes a separate parcel of real estate that is owned in fee simple and may be transferred to whomever the owner chooses, unless the condominium association provides for a right of first refusal. p. 133

19. **True.** Living trusts have become a major estate planning tool used to minimize the time and costs of probate. p. 131

20. **False.** A *town house* is a type of housing connected by common walls and is usually located on a small lot. p. 136

Multiple Choice

1. **d.** Because a corporation continues indefinitely until terminated by legal action, a corporation may never take title as a joint tenant. It would never die. p. 127–128

2. **b.** When two or more people buy property together, it is called *co-ownership*. A *joint venture* is a form of partnership in which two or more people carry out a single business project with no intention of establishing an ongoing relationship. p. 128

3. **c.** The brothers are presumed to be tenants in common because they did not indicate as *joint tenants with right of survivorship*. Joint tenancy requires extra wording; it is sometimes called *the poor man's will*. Severalty ownership indicates one owner. p. 126–127

4. **c.** A trust is a device by which one person transfers ownership of property to someone else to hold or manage for the benefit of a third party. Severalty indicates one owner. Joint tenancy is a form of ownership whereby, as joint owners die, the surviving owners acquire the deceased tenant's interest. p. 130

5. **d.** Because the choice of ownership affects the ability to transfer the real estate, has tax implications, and decides rights to future claims, real estate licensees should tell their clients to discuss the issue with an attorney. Real estate licensees and their brokers are not permitted to give legal advice. p. 126

6. **a.** A testamentary trust is established by will after the trustor's death. A living trust is established during the trustor's lifetime. Real estate is the only asset in a land trust. Trust deed is another name for a deed of trust, which is a financing instrument. p. 131

7. **b.** Condominiums are regulated by the horizontal property acts enacted in most states. p. 133

8. **c.** The proprietary lease is part of the ownership of the cooperative stock and gives the owner the right to occupy a specific apartment. Common elements refer to the property owned jointly by condominium owners. p. 135

9. **d.** The owner of membership camping purchases the right to use the developer's facilities, which is similar to time-sharing; however, the owner may not be limited to a specific time as in the case of a typical time-share arrangement. p. 137

10. **c.** The property that condominium owners own together is referred to as common elements. Community property is a system of property ownership based on the theory that each spouse has an equal interest in property acquired during the marriage, making a distinction from property acquired before marriage, that is, separate property. p. 133

11. **b.** A co-owner can sell whatever the co-owner owns. However, once the unities of time, title, and interest are destroyed, as they are when the woman sells her interest to the man, there can no longer be a joint tenancy. p. 128

12. **c.** Because there are two deeds made at different times, the four unities of joint tenancy have not been met. Therefore, the man and woman are tenants in common. p. 127–128

13. **a.** When co-owners cannot come to an agreement, they must file for partition in court. The property will not physically be divided; rather, one or more will be given the opportunity to buy the others out. If this is not possible, then the property will be sold, and the money will be divided appropriately. p. 128–129

14. **c.** It appears that the man has condominium ownership, because he owns the cottage as well as the interest in the common elements. Cooperative ownership is ruled out, because he does not have a proprietary lease. It is not a time-share, because he clearly owns more than the right to use at specific times. p. 133, 135

15. **b.** A limited partnership limits the participation of the silent partners, as well as limiting their liability. A general partnership would require that all are equally involved in running the operation and all are exposed to liability. p. 132

16. **b.** The limited partners are limited in liability to the $50,000 amount of their original investment. p. 132

17. **b.** To create joint tenancy ownership, four unities are required: possession, interest, time, and title; not ownership. p. 127–128

18. **d.** Under tenancy by the entirety, title may be conveyed only by a deed signed by both parties, each spouse owns an equal, undivided interest in the property, and the surviving spouse automatically becomes the owner upon the death of the other. p. 129

19. **c.** The man is the owner-trustor, the broker is the beneficiary, and the woman is the person who manages the trust—that is, the trustee. p. 130

20. **c.** The corporation would not be affected if one of the directors dies. The particular tip-off to this answer is *double taxation*, which applies to corporations. p. 133

21. **d.** Corporations are artificial persons, and therefore, hold ownership in severalty. p. 126

22. **b.** The deed creating a tenancy in common may or may not state the fractional interest held by each co-owner; if no fractions are stated, the tenants are presumed to hold equal shares. p. 126

23. **a.** In the case of land trusts, the beneficiary is usually also the trustor. The beneficiary retains management and control of the real property and has the right of possession and the right to any income. p. 131

Activity: Types of Ownership

Condominium
- ✓ undivided interest in common elements
- ✓ fee simple ownership of units

Cooperative
- ✓ corporate ownership
- ✓ proprietary lease

Time-Share
- ✓ undivided interest in common elements
- ✓ occupancy and use for limited periods
- ✓ fee simple ownership of units

CHAPTER 9

Legal Descriptions

■ **LEARNING OBJECTIVES**   *Before you answer these questions, you should be able to*

- ■ **identify** the three methods used to describe real estate;
- ■ **describe** how a survey is prepared;
- ■ **explain** how to read a rectangular survey description;
- ■ **distinguish** the various units of land measurement; and
- ■ **define** the following *key terms*:

air lots	metes-and-bounds description	rectangular (government) survey system
base lines	monuments	sections
benchmarks	plat map	survey
datum	point of beginning (POB)	township lines
legal description	point of ending (POE)	townships
lot-and-block (recorded plat) system	principal meridians	township tiers
	ranges	

MATCHING   *Write the letter of the matching term on the appropriate line.*

a. metes-and-bounds

b. rectangular survey system

c. sections

d. monuments

e. lot-and-block

f. benchmarks

g. datum

h. POB

i. township lines

j. ranges

1. ___ The type of legal description that relies on a property's physical features to determine and to describe the boundaries and measurements of the parcel

2. ___ The designated starting point for a metes-and-bounds description

3. ___ Fixed objects used to identify significant points of measurement in a metes-and-bounds description

4. ___ A land description system based on principal meridians and base lines

5. ___ Lines running six miles apart and parallel to the base line

6. ___ Strips of land running parallel to the meridian

7. ___ Numbered squares of land within a township square

8. ___ A system of description that uses numbered areas referred to in a plat map

9. ___ A point, line, or surface from which elevations are measured

10. ___ Permanent reference markers, usually found on embossed brass markers set in concrete or asphalt

TRUE OR FALSE   *Circle the correct answer.*

1. T F The metes-and-bounds description was established by Congress in 1785.

2. T F In the metes-and-bounds system, a monument may be either a natural object or a human-made marker.

3. T F For a parcel described under the lot-and-block system, the lot refers to the numerical designation of any particular parcel.

4. T F Principal meridians run east and west.

5. T F Township lines and base lines are parallel.

6. T F Ranges are strips of land six miles wide that run parallel to the base line.

7. T F When the horizontal township lines and the vertical range lines intersect, they form township squares.

8. T F Every township contains 36 sections of 640 acres each.

9. T F A datum is a permanent reference point, which is usually found on an embossed brass marker set into a solid concrete or asphalt base.

10. T F Section 6 is always in the northeast, or upper-left corner.

11. T F Air lots are composed of the airspace within specific boundaries located over a parcel of land.

12. T F When preparing a plat map of a new condominium, the surveyor shows the elevations of floor and ceiling surfaces.

MULTIPLE CHOICE   *Circle the correct answer.*

1. All of the following systems are used to express a legal description *EXCEPT*
    a. lot-and-block.
    b. metes-and-bounds.
    c. rectangular survey.
    d. benchmarks.

2. Air lots, condominium descriptions, and other vertical measurements may be computed from the U.S. Geological Survey
    a. datum.
    b. benchmark.
    c. principal meridian.
    d. base line.

3. A man sells six acres of prime undeveloped property to a woman for $2.25 per square foot. How much did the woman pay?
    a. $466,560
    b. $588,060
    c. $612,360
    d. $733,860

4. Which township section number is directly north of Section 7?
    a. Section 1
    b. Section 6
    c. Section 5
    d. Section 8

5. Which of the following *MOST* accurately describes the dimensions of a quarter-section?
    a. 1/4 mile by 1/4mile
    b. 1/2 mile by 1/2 mile
    c. 1/2 mile by 1 mile
    d. 1/8 mile by 1/8 mile

6. A man is willing to pay $1,200 per acre. He is planning to buy the SE 1/4 of the SE 1/4 of the SE 1/4 of Section 11. How much will he pay for the land?
    a. $3,000
    b. $6,000
    c. $12,000
    d. $24,000

7. Years ago, a farm was typically a quarter section. How many acres is that?
    a. 20 acres
    b. 80 acres
    c. 160 acres
    d. 320 acres

8. How many acres are contained in a parcel described as follows: The NE 1/4 of the NW 1/4; the N 1/2 of the NW 1/4, NE 1/4, of Section 10?
    a. 40 acres
    b. 60 acres
    c. 70 acres
    d. 74 acres

9. The basic units of the rectangular survey system are the
    a. base lines.
    b. principal meridians.
    c. ranges.
    d. township squares.

10. Metes-and-bounds descriptions may be required in rectangular survey system descriptions in all of the following situations *EXCEPT*
    a. when a tract is too large to be described by quarter sections.
    b. when describing an irregular tract.
    c. when a tract is too small to be described by quarter-sections.
    d. when a tract does not follow the lot or block lines of a recorded subdivision or section.

11. What is the square footage for the following property described by the metes-and-bounds method?

    Beginning at a point on the southerly side of Smith Street, 200 feet easterly from the corner formed by the intersection of the southerly side of Smith Street and the easterly side of Johnson Street; then East 200 feet; then South 100 feet; then West 200 feet; then North 100 feet to the POB.
    a. 5,000 square feet
    b. 10,000 square feet
    c. 15,000 square feet
    d. 20,000 square feet

12. The end of a metes-and-bounds land description is always a
    a. monument.
    b. benchmark.
    c. point of beginning.
    d. base line.

13. The lot-and-block system starts with the preparation of a(n)
    a. subdivision plat.
    b. range map.
    c. survey.
    d. air lot.

MULTIPLE CHOICE   *(Continued)*

Refer to the example plat for Honeysuckle Hills Subdivision when answering Questions 14 through 20.

14. Which lot in Block A has the *MOST* frontage on Jasmine Lane?

    a. 1   c. 7
    b. 2   d. 11

15. How many lots have easements?

    a. 1   c. 4
    b. 3   d. 6

16. Which road or roads run east and west?

    a. Wolf and Jasmine
    b. Carney and Goodrich
    c. Wolf only
    d. Goodrich only

17. Which lot has the *LEAST* street exposure?

    a. Lot 3, Block A   c. Lot 9, Block A
    b. Lot 15, Block B   d. Lot 10, Block B

18. Beginning at the intersection of the West line of Carney Street and the North line of Wolf Road, running west 140 feet, then North 120 feet, then North 50 degrees East 120 feet, then following the southeasterly curvature of the South line of Jasmine Lane for 100 feet, then South 120 feet to POB.

    To which lot does this description refer?

    a. Lot 15, Block B
    b. Lot 8, Block A
    c. Lot 7, 8, and 9, Block A
    d. Lot 8 and 9, Block A

19. If lot 13 and lot 14, Block A were combined into one parcel, how many square feet would it contain?

    a. 1,020   c. 22,800
    b. 19,800   d. 21,600

20. If a woman is willing to pay $3 per square foot for lot 10, Block A, how much would she pay for the land?

    a. $20,600   c. $28,000
    b. $24,000   d. $32,400

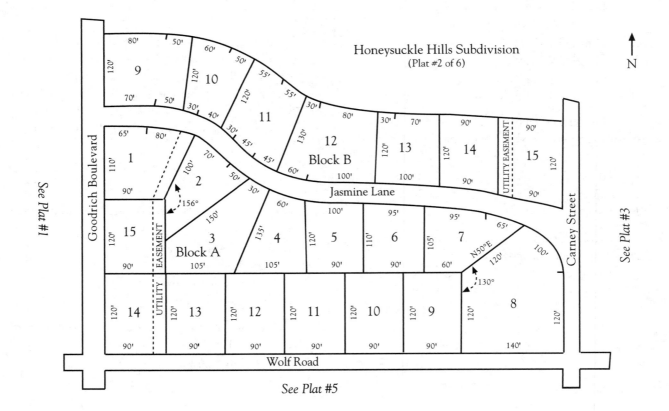

Honeysuckle Hills Subdivision
(Plat #2 of 6)

See Plat #5

ANSWER KEY

Matching

1. a **2.** h **3.** d **4.** b **5.** i **6.** j **7.** c **8.** e
9. g **10.** f

True or False

1. **False.** The *rectangular survey system* was established by Congress in 1785 to standardize the description of land acquisition. p. 146

2. **True.** The oldest type of legal description is metes-and-bounds, which relies on a property's physical features to determine the boundaries and measurements of the parcel. It may include natural and artificial landmarks called monuments. p. 145

3. **True.** The lot-and-block (recorded plat) system of land description, which uses lot and block numbers referred to in a plat map, and that indicates the location and boundaries of individual properties, is filed in the public records of the county where the land is located. p. 151

4. **False.** A principal meridian runs *north and south*, and base lines run east and west. p. 146

5. **True.** Lines running east and west, parallel to the base line, and six miles apart, are referred to as township lines. p. 147

6. **False.** Range lines are strips of land six miles wide that run parallel to the *principal meridian*. p. 146

7. **True.** When the horizontal township lines and the vertical range lines intersect, they form township squares, which are the basic units of the rectangular survey system. p. 147

8. **True.** Townships are 6 miles square and contain 36 square miles. They are further subdivided into 36 sections, each containing 640 acres. p. 147

9. **False.** A *benchmark* is a permanent reference point that is usually found on an embossed brass marker set into a solid concrete or asphalt base. It is used for marking datums, the point, line, or surface from which elevations are measured or indicated. p. 154

10. **False.** Section 6 is always in the *northwest* or upper-left corner. p. 148

11. **True.** In the same way land may be measured and divided into parcels, the air may also be divided; air lots are composed of the airspace within specific boundaries located over a parcel of land. p. 153

12. **True.** The condominium laws passed in all states require that a registered land surveyor prepare a plat map that shows the elevations of floor and ceiling surfaces, and the vertical boundaries of each unit with reference to an official datum. p. 153

Multiple Choice

1. **d.** A *benchmark* is a permanent reference point used as a reference for marking datums, not for expressing a legal description. p. 154

2. **a.** The U.S. Geological Survey *datum* is defined as the mean sea level at New York Harbor. A surveyor uses the datum to determine the height of a structure or to establish the grade of a street. p. 154

3. **b.** The woman paid $588,060:

   43,560 square feet × 6 = 261,360 square feet

   261,360 square feet × $2.25 = $588,060

4. **b.** A township is numbered in an "s" fashion: 1 through 6, right to left; and 7 to 12, left to right. Section 7 is directly south of Section 6. p. 148

5. **b.** A *section* is one square mile. p. 148

6. **c.** The man paid $12,000:

   1/4 × 640 = 160

   160 × 1/4 = 40

   40 × 1/4 = 10 acres

   10 acres × $1,200 = $12,000. p. 149

7. **c.** A quarter of 640 acres is 160 acres. p. 146

8. **b.** There are two parcels in this description denoted by the semicolon (;).

    The first: 1/4 × 640 = 160;

    1/4 × 160 = 40.

    The second: 1/4 × 640 = 160;

    160 × 1/4 = 40;

    40 × 1/2 = 20.

    40 + 20 = 60 acres. p. 149–150

9. **d.** Township squares are the basic units of the rectangular survey system. Principal meridians and base lines are the two sets of intersecting lines in the system. Ranges are the six-mile strips of land on either side of a principal meridian. p. 147

10. **a.** Metes-and-bounds descriptions within the rectangular survey system usually occur when describing an irregular tract, when a tract is too small to be describe by quarter-sections, or when a tract does not follow the lot or block lines of a recorded subdivision or section, quarter-section lines, or other fractional section lines. p. 150

11. **d.** The property is 200 × 100 = 20,000 square feet. p. 150

12. **c.** A metes-and-bounds description must always begin and end at the point of beginning, thus *encircling* the described property. p. 145

13. **a.** The lot-and-block system starts with the preparation of a subdivision plat by a licensed surveyor or an engineer. p. 151

14. **c.** In Block A, Lot 7 has the longest frontage with 160 feet. p. 151

15. **c.** Four lots have easements: Lots, 1, 14, and 15, Block A. Lot 15, Block B. p. 151

16. **a.** Wolf and Jasmine roads run east and west. p. 151

17. **a.** Lot 3, Block A with 30 feet has the least street exposure. p. 151

18. **b.** The description refers to Lot 8, Block A. p. 151

19. **d.** The combined parcel would have 21,600 square feet. The parcel would be 180 × 120 = 21,600. p. 151

20. **d.** The woman would pay $32,400:

    90 × 120 = 10,800 square feet;

    10,800 square feet × $3 = $32,400.

CHAPTER 10

Real Estate Taxes and Other Liens

■ **LEARNING OBJECTIVES**   *Before you answer these questions, you should be able to*

- **identify** the various classifications of liens;

- **describe** how real estate taxes are applied through assessments, tax liens, and the use of equalization ratios;

- **explain** how nontax liens, such as mechanics' liens, mortgage liens, and judgment liens are applied and enforced;

- **distinguish** the characteristics of voluntary, involuntary, statutory, and equitable liens; and

- **define** the following *key terms*:

ad valorem tax	general real estate tax	redemption
assessment	inheritance taxes	special assessments
attachment	involuntary lien	specific liens
equalization factor	judgment	statutory lien
equitable lien	lien	subordination agreements
equitable right of redemption	lis pendens	tax liens
	mechanic's lien	tax sale
estate tax	mill	vendor's lien
general liens	mortgage lien	voluntary lien

MATCHING A   *Write the letter of the matching term on the appropriate line.*

a. *ad valorem*

b. *equitable lien*

c. *subordination*

d. *statutory lien*

e. *lien*

f. *priority*

g. *specific lien*

h. *general lien*

i. *taxes*

j. *voluntary lien*

1. ___ A charge or claim against a person's property, to enforce the payment of money

2. ___ A lien that is created intentionally by the property owner's action

3. ___ A lien created by law

4. ___ A lien created by a court judgment

5. ___ A lien that affects all the real and personal property owned by a debtor

6. ___ A lien that is secured by and only affects certain property of the debtor

7. ___ The order in which claims against property will be satisfied

8. ___ A written agreement between lienholders to change the priority of a lien

9. ___ Charges imposed by state and local governments to fund their functions and services

10. ___ A type of tax based on the assessment of a property

Matching B   *Write the letter of the matching term on the appropriate line.*

a. *assessment*

b. *money judgment*

c. *equalization factor*

d. *equitable right of redemption*

e. *lis pendens*

f. *attachment*

g. *mechanic's lien*

h. *mill*

i. *special assessments*

j. *statutory right of redemption*

1. ___ The official process of valuing real estate for tax purposes

2. ___ A device to achieve uniformity in statewide assessments

3. ___ $1/_{1,000}$ of a dollar, or $0.001

4. ___ The right of a delinquent taxpayer to recover property before a tax sale

5. ___ The right of a delinquent taxpayer to recover property after a tax sale

6. ___ Taxes levied on specific properties that benefit from public improvement

7. ___ A specific, involuntary lien that gives security to persons or companies who perform labor, or who furnish material to improve real property

8. ___ A court decree that establishes the amount owed by a debtor and provides for money to be awarded

9. ___ A notice of a possible future lien based on a lawsuit

10. ___ A writ that permits a court to retain custody of a debtor's property until the creditor's lawsuit is concluded

TRUE OR FALSE   *Circle the correct answer.*

1. T F A voluntary lien may be classified as either statutory or equitable.

2. T F A charge or claim against a person's property by a creditor, which is made to enforce the payment of money, is referred to as a *lien*.

3. T F All encumbrances are liens.

4. T F Both federal estate taxes and state inheritance taxes are general, statutory, and involuntary liens.

5. T F Taking out a mortgage loan is an example of creating an equitable lien.

6. T F A lien attaches to real property at the time the lien is filed.

7. T F A special assessment is always a general and statutory lien.

8. T F A court's decree that establishes the amount owed by a debtor and also directs the sheriff to seize and sell the debtor's property.

9. T F Mechanics' liens never take priority over tax or special assessment liens.

10. T F *Ad valorem* taxes apply to the difference between the assessed value of a property and the value added by resale or improvement.

11. T F All liens are encumbrances.

12. T F The presence of a lien on real property does not prevent the owner from conveying title to another party.

13. T F A taxing body determines the appropriate tax rate by dividing the total monies needed for the coming fiscal year by the total assessments of all taxable real estate located within the taxing body's jurisdiction.

14. T F A delinquent taxpayer may redeem property at any time prior to a tax sale by exercising a statutory right of redemption.

15. T F A mechanic's lien is a specific, involuntary lien.

MULTIPLE CHOICE   *Circle the correct answer.*

1. Generally, in a court-ordered sale, which of the following is paid first?
   a. First mortgage
   b. Mechanics' liens
   c. Child support liens
   d. Real estate taxes

2. Which of the following is an example of a specific lien?
   a. Decedent's debts
   b. Internal Revenue Service liens
   c. Mortgage lien
   d. Corporate franchise liens

3. The millage breakout for ad valorem taxes are: library: .5; school: 1; school debt service: .5; community college: 1; vocational school: .5; and all others: 5. If the property is assessed at $165,000, how much is the tax bill?
   a. $1,200.25   c. $1,405.75
   b. $1,402.50   d. $1,800.50

4. All of the following are liens against real property *EXCEPT*
   a. a mortgage.
   b. real estate taxes.
   c. lis pendens.
   d. home improvement loan of a deceased property owner.

5. Which of the following characteristics apply to a real estate tax lien?
   a. Specific, involuntary lien
   b. Specific, voluntary lien
   c. General, involuntary lien
   d. General, voluntary lien

6. Which of the following would permit a law enforcement officer to seize and sell a debtor's property?
   a. Lis pendens
   b. Satisfaction of judgment
   c. Writ of execution
   d. Writ of attachment

7. Which of the following is a general, statutory, and involuntary lien on both real and personal property?
   a. Federal tax lien
   b. Mechanic's lien
   c. Special assessment
   d. Consumer loan lien

8. In February, a homeowner contracted with a general contractor to have his billiard room converted to a sauna, but he never paid for the work. The homeowner stopped making mortgage payments to his mortgage company in June. The owner is two years delinquent in property taxes to the county. The state gives mechanics' liens priority. If all of these creditors obtain judgments against the owner in November, what will be the priority of their liens (first to last)?
   a. Contractor → mortgage company → county
   b. County → mortgage company → contractor
   c. Contractor → county → mortgage company
   d. County → contractor → mortgage company

9. A town wants to construct new concrete curbs in a residential neighborhood. How will the town most likely raise the money necessary for the improvement?
   a. Ad valorem tax
   b. Special assessment
   c. Equalized assessment
   d. Utility lien

10. All of the following liens must be recorded to be effective *EXCEPT*
   a. money judgment.
   b. mechanic's lien.
   c. real estate tax lien.
   d. voluntary lien.

11. The market value of an undeveloped parcel is $40,000. Its assessed value is 40 percent of market value, and properties in its county are subject to an equalization factor of 1.50. If the tax rate is $4 per $100, what is the amount of the tax owed on the property?
   a. $480   c. $1,080
   b. $960   d. $1,800

MULTIPLE CHOICE *(Continued)*

12. To give notice of a potential claim against the property and to establish priority, a creditor may file a(n)

    a. lis pendens.

    b. attachment.

    c. general lien.

    d. specific lien.

13. A man was considering having a new garage built. He talked about the project with a contractor. In April, while the man was on vacation, the contractor began building the garage according to the man's specifications. Work was complete by the end of May. In June, the man returned from vacation and refused to pay for the garage. The contractor decides to file a mechanic's lien in July. Is the contractor entitled to a lien?

    a. Yes, because the garage was constructed according to the man's specifications.

    b. Yes, because the garage is not a part of an owner-occupied residence.

    c. No, because notice of the lien should have been filed in May, when the work was completed.

    d. No, because there was no express or implied contract between the man and the contractor.

FILL-IN-THE-BLANK   *Select the word or words that best complete the following statements:*

assessed value

certificate of sale

golf course

hospital

Local Improvement
  District (LID)

mechanic's lien

satisfaction of judgment

subordination agreement

tax levy

tax lien

title search

voluntary lien

writ of attachment

1. To reveal any recorded liens, a property buyer should require a(n) _____ before closing the real estate transaction.

2. A county assessor usually bases a property's _____ on the sale prices of comparable properties.

3. Usually, a vote of the taxing district's governing body is needed to impose a(n) _____.

4. In many states, when a purchaser at a tax sale receives the _____, the purchaser gains the right to take possession of the property.

5. A lien that is created intentionally by the property owner's action, such as taking out a mortgage loan, is called a(an) _____.

6. The priority of a(n) _____ may be established as of the date construction began or materials were first furnished.

7. A court order against the property of another person that directs the sheriff to take control of a property is called a(n) _____.

8. When real property is sold to pay off a debt, the debtor should get a legal document known as a(n) _____.

9. An example of a property that is exempt from taxation is a(n) _____.

10. When a large-scale improvement project, such as sewer construction, is planned, it may be funded by creating a(an) _____.

ACTIVITY: Lien Characteristics

Identify the characteristics of liens by placing check marks in the appropriate columns.

Type of Lien	General	Specific	Voluntary	Involuntary	Equitable	Statutory
Mechanic's Lien						
Mortgage						
Bail Bond						
Municipal Utility Lien						
Federal Estate Tax Lien						
Corporate Franchise Tax						
State Inheritance Tax						
Judgment						
Real Property Tax						

ANSWER KEY

Matching A

1. e   **2.** j   **3.** d   **4.** b   **5.** h   **6.** g   **7.** f   **8.** c
9. i   **10.** a

Matching B

1. a   **2.** c   **3.** h   **4.** d   **5.** j   **6.** i   **7.** g   **8.** b
9. e   **10.** f

True or False

1. **False.** An *involuntary* lien may be classified as either statutory or equitable. Voluntary liens are never statutory. p. 161

2. **True.** A lien is a charge or claim against a person's property made to enforce the payment of money; a lien represents an interest only in ownership; it does not constitute actual ownership of the property. p. 161

3. **False.** Although all liens are encumbrances, not all encumbrances are liens. An encumbrance is any charge or claim that attaches to real property and lessens its value or impairs its use, but does not prevent the transfer of the property. p. 161

4. **True.** General liens affect all property owned by the debtor. State and federal taxes are imposed involuntarily by statute. p. 162

5. **False.** A voluntary lien is created intentionally by the property owner's action, such as when someone takes out a mortgage loan. p. 161, 167

6. **True.** A lien attaches to real property at the moment it is filed and recorded; in contrast, a lien does not attach to personal property until the personal property is seized. p. 162

7. **False.** A special assessment is always a specific and statutory lien. p. 162

8. **False.** A court's decree that establishes the amount owed by a debtor is enforced by the creditor obtaining a *writ of execution* directing the sheriff to seize and sell the debtor's property. p. 168

9. **True.** Real estate taxes and special assessments generally take priority over all other liens, regardless of the order in which the liens are recorded. p. 163

10. **False.** *Ad valorem* taxes are based on the value of the property being taxed and are specific, involuntary, statutory liens. p. 163

11. **True.** A lien is a charge or claim against a person's property made to enforce the payment of money; a lien represents an interest only in ownership; it does not constitute actual ownership of the property. p. 161

12. **True.** Although the existence of a lien does not necessarily prevent a property owner from transferring title to someone else, once in place, the lien runs with the land and will bind all successive owners until the line is paid and cleared. p. 162

13. **True.** After determining the budget, the taxing body authorizes the expenditure of funds. The tax rate is determined by dividing the total monies needed for the coming fiscal year by the total assessments of all real estate located within the taxing body's jurisdiction. p. 165

14. **False.** A delinquent taxpayer may redeem property any time prior to a tax sale by exercising an *equitable* right of redemption. p. 166

15. **True.** Specific liens are secured by specific property and affect only that particular property; examples include mechanics' liens, vendors' liens, mortgages, and real estate tax liens. p. 162

Multiple Choice

1. **d.** Real estate taxes do not have to be recorded to be effective, and they take precedence over all other liens. p. 163

2. **c.** A mortgage lien is a specific, voluntary lien. p. 161, 162

3. **b.** The tax bill is $1402.50:

   .5 + 1 + .5 + 1 + .5 + 5 = 8.5 mills or $.0085 per dollar of valuation

   $165,000 × .0085 = $1,402.50. p. 165

4. **c.** A lis pendens is only the notice of a possible future lien. However, if it becomes a lien, the priority is established by the date and time that the lis pendens was originally filed. p. 169

5. **a.** A real estate tax is levied on an individual property; few would argue that individuals choose to have the tax levied, hence, an involuntary lien. p. 163

6. **c.** A *writ of execution* directs the sheriff to seize and sell as much of the debtor's property as necessary to pay both the debt and the expenses of the sale. p. 168

7. **a.** An Internal Revenue Service lien is a general lien against the person, which is against the real and personal property owned by the delinquent taxpayer. p. 162

8. **d.** The priority is taxes, mechanic's lien, and then first mortgage. Although the mortgage was filed first, property taxes always have first priority, and the state has given second priority to mechanic's liens. p. 163

9. **b.** The town will levy a special assessment against the benefiting properties to pay for the new concrete curbs. p. 166–167

10. **c.** Ad valorem real estate tax liens do not have to be recorded to be effective, and they always take precedence over all other liens. This is why many lenders collect $1/12$ of the taxes each month, so that the lender can pay the taxes when due. Unpaid taxes take priority over mortgage liens. p. 163

11. **b.** The tax owned on the property is $960: $40,000 × 40% × 1.5 ÷ 100 × 4 = $960. p. 165

12. **a.** A *lis pendens* is a notice of a possible future lien. If it becomes an actual lien, the effective date of the lien is the date and time that the lis pendens was filed. p 169

13. **d.** Because the contractor was in no way given authority to act, he has no right to file a mechanic's lien. p. 168

Fill-in-the-Blank

1. To reveal any recorded liens, a property buyer should require a *title search* before closing the real estate transaction.

2. A county assessor usually bases a property's *assessed value* on the sales prices of comparable properties.

3. Usually, a vote of the taxing district's governing body is needed to impose a *tax levy*.

4. In many states, when a purchaser at a tax sale receives the *certificate of sale*, the purchaser gains the right to take possession of the property.

5. A lien that is created intentionally by the property owner's action, such as taking out a mortgage loan, is called a *voluntary lien*.

6. The priority of a *mechanic's lien* may be established as of the date construction began or materials were first furnished.

7. A court order against the property of another person that directs the sheriff to take control of a property is called a *writ of attachment*.

8. When real property is sold to pay off a debt, the debtor should get a legal document known as a *satisfaction of judgment*.

9. An example of a property that is exempt from taxation is a *hospital*.

10. When a large-scale improvement project, such as sewer construction, is planned, it may be funded by creating a *Local Improvement District (LID)*.

Activity: Lien Characteristics

Type of Lien	General	Specific	Voluntary	Involuntary	Equitable	Statutory
Mechanic's Lien		✓		✓		✓
Mortgage		✓	✓		✓	
Bail Bond		✓	✓			✓
Municipal Utility Lien		✓		✓	✓	
Federal Estate Tax Lien	✓			✓		✓
Corporate Franchise Tax	✓			✓		✓
State Inheritance Tax	✓			✓		✓
Judgment	✓			✓	✓	
Real Property Tax		✓		✓		✓

CHAPTER 11

Real Estate Contracts

■ **LEARNING OBJECTIVES** *Before you answer these questions, you should be able to*

■ **identify** the requirements for a valid contract;

■ **describe** the various types of contracts used in the real estate business;

■ **explain** how contracts may be discharged;

■ **distinguish** among bilateral and unilateral, executed and executory, and valid, void, and voidable contracts; and

■ **define** the following *key terms*:

addendum	equitable title	statute of frauds
amendment	executed contract	suit for specific
assignment	executory contract	performance
bilateral contract	express contract	"time is of the essence"
breach of contract	implied contract	unenforceable contract
consideration	land contract	unilateral contract
contingencies	liquidated damages	valid contract
contract	novation	void contract
counteroffer	offer and acceptance	voidable contract
disclosure	option	
earnest money	rescission	

MATCHING A   *Write the letter of the matching term on the appropriate line.*

a. *bilateral contract*

b. *consideration*

c. *contract*

d. *executed contract*

e. *executory contract*

f. *express contract*

g. *implied contract*

h. *mutual assent*

i. *offeree*

j. *unilateral contract*

1. ___ A voluntary, legally enforceable promise between legally competent parties to perform (or refrain from performing) some legal act

2. ___ A contract in which the parties show their intentions in words

3. ___ A contract established by the acts and conduct of the parties

4. ___ A contract in which both parties promise to perform some act

5. ___ A one-sided agreement

6. ___ A contract that has been completely performed

7. ___ The status of a real estate sales contract prior to closing

8. ___ The person who accepts the offer in a contract

9. ___ Complete agreement about the purpose and terms of a contract

10. ___ Something of legal value offered by one party and accepted by another as an inducement to act or refrain from acting

MATCHING B   *Write the letter of the matching term on the appropriate line.*

a. *void*

b. *assignment*

c. *breach*

d. *contingencies*

e. *earnest money*

f. *land contract*

g. *liquidated damages*

h. *equitable title*

i. *listing agreement*

j. *novation*

1. ___ A contract that is without legal force or effect because it lacks one or more essential elements

2. ___ The transfer of rights or duties under a contract

3. ___ The substitution of a new contract to replace an earlier one

4. ___ A violation of any of the terms or conditions of a contract without legal excuse

5. ___ An employment contract between a broker and a seller

6. ___ A deposit customarily made by a prospective purchaser when making an offer

7. ___ The interest held by a buyer prior to delivery and acceptance of the deed

8. ___ An amount of money that the parties agree will be the complete compensation available in the event of a breach

9. ___ Additional conditions that must be satisfied before a property sales contract is fully enforceable

10. ___ A contract under which the seller retains legal title to property and, until the terms of the contract are satisfied, the buyer obtains possession only

TRUE OR FALSE   *Circle the correct answer.*

1. T F An agreement to be bound by most of the terms proposed in an offer constitutes acceptance.

2. T F All contracts must be in writing to be enforceable.

3. T F A listing agreement is the same as a contract for the sale of real estate.

4. T F *Consideration* is something of legal value offered by one party and accepted by the other as an inducement to act.

5. T F In an implied contract, the actual agreement between the parties is inferred from general or vague statements in the written agreement itself.

6. T F The difference between a bilateral and a unilateral contract is the number of parties involved.

7. T F A sales contract is an executory contract from the time it is signed until closing; at closing, it becomes an executed contract.

8. T F A contract that may be rescinded or disaffirmed by one or both of the parties based on some legal principle is void, even though it may appear to be valid.

9. T F The person who makes an offer is the offeree; the person who accepts or rejects the offer is the *offeror*.

10. T F A contract entered into by a mentally ill person is voidable during the illness and for some time after the individual is cured.

11. T F An oral agreement for the sale of real estate is unenforceable.

12. T F Under a *land contract*, the buyer obtains both possession and legal title to the property by agreeing to make regular monthly payments to the seller over a number of years.

13. T F *Assignment* is the substitution of a new contract in place of the original one, while *novation* is a transfer of rights or duties under a contract.

14. T F An offer or counteroffer may be revoked at any time prior to its acceptance.

15. T F An *option contract* is an agreement by which the *optionee* gives the *optionor* the right to buy or lease property at a fixed price within a specific period of time.

16. T F *Commingling* occurs when a broker mixes personal funds with a buyer's earnest money deposit.

17. T F The interest held by a buyer during the time between the signing of a sales contract and the transfer of title is known as *equitable title*.

18. T F An example of an addendum to a real estate sales contract is an attached page that adds a detailed provision that the purchase is contingent on the sale of the buyer's current home within 90 days.

19. T F An option agreement is a unilateral contract.

20. T F A real estate contract entered into by a minor is void.

MULTIPLE CHOICE   *Circle the correct answer.*

1. Which of the following is an example of a unilateral contract?

   a. Lease
   b. Agreement of sale
   c. Option
   d. Listing agreement

2. A seller accepted all of the terms that the buyer offered, making only one small change in the amount of the earnest money. At the moment, these agreements constitute a(n)

   a. offer.
   b. counteroffer.
   c. acceptance.
   d. executed contract.

3. The buyer changed her mind about buying a particular lot. She called her agent and said, "Withdraw my offer." Her action is called a

   a. counteroffer.
   b. rejection.
   c. breach of contract.
   d. revocation.

4. A real estate broker announces to the salespeople in her office that she will pay a $1,000 bonus to the top-selling salesperson each quarter. This contract is a(n)

   a. implied bilateral contract.
   b. express unilateral contract.
   c. implied unilateral contract.
   d. express bilateral contract.

5. A buyer makes an offer on a house, and the seller accepts. What is the current status of this relationship?

   a. The buyer and seller do not have a valid contract until the seller delivers title at closing.
   b. The buyer and seller have an express, bilateral executed contract.
   c. The buyer and seller have an express, bilateral executory contract.
   d. The buyer and seller have an implied, unilateral executory contract.

6. A woman offers to buy a man's house for the full $215,000 asking price. The offer contains the following clause: "Possession of the premises on August 1." The man is delighted to accept the woman's offer and signs the contract. First, however, The man crosses out "August 1" and replaces it with "August 3," because he won't be back from vacation on the first of the month. He then begins scheduling movers. What is the status of this agreement?

   a. Because the man changed the date of possession rather than the amount, the man and woman have a valid contract.
   b. The man has accepted the woman's offer. Because the reason for the change was out of the man's control, the change is of no legal effect once he signed the contract.
   c. The man has rejected the woman's offer and made a counteroffer, which the woman is free to accept or reject.
   d. While the man technically rejected the woman's offer, his behavior in scheduling movers creates an implied contract between the parties.

7. A contract that is entered into by a person who is under the age of contractual capacity is

   a. unenforceable.
   b. void.
   c. voidable.
   d. valid.

8. A woman is buying a man's house and wants to take over the mortgage. The lender releases the man from the obligation, substituting the woman as the party liable for the debt. This new agreement is called a(n)

   a. assignment.
   b. novation.
   c. conversion.
   d. consideration.

MULTIPLE CHOICE   *(Continued)*

9. A buyer and a seller enter into a sales contract for the sale of a home. The seller changes his mind at the last minute, and the buyer suffers a financial loss of $1,500 and must rent a home in which to live. Unless the contract provides otherwise, all of the following are legal actions that are likely to succeed *EXCEPT*

   a. the buyer may sue the seller for specific performance, forcing the sale of the home to the buyer.

   b. the buyer may sue the seller for damages to recover the $1,500 loss.

   c. the seller is not liable because the buyer should not have incurred the $1,500 cost before the sale.

   d. the buyer may sue the seller for the rent he paid.

10. On March 7, a buyer and a seller execute a contract for the purchase of the seller's property. Closing is set for June 10. On April 15, the property is struck by lightning and virtually destroyed by the resulting fire. If the Uniform Vendor and Purchaser Risk Act has been adopted by the state in which the property is located, which party bears liability for the loss?

    a. Under the Act, the buyer and the seller share the loss equally.

    b. Under the Act, the seller bears the loss alone.

    c. The Act does not apply. The buyer bears the loss alone, by virtue of his equitable title.

    d. Under the Act, neither the buyer nor the seller bears the loss. A state fund covers the loss.

11. A seller is having difficulty finding a buyer for his house. A woman wants to buy the house but is not sure whether she will be transferred out of the country by her employer. The seller agrees to accept a $500 payment from the buyer, in return for which the house will be taken off the market for three months. The buyer may purchase the house for a certain price any time during that period. This is a(n)

    a. unenforceable contract.

    b. land contract.

    c. sales contract.

    d. option contract.

12. All the following are essential to a valid real estate sales contract *EXCEPT*

    a. an adequate description of the property.

    b. consideration.

    c. an earnest money deposit, held in an escrow account.

    d. legally competent parties.

13. A 14-year-old comes into a brokerage office and says, "I want to make an offer on this property. Here is a certified check for 10 percent of the asking price. Please help me with the paperwork." Why should the broker be concerned?

    a. Because one of the parties is a minor, the contract is illegal.

    b. The earnest money deposit must be at least 20 percent of the asking price when a minor is involved in the transaction.

    c. The sales contract may be disaffirmed by the minor.

    d. The sales contract will be void because the minor's age is a matter of public record.

14. In case the buyer decides not to buy for no legal reason, the contract may provide that the earnest money is there as

    a. actual damages.

    b. nominal damages.

    c. punitive damages.

    d. liquidated damages.

MULTIPLE CHOICE   *(Continued)*

15. The buyer and seller agreed to a closing date of September 7 and that *time is of the essence*. Which of the following is the closest meaning of the phrase?

    a. The date of closing may only be delayed by one day at a time.

    b. If closing is not held on September 7, there is an automatic extension built in.

    c. Closing must be on or before September 7.

    d. If either party gives notice, the date can be moved back.

16. If either party gives notice, the date can be moved back. A promise made by one party, requesting something in exchange for that promise is called a(n)

    a. offer.   c. consideration.

    b. acceptance.   d. rescission.

17. If a man threatens another man to get him to sign a contract to sell property for a low price, the contract is voidable because it violates the doctrine of

    a. reality of consent.
    b. legally competent parties.
    c. consideration.
    d. offer and acceptance.

18. If a contract seems to be valid, but neither party can sue the other to force performance, the contract is said to be

    a. voided.   c. rescinded.

    b. breached.   d. unenforceable.

19. What is minimum consideration in a valid contract?

    a. One dollar

    b. Any item that can be appraised with a market value

    c. Specified goods or services

    d. Anything the parties agree is *good and valuable*

20. If a contract does NOT contain a time or date for performance, when should the act be done?

    a. Within a reasonable time
    b. Within one week
    c. Within two weeks
    d. Within one month

21. If a man allows a woman to back out of a contract, returns the earnest money to her, and both are back to the positions they held before the contract, the contract has been

    a. cancelled.   c. assigned.

    b. rescinded.   d. executed.

22. When is an offer considered to be accepted?

    a. When the broker notifies the buyer that the seller has accepted the offer

    b. When the buyer gives a signed receipt to the broker to show the buyer has received the acceptance

    c. The moment the seller accepts the buyer's offer

    d. One business day after the offer is accepted and signed by the seller

23. Additional conditions that must be satisfied before a sales contract is fully enforceable are called

    a. binders.   c. addendums.

    b. amendments.   d. contingencies.

24. The amount of the earnest money in a sales contract should accomplish what purpose?

    a. Cover any expenses the buyer might incur if the seller defaults

    b. Discourage the buyer from walking away from the agreement

    c. Pay the broker's commission

    d. Pay for any required inspections

25. The purchaser's right to inspect the property shortly before closing the sale is called the

    a. walk-through.
    b. open house.
    c. title search.
    d. subordination agreement.

ACTIVITY: Sales Contract

The document on the following page is the first page of a standard real estate sales contract. Complete the document using information from the following narrative.

You are the buyer. The date is today. The property is 1105 Azalea Street in Poleduck County, City of Pleasant Valley, Virginia 98675. The lot dimensions are 70 feet by 160 feet. The sellers are Paul and Polly Purveyor, who currently live in the house being sold.

The buyer is particularly insistent that the kitchen appliances (a stove, dishwasher, and refrigerator) convey with the property, and that an outdoor gas cooker and swing set stay as well. The earnest money deposit is 15 percent of the purchase price of $317,500, paid by check, with an additional 10 percent of the balance due in one business week.

The closing will take place exactly 64 days from today at the office of the buyer's attorney, R. Tassel. The financing will be by conventional, fixed-rate mortgage, in the amount of the balance due. The buyer will not accept an interest rate greater than 7.5 percent. The commitment date is two weeks from today. The listing broker is F. J. Broker.

Agreement for Sale of Real Estate

BUYER(S): _____

    Address: _____

        City: _____ State: ___ Zip _____ agrees to purchase, and

SELLER(S): _____

    Address: _____

        City: _____ State: ___ Zip _____ agrees to sell to Buyer(s)

at the Price of : _____ Dollars ($_____)

the Property commonly described as _____

(City of _____, County of _____ State of _____)

1. **PROPERTY DESCRIPTION:** "the Property," a complete legal description of which may be attached to this contract by either party. The Property has approximate lot dimensions of _____, together with all existing improvements and fixtures, if any, to be transferred to the Buyer(s) by Bill of Sale at the time of closing, including (but not limited to): hot water heater, furnace, plumbing and electrical fixtures, sump pumps, central heating and cooling systems, fixed floor coverings, built-in kitchen appliances and cabinets, storm and screen windows and doors, window treatment hardware, shelving systems, all planted vegetation, garage door openers and car units, and the following items of personal property:

2. **EARNEST MONEY:** Buyer has paid $_____ by check by note (*delete one*), and will pay within _____ days the further sum of $_____, as earnest money to be applied against the purchase price. The earnest money shall be held by the Listing Broker for the mutual benefit of the parties. The balance of the purchase price, $_____, shall be paid in full at closing.

3. **CLOSING DATE:** The closing date shall be _____, 20___, at _____.

4. **POSSESSION:** Possession shall be at closing.

5. **COMMISSION:** Seller(s) agree that _____, Listing Broker, brought about this sale and agrees to pay a Broker's commission as agreed in the listing agreement.

6. **FINANCING:** This contract is subject to the condition that Buyer(s) shall, by _____, 20 ___, obtain a written commitment for a loan secured by a mortgage or deed of trust on the Property in the amount of $ _____. Financing shall be secured in the form of a mortgage of the following type: (delete those items that do not apply); Conventional (fixed or adjustable rate); FHA mortgage; VA mortgage; assumption of existing mortgage; financing by Seller(s).

ANSWER KEY

Matching A

1. c **2.** f **3.** g **4.** a **5.** j **6.** d **7.** e **8.** i
9. h **10.** b

Matching B

1. a **2.** b **3.** j **4.** c **5.** i **6.** e **7.** h **8.** g
9. d **10.** f

True or False

1. **False.** An agreement to be bound by *all* of the terms proposed in an offer constitutes *acceptance*. p. 177

2. **False.** While a contract may be written or oral, only certain types of contracts must be in writing to be enforceable. p. 176

3. **False.** A contract is a voluntary agreement or promise between legally competent parties, supported by legal consideration, to perform or refrain from performing some legal act. p. 176

4. **True.** Consideration is some interest or benefit accruing to one party, or some loss or responsibility by another party as inducements to perform or to refrain from performing some act. p. 178

5. **False.** In an implied contract, the actual agreement between the parties is *demonstrated by their acts and conduct*. p. 176

6. **False.** The difference between a bilateral and a unilateral contract is the number of parties bound to perform; both parties to a bilateral contract are obligated to perform, but in a unilateral contract, the second party is not legally obligated to act. p. 177

7. **True.** An executory contract exists when one or both parties sill have an act to perform; a sales contract is executory from the time it is signed until closing. p. 177

8. **False.** A contract that may be rescinded or disaffirmed by one or both of the parties based on some legal principle is *voidable*, even though it may appear to be valid. p. 179

9. **False.** The person who makes an offer is the *offeror*; the person who accepts or rejects the offer is the *offeree*. p. 177

10. **True** A voidable contract is considered by the courts to be valid if the party who has the option to disaffirm the agreement does not do so within a period of time. A contract entered into by a mentally ill person is voidable during the illness and for some time after the individual is cured. p. 179

11. **True.** Because the statute of frauds requires that any transfer of real property interests must be in writing, an oral purchase agreement is unenforceable. p. 179

12. **False.** Under a *land contract*, the buyer obtains possession, but the seller retains legal title until the terms of the contract have been satisfied. p. 187

13. **False.** *Novation* is the substitution of a new contract in place of the original one, while *assignment* is a transfer of rights or duties under a contract. p. 180

14. **True.** The offeror may revoke the offer any time before notification of acceptance, but the revocation must be communicated to the offeree by the offeror, either directly or through the parties' agents. p. 178

15. **False.** An *option contract* is an agreement by which the *optionor* gives the *optionee* the right to buy or lease property at a fixed price within a specific period of time. p. 187

16. **True.** Earnest money may not be mixed with the broker's personal funds, called commingling. In addition, the funds cannot be used for personal use, called conversion. p. 184

17. **True.** After both buyer and seller have executed a sales contract, the buyer acquires an interest in the land, known as equitable title. p. 185

18. **True.** An addendum is any provision added to an existing contract without altering the content of the original; it is essentially a new contract between parties that includes the provisions of the original contract by reference. p. 187

19. **True.** Because an option is enforceable by the optionee only, it is a unilateral contract. p. 187

20. **False.** A voidable contract is considered by the courts to be valid if the party who has the option to disaffirm the agreement does not so within a period of time. A contract entered into by a minor is *voidable*. p. 179

Multiple Choice

1. **c.** In a unilateral contract, only one party is obligated to perform. The optionor-owner of the property must sell at the agreed-upon price only if the optionee decides to buy. p. 177

2. **b.** Proposing any deviation from the terms of the offer is considered a rejection of the original offer and is known as a counteroffer. p. 178

3. **d.** The buyer may revoke her offer anytime until she is notified that the seller has accepted the offer. p. 178

4. **b.** The offer of a bonus to the top-selling sales-person each quarter is an *express contract* because the broker clearly stated her intentions in words to the salespeople. It is a *unilateral contract* because she is obligated to keep her promise, but the salespeople are not obligated to perform. p. 176–77

5. **c.** Because the seller has promised to sell and the buyer has promised to buy, it is clearly a *bilateral contract*. It is *express* because they announced their intentions in writing. The contract is *executory* because the sale has not yet closed. p. 176–177

6. **c.** Even changing the smallest of terms, for what-ever reason, constitutes a rejection and counter-offer that the other party is not under obligation to accept. p. 178

7. **c.** The underage party may void the contract, but the older party who entered into the contract with the minor cannot. p. 179

8. **b.** Substituting a new contract where the intent is to discharge the old obligation is known as *novation*. In this situation, it is also called *release of liability*. p. 180

9. **c.** In this case, the seller breached the contract without legal excuse. The buyer is likely to be successful if he sues the seller for specific per-formance, for the $1,500 loss, and for the cost of rent as a hardship. However, many contracts limit the remedies available to parties. p. 181

10. **b.** In states that have adopted the Uniform Vendor and Purchaser Act, the seller remains responsible for the property until the day of closing. p. 185

11. **d.** The buyer has the right to buy at an agreed-upon price within a certain timeframe, but she is not obligated to do so. The seller must sell to the buyer within that timeframe whether or not he receives a higher offer from another prospect. p. 186

12. **c.** Earnest money is an option to a contract, not a requirement; it is available for liquidated damages. The *consideration* is the exchange of promises; that is, the seller promises marketable title and the buyer promises a certain amount of money. p. 184

13. **c.** A minor may void the contract citing, "I am underage." A minor's guardian may purchase for the minor. p. 179

14. **d.** Liquidated damages limit the compensation available to the injured party should a breach of contract occur. p. 185

15. **c.** *Time is of the essence* requires that the contract be completed during that time frame; otherwise, the party who fails to perform on time is liable for breach of contract. p. 180

16. **a.** An offer is a promise made by one party, requesting something in exchange for that promise. An offer must be made before it can be accepted. Consideration is something of legal value. Rescission refers to cancellation of a contract. p. 178

17. **a.** Because a contract must be entered into by consent as a free and voluntary act of each party, a contract made under duress deprives a person of that ability. The contract is voidable by the injured party. p. 178–179

18. **d.** An unenforceable contract may appear to be valid; however, neither party can sue the other to enforce performance. p. 178

19. **d.** The parties must agree that the consideration is *good and valuable*. The courts do not consider whether the consideration is adequate. p. 178

20. **a.** Interpretation of what is a *reasonable time* depends on the situation. However, courts have sometimes declared contracts invalid if they did not contain a time or date for performance. p. 180

21. **b.** Rescission allows both parties to return to their original positions before the contract, so any monies exchanged must be returned. p. 181

22. **a.** Buyer notification is the key. It is not an accepted offer until the buyer is notified, and there is no lag time after that point. p. 178

23. **d.** A contingency is any additional condition that must be satisfied before a sales contract is fully enforceable. A *binder* is a short version of a sales contract that is used until a more complete version is composed by a lawyer. *Amendments* are changes to the existing content of a contract. p. 186

24. **b.** The amount of earnest money should be sufficient that the seller feels reassured that the buyer is committed to the purchase. Money is not used to pay for inspections or the broker's commission. p. 184

25. **a.** The purchaser's right to inspect the property shortly before the closing or settlement is called the walkthrough. The right to a walkthrough is typically agreed upon in the original purchase agreement. p. 186

Activity: Sales Contract

Agreement for Sale of Real Estate

BUYER(S): _Student's Name_

Address: _Student's Address_

City: _____ State: ___ Zip _____ agrees to purchase, and

SELLER(S): _Paul and Polly Purveyor (h/w)_

Address: _1105 Azalea St._

City: _Pleasant Valley_ State: _VA_ Zip _98765_ agrees to sell to Buyer(s)

at the Price of : _Three Hundred Seventeen Thousand Five Hundred_ Dollars ($ _317,500_)

the Property commonly described as _1105 Azalea St._

(City of _Pleasant Valley_ , County of _Poleduck_ State of _Virginia_)

1. PROPERTY DESCRIPTION: "the Property," a complete legal description of which may be attached to this contract by either party. The Property has approximate lot dimensions of _70' by 160'_ , together with all existing improvements and fixtures, if any, to be transferred to the Buyer(s) by Bill of Sale at the time of closing, including (but not limited to): hot water heater, furnace, plumbing and electrical fixtures, sump pumps, central heating and cooling systems, fixed floor coverings, built-in kitchen appliances and cabinets, storm and screen windows and doors, window treatment hardware, shelving systems, all planted vegetation, garage door openers and car units, and the following items of personal property:

    Kitchen stove, dishwasher, refrigerator, outdoor gas cooker and swing set

2. EARNEST MONEY: Buyer has paid $_47,625.00_ by check ~~by note~~ (*delete one*), and will pay within _5_ days the further sum of $_26,987.50_ , as earnest money to be applied against the purchase price. The earnest money shall be held by the Listing Broker for the mutual benefit of the parties. The balance of the purchase price, $_242,887.50_ , shall be paid in full at closing.

3. CLOSING DATE: The closing date shall be _today + 64 days_ ,20__, at _Law Office of R. Tassel_ .

4. POSSESSION: Possession shall be at closing.

5. COMMISSION: Seller(s) agree that _F. J. Broker_ , Listing Broker, brought about this sale and agrees to pay a Broker's commission as agreed in the listing agreement.

6. FINANCING: This contract is subject to the condition that Buyer(s) shall, by _today + 2 wks_ , 20__, obtain a written commitment for a loan secured by a mortgage or deed of trust on the Property in the amount of $ _242,887.50_ . Financing shall be secured in the form of a mortgage of the following type: (delete those items that do not apply); Conventional (fixed ~~or adjustable~~ rate); ~~FHA mortgage; VA mortgage; assumption of existing mortgage; financing by Seller(s).~~ *Not to exceed 7.5%.*

CHAPTER 12

Transfer of Title

■ **LEARNING OBJECTIVES**   *Before you answer these questions, you should be able to*

- ■ **identify** the basic requirements for a valid deed;

- ■ **describe** the fundamental types of deeds;

- ■ **explain** how property may be transferred through involuntary alienation;

- ■ **distinguish** transfers of title by will from transfers by intestacy; and

- ■ **define** the following *key terms*:

acknowledgment	grantor	testate
adverse possession	habendum clause	testator
bargain and sale deed	heirs	title
deed	intestate	transfer tax
deed of trust	involuntary alienation	trustee's deed
devise	probate	voluntary alienation
general warranty deed	quitclaim deed	will
grantee	reconveyance deed	
granting clause	special warranty deed	

MATCHING A   *Write the letter of the matching term on the appropriate line.*

a. acknowledgment

b. deed

c. deed in trust

d. grantee

e. quiet enjoyment

f. grantor

g. granting clause

h. seisin

i. title

j. voluntary alienation

1. ___ The right to, and evidence of, ownership of land

2. ___ The transfer of title by gift or sale

3. ___ A written instrument by which an owner intentionally conveys the right, title, or interest in a parcel of real estate to someone else

4. ___ The person who transfers title

5. ___ The person who acquires title by gift or sale

6. ___ A statement of the intention to convey property by deed

7. ___ A formal declaration, made before a notary public, that the person who is signing the deed is doing so voluntarily and that the signature is genuine

8. ___ A covenant in a deed that warrants that the grantor is the owner of the property and has the right to convey it

9. ___ A guarantee in a deed that the grantee's title will be good against any third party who might bring legal action to establish superior title

10. ___ A conveyance by deed from a trustor to a trustee for the benefit of a beneficiary

MATCHING B   *Write the letter of the matching term on the appropriate line.*

a. reconveyance deed

b. devise

c. involuntary alienation

d. probate

e. quitclaim

f. special warranty

g. bargain and sale

h. testate

i. testator

j. trustee's deed

1. ___ A type of deed that warrants only that the grantor received title and that the property has not been encumbered during the grantor's ownership

2. ___ A deed that contains no express warranties against encumbrances, but implies that the grantor holds title and possession of the property

3. ___ A deed that contains no covenants, warranties, or implications, and that provides the least amount of protection of any deed

4. ___ A conveyance by deed from a trustee to anyone other than the trustor

5. ___ A conveyance by deed from a trustee to the trustor

6. ___ The transfer of title without the owner's consent

7. ___ Having prepared a will indicating how property is to be disposed of after death

8. ___ The gift of real property by will

9. ___ The person who makes a will

10. ___ A formal judicial process to confirm a will's validity and to see that assets are distributed correctly

TRUE OR FALSE   *Circle the correct answer.*

1. T F A *title* to real estate is a printed document signed by the secretary of state.

2. T F A *deed* is the written instrument by which an owner of real estate intentionally conveys the right, title, or interest in a parcel to someone else.

3. T F To be valid, a deed must include a recital of consideration, an identifiable grantee, and a recital of exceptions and reservations.

4. T F A title is considered transferred when the deed is actually signed and acknowledged by the grantor.

5. T F To be valid, a deed must be signed by both the grantor and the grantee.

6. T F In a special warranty deed, the covenant of seisin warrants that the grantor's title will be good against third parties.

7. T F In a general warranty deed, the covenant of further assurance represents a promise by the grantor that the grantor will obtain and deliver any instrument needed to ensure good title.

8. T F A bargain and sale deed does not contain any express warranties against encumbrances.

9. T F If a trustee wanted to convey real estate back to the trustor, the trustee would use a trustee's deed.

10. T F In a deed executed under a court order, the full amount of consideration is stated in the deed.

11. T F Adverse possession is an example of involuntary alienation of property.

12. T F When a property owner dies, the owner's heirs by descent or by will may immediately take possession of any real estate.

13. T F While a deed must be delivered during the grantor's lifetime, a will takes effect only after the owner's death.

14. T F A person who receives real property through a testamentary transfer is referred to as the *devisee*.

15. T F Real property of an owner who dies intestate is distributed according to the laws of the state in which the owner resided at the time of death.

16. T F The type of ownership under which the grantees to a deed will receive the property is stated in the deed.

17. T F Encumbrances that run with the land, such as an easement, are stated in the sale disclosures rather than the deed.

18. T F One of the functions of probate is to determine the precise assets of the deceased person.

19. T F Many states have laws establishing a transfer tax that must be paid on conveyances of real estate.

20. T F When an estate is probated, the court usually selects the executor to distribute the assets to the heirs.

MULTIPLE CHOICE   *Circle the correct answer.*

1. The grantor is conveying an interest that is less than fee simple absolute. This explanation of the extent of ownership will be found in the
   a. seisin clause.
   b. granting clause.
   c. habendum clause.
   d. exceptions and reservations.

2. A woman conveys property to a buyer by a written document that contains five covenants protecting the buyer's title. What is the woman's role in this transaction?
   a. Grantee
   b. Grantor
   c. Devisor
   d. Devisee

3. The verification that the grantor's signature is both genuine and voluntary is a(n)
   a. judgment.
   b. attachment.
   c. consideration.
   d. acknowledgment.

4. Which of the following is an example of involuntary alienation?
   a. Sale
   b. Gift
   c. Escheat
   d. Will

5. The transfer of any interest in a parcel of real estate is typically in a document called the
   a. title.
   b. deed.
   c. attachment.
   d. mortgage.

6. All of the following are necessary to a valid deed *EXCEPT*
   a. recital of consideration.
   b. words of conveyance.
   c. the grantee's signature.
   d. delivery.

7. "I do hereby convey to my nearest relative all my interest in the property known as 123 Main Street, Bismarck, North Dakota, to have and to hold, in consideration of receipt of the amount of $10 and other good and valuable consideration." When signed, this document is a(n)
   a. valid conveyance by deed.
   b. invalid conveyance by deed, because the property conveyed is inadequately described.
   c. invalid conveyance by deed, because there is no recital of exceptions and reservations.
   d. invalid conveyance by deed, because the grantee is inadequately identified.

8. The type of deed that imposes the least liability on the grantor is a
   a. special warranty deed.
   b. bargain and sale deed.
   c. quitclaim deed.
   d. general warranty deed.

9. Title is *NOT* considered transferred until the deed is
   a. signed by the grantor.
   b. delivered to and accepted by the grantee.
   c. delivered to the grantee.
   d. released from escrow.

10. Which of the following is a guarantee that the grantor has the right to convey the property?
    a. Covenant against encumbrances
    b. Covenant of seisin
    c. Covenant of further assurance
    d. Covenant of quiet enjoyment

11. A bargain and sale deed contains how many express warranties?
    a. 0
    b. 2
    c. 3
    d. 5

12. Which type of deed is used by a grantor whose interest in the real estate may be unknown?
    a. Bargain-and-sale deed
    b. Special warranty deed
    c. General warranty deed
    d. Quitclaim deed

MULTIPLE CHOICE *(Continued)*

13. Under state law, one-half of an intestate decedent's property goes to the decedent's spouse, one-fourth is divided equally among the decedent's children, and one-fourth goes to the state. If there is no spouse, the children divide three-fourths equally. A citizen of this state dies intestate, survived by an ex-spouse and seven adult children. If the estate is $865,550, how much will each child receive under state law?
    a. $0
    b. $92,737.50
    c. $61,825.25
    d. $123,650.00

14. In one state, transfer tax is $1.20 for each $300 (or fraction of $300) of the sales price of any parcel of real estate. If a seller's property sold for $250,000, what will be the amount of the transfer tax due?
    a. $97.00
    b. $999.99
    c. $1,000.80
    d. $1,250.50

15. In front of witnesses, a woman says to a man, "I never made a will, but I want you to have my property when I die." If the man becomes the owner of the property, it is because the state recognizes what kind of will?
    a. Holographic
    b. Testamentary
    c. Nuncupative
    d. Probated

16. In one state, the transfer tax is $0.80 per $500 or fraction thereof. There is no tax charged on the first $500 of the price. What tax must the seller pay if the property sells for $329,650?
    a. $525.60
    b. $526.40
    c. $527.20
    d. $528.00

17. A modification to the original will is called a(n)
    a. addendum.
    b. amendment.
    c. probate.
    d. codicil.

18. All of the following are reasons for probate *EXCEPT*
    a. to ensure that the heirs do not fight among themselves.
    b. to confirm that the will is valid.
    c. to determine the exact assets of the deceased person.
    d. to identify which persons get any of the estate.

19. When a corporation transfers ownership of property, the deed must be signed by a(n)
    a. authorized officer.
    b. shareholder.
    c. broker.
    d. grantee.

20. The granting clause in a special warranty deed generally contains the words
    a. "grantor conveys and warrants."
    b. "grantor grants, bargains, and sells."
    c. "grantor remises, releases, and quitclaims."
    d. "grantor remises, releases, alienates, and conveys."

21. If a person dies intestate, the estate passes to the deceased person's heirs according to the
    a. deceased person's will.
    b. judgment of the executor.
    c. federal escheat laws.
    d. state's statute of descent and distribution.

22. What limits are set by the covenants in a general warranty deed?
    a. None.
    b. The covenants are limited to matters that occurred during the time the grantor owned the property.
    c. The covenants are limited to the matters that occurred within the last 10 years.
    d. The covenants are limited to the matters that occurred before the grantor owned the property.

ACTIVITY: Deed Characteristics

Identify the characteristics of deeds by placing check marks in the appropriate columns.

Characteristics	Types of Deeds			
	General Warranty	Special Warranty	Bargain and Sale	Quitclaim
Covenant of Warranty Forever				
Covenant of Further Assurance				
Covenant of Quiet Enjoyment				
Covenant Against Encumbrances				
Covenant of Seisin				
Express Warranties				
Implied Warranties				
Delivery and Acceptance				
Legal Description				
Habendum Clause				
Granting Clause				
Identifiable Grantee				
Signature of Grantor				
Consideration				
Grantor of Sound Mind				
Grantor of Lawful Age				

ANSWER KEY

Matching A

1. i   **2.** j   **3.** b   **4.** f   **5.** d   **6.** g   **7.** a   **8.** h
9. e   **10.** c

Matching B

1. f   **2.** g   **3.** e   **4.** j   **5.** a   **6.** c   **7.** h   **8.** b
9. i   **10.** d

True or False

1. **False.** Title to real estate is a way of referring to ownership; it is not an actual printed document. p. 194

2. **True.** A *deed* is the written instrument by which an owner of real estate intentionally conveys the right, title, or interest in a parcel to someone else. p. 194

3. **False.** To be valid, a deed must include a recital of consideration and an identifiable grantee; a deed *may* contain a recital of exceptions and reservations. p. 194

4. **False.** A title is considered transferred when the deed is actually *delivered to the grantee by the grantor.* p. 197

5. **False.** To be valid, a deed must be signed by all grantors named in the deed. Grantees are not required to sign the deed. p. 197

6. **False.** In a *general warranty deed,* the covenant of seisin warrants that the grantor is the owner of the property and has the right to convey it. p. 198

7. **True.** The covenant of further assurance represents a promise by the grantor that the grantor will obtain and deliver any instrument needed to ensure good title. p. 198

8. **True.** Although bargain and sale deed does not contain any express warranties against encumbrances, it does imply that the grantor holds title and possession of the property. p. 199

9. **False.** A trustee uses a reconveyance deed to return title to the trustor. p. 200

10. **True.** One common characteristic of deeds executed pursuant to court order is that the full consideration is usually stated in the deed, instead of "$10 and other valuable consideration." p. 200

11. **True.** Adverse possession is another means of involuntary transfer; it may take title away from an owner who fails to use or inspect the property for a number of years. p. 202

12. **False.** When a property owner dies, the owner's heirs by descent or will immediately take *title* to the property, but they may take possession *only after probate.* p. 204

13. **True.** A will is made by an owner to convey title to real or personal property after the owner's death. A deed must be delivered during the lifetime of the grantor that conveys a present interest in property. p. 203

14. **True.** The gift of real property by will is known as a devise, and a person who receives real property by will is known as a devisee. p. 203

15. **False.** Real property of an owner who dies intestate is distributed according to the laws of the state in which *the property is located.* p. 204

16. **True.** When it is necessary to define or explain the ownership to be enjoyed by the grantee, a habendum clause may follow the granting clause. p. 196

17. **False.** A deed must note any encumbrances that affect the title being conveyed. p. 196

18. **True.** Probate is a formal judicial process that proves or confirms the validity of a will, determines the precise assts of the deceased person, and identifies the people to whom the assets are to pass. p. 204

19. **True.** Many states have enacted laws providing for a state transfer tax on conveyances of real estate; the tax is usually payable when the deed is recorded. p. 201

20. **False.** The executor is usually named in the will. p. 205

Multiple Choice

1. **c.** The *habendum clause* is the *to have and to hold* clause that defines the extent of ownership that is being conveyed. p. 196

2. **b.** Because the woman is conveying her interest, she is the *grantor*. The person who receives the interest is the *grantee*. p. 195

3. **d.** An acknowledgment is a formal declaration under oath that the person who signs a written document does so voluntarily, and that the signature is genuine. p. 197

4. **c.** Dying may not be voluntary, but writing a will is. When a person dies intestate and leaves no heirs, the estate will *escheat* to the state. p. 203

5. **b.** A *deed* is the written document that transfers a real estate interest. Evidence of ownership (*title*) is written in the deed. An *attachment* is the process of taking a person's property into legal custody by a court order. A mortgage provides the security for a loan. p. 194

6. **c.** The grantee does not need to sign the deed, because the grantee receives the property (refer to answer 5). p. 197

7. **d.** Although the property may be adequately described, the grantee is not sufficiently identified. There is no transfer. p. 195

8. **c.** A quitclaim deed offers little or no protection. It transfers an interest, if any. p. 199

9. **b.** The most complete answer is delivered to and accepted by the grantee during the grantor's lifetime. p. 197

10. **b.** The *covenant against encumbrances* is a warranty that the property is free from encumbrances, except as so noted. The grantor further assures that everything will be done to make the title good. *Quiet enjoyment* guarantees that the title will be good against third parties who might try to bring legal action to gain the property. p. 198

11. **a.** A bargain and sale deed contains no express warranties against encumbrances; however, it does imply that the grantor holds title and possession of the property. p. 199

12. **d.** A quitclaim deed clears up clouds on the title. The grantor *quits* claim, if any. p. 199

13. **b.** The ex-spouse gets nothing. The state gets one-fourth; and three-fourths will be divided equally among the seven children: $865,550 ÷ 4 = $216,387.50 to the state. The remaining amount, $649,162.50, is divided seven ways, leaving $92,737.50 per child.

14. **c.** The transfer tax due is $1,000.80:

    $250,000 ÷ $300 = 833.33, which is rounded up to 834.

    834 × $1.20 = $1,000.80. p. 201

15. **c.** A holographic will is completely handwritten. A testamentary trust is established by will after the owner's death. *Probate* is the process of determining the validity of the will and distributing the assets of the estate. p. 202–204

16. **c.** The seller must pay $527.20:

    $329,650 – the free $500 = $329,150;

    $329,150 ÷ $500 = 658.3, which is rounded up to 659.

    659 × $0.80 = $527.20. p. 201

17. **d.** Any modification to a previously executed will is contained in a separate document called a codicil. Additional agreements attached to an agreement of sale are *addenda*; an *amendment* is a change to the existing content of a contract. *Probate* is the process of determining the validity of a will. p. 204

18. **a.** Hopefully, the probate process will not anger too many heirs, but keeping them happy is not the reason for probate. p. 204

19. **a.** Proper authority for the sale must be given by bylaws or by a resolution passed by the board of directors. Shareholders are not necessarily officers, nor are brokers. A grantee does not sign a deed. p. 197

20. **d.** The granting clause in a special warranty deed generally contains the words *grantor remises*, *releases*, *alienates*, and *conveys*. p. 199

21. **d.** A person who dies intestate does not have a will nor an executor named in a will. State escheat laws revert property ownership to the state if no heirs are determined by the statute of descent and distribution. p. 202

22. **a.** No limits are set by the covenants in a general warranty deed; the grantor defends the title against the grantor and all those who previously held title. p. 198

Activity: Deed Characteristics

Characteristics	Types of Deeds			
	General Warranty	Special Warranty	Bargain and Sale	Quitclaim
Covenant of Warranty Forever	✓			
Covenant of Further Assurance	✓			
Covenant of Quiet Enjoyment	✓			
Covenant Against Encumbrances	✓	✓		
Covenant of Seisin	✓	✓		
Express Warranties	✓	✓		
Implied Warranties	✓	✓	✓	
Delivery and Acceptance	✓	✓	✓	✓
Legal Description	✓	✓	✓	✓
Habendum Clause	✓	✓	✓	✓
Granting Clause	✓	✓	✓	✓
Identifiable Grantee	✓	✓	✓	✓
Signature of Grantor	✓	✓	✓	✓
Consideration	✓	✓	✓	✓
Grantor of Sound Mind	✓	✓	✓	✓
Grantor of Lawful Age	✓	✓	✓	✓

Note: The check marks in the top two boxes of the **Special Warranty Deed** column show that its basic warranties are similar to the **General Warranty's** covenants of seisin and against encumbrances. Remember that a **Special Warranty Deed contains two warranties** (1) that the grantor received title, and (2) that the property was not encumbered during the time the grantor held it.

Title Records

■ **identify** the various proofs of ownership;

■ **describe** recording, notice, and chain of title issues;

■ **explain** the process and purpose of a title search;

■ **distinguish** constructive and actual notice; and

■ **define** the following *key terms:*

abstract of title	chain of title	recording
actual notice	constructive notice	suit to quiet title
attorney's opinion of title	marketable title	title insurance
certificate of title	priority	title search

MATCHING   Write the letter of the matching term on the appropriate line.

a. *abstractor*

b. *actual notice*

c. *chain of title*

d. *constructive notice*

e. *title insurance*

f. *recording*

g. *cloud on the title*

h. *priority*

i. *suit to quiet title*

j. *title search*

1. ___ The act of placing documents in the public record

2. ___ The legal presumption that information may be obtained through diligent inquiry

3. ___ A type of notice also known as *direct knowledge*

4. ___ The order of rights in time, such as who recorded first, which party was in possession first, etc.

5. ___ The record of a property's ownership

6. ___ A legal action to remove a cloud on the title and establish legal ownership

7. ___ An examination of all the public records to determine if any defects exist in a property's history of ownership

8. ___ The individual who prepares a summary report of the results of a title search

9. ___ A contract under which a policyholder is protected from losses arising from defects in title

10. ___ Title problem that is created by a gap in the chain or other dispute of ownership

TRUE OR FALSE   Circle the correct answer.

1. T F Any individual who is interested in a particular property may review the public records to learn about the documents, claims, and other issues that affect its ownership.

2. T F Any written document that affects any estate, right, title, or interest in land must be recorded in the county in which the property owner resides.

3. T F To be eligible for recording, a document pertaining to real estate must be drawn and executed in accordance with the requirements of the federal government.

4. T F *Constructive notice* means that information about a property is not only available, but that someone has been given access to that information.

5. T F A search of the public records will disclose all liens that exist against a property.

6. T F The term *chain of title* refers to the record of a property's ownership.

7. T F In a typical title search, the chain of title is examined, beginning with the earliest records of ownership and proceeding forward up to the present owner.

8. T F An extended standard coverage title insurance policy protects a homeowner against rights of parties in possession and unrecorded liens.

9. T F One of the requirements of marketable title is that it could convince a reasonably well-informed and prudent purchaser, acting on business principles and with full knowledge of the significant facts, that the property could be resold or mortgaged at a later time.

10. T F A certificate of title is a guarantee of legal ownership.

MULTIPLE CHOICE   *Circle the correct answer.*

1. All of the following are acceptable evidence of an owner's title *EXCEPT*
   a. a recorded deed.
   b. an abstract of title and attorney's opinion.
   c. a title insurance policy.
   d. a certificate of title.

2. To serve as public notice, where is a deed recorded?
   a. The city where the owner lives
   b. The county or, in some states, the town where the property is located
   c. The state capital
   d. The largest city in the state

3. Five years ago, a lien was recorded against a parcel of property by a construction company. When the lien was recorded, a man was the owner of the property and a woman was an active partner in the construction company. The property is in county A, but the lien was recorded in county B. Now, the woman is trying to buy the property from the man. A title search in county A disclosed no liens against the property. Which of the following is *TRUE*?
   a. The woman has constructive notice of the lien but not actual notice, because of the mistake in recording.
   b. The woman has actual notice of the lien but not constructive notice, because of the mistake in recording.
   c. The woman has both actual and constructive notice of the lien, because of her association with the construction company and the recorded lien.
   d. The woman has no notice of the lien.

4. A woman purchased property from a man. Shortly after closing, the woman discovered that there were serious flaws in the title that made it unlikely that the property could be resold in the future. What can she do now?
   a. Because the title was flawed, the woman can legally void the sale, and the man must return any consideration.
   b. The woman has no recourse.
   c. Because the man conveyed unmarketable title, the woman is entitled to a new title report.
   d. Because the woman has accepted the deed, her only recourse is to sue the man under any covenants contained in the deed.

5. The reason that deeds and liens and other claims are recorded is to give
   a. constructive notice.
   b. actual notice.
   c. direct notice.
   d. nominal notice.

6. A history of all recorded liens and encumbrances is revealed in the
   a. title insurance policy.
   b. unrecorded documents.
   c. chain of title.
   d. abstract.

7. The person who prepares a certificate of title is the
   a. broker.   c. buyer.
   b. abstractor. d. seller.

8. Which of the following would be covered in a standard title insurance policy?
   a. Defects discoverable by physical inspection
   b. Unrecorded liens
   c. Forged documents
   d. Easements and restrictive covenants

9. A title insurance policy that protects the interests of a mortgagee is referred to as a(n)
   a. leasehold policy.
   b. lender's policy.
   c. certificate of sale policy.
   d. ALTA policy.

MULTIPLE CHOICE   *(Continued)*

10. What is an effect of the Marketable Title Act in the states in which it has been adopted?
    a. Establishes standardized forms for abstracts of title
    b. Disqualifies use of an attorney's opinion of title as acceptable evidence of title
    c. Limits the time beyond which title records must be searched
    d. Provides a certification system for qualifying title insurance companies

FILL-IN-THE-BLANK   *Select the word or words that best complete the following statements:*

abstract of title

actual notice

opinion of title

constructive notice

exclusions

improperly delivered deeds

marketable title

once, at closing

preliminary title search

*rights of parties in
    possession*

suit to quiet title

Torrens system

*twice, at purchase
    and resale*

1. To protect the buyer, in some states, a(n) _____ is conducted as soon as an offer to purchase has been accepted.

2. The type of notice that means the information is not only available, but that someone has been given the information and is aware of, it is called _____.

3. If a title has no serious defects, does not expose a purchaser to litigation, and does not cause the property to have a poor likelihood of resale, it is called _____.

4. Rather than a certificate of title, in some parts of the country, an attorney's _____ is used as evidence of title.

5. The premium for a title insurance policy is paid _____.

6. Uninsurable losses, such as zoning ordinances, named in a title insurance policy, are called _____.

7. A summary report of what a title search found in the public record is called a(an) _____.

8. The standard coverage title policy insures against hidden defects, such as _____.

9. Registration in the _____ provides evidence of title without needing to make an additional search of public records.

10. The legal presumption that information about rights in a property may be obtained by a person through diligent questioning and research is called _____.

ACTIVITY: Tracing the Chain of Title

The following abstract illustrates the complete title record for Lot 27, Block 6 of a subdivision. Mark the point at which the chain of title is broken.

Grantor	Grantee	By Instrument	Conveyance Date
Ferris-Bumper Builders, Inc.	Barton Doyle and Jane Doyle	Warranty Deed	January 19, 1909
Barton Doyle and Jane Doyle	Market Title & Trust Company	Trust Deed	January 20, 1909
Market Title & Trust Company	Barton Doyle and Jane Doyle	Reconveyance Deed	June 10, 1935
Barton Doyle and Jane Doyle	Anton Feldspar	Bargain and Sale Deed	March 7, 1940
Peter Parker and Mary Parker	Lamont Cranston and Gloria Reeve	Warranty Deed	November 16, 1958
Lamont Cranston and Gloria Reeve	Brookfield Bank and Trust Company	Mortgage	November 8, 1958
Lamont Cranston and Gloria Reeve	Gerald Carlos and Lydia Carlos	Warranty Deed	September 4, 1979
Brookfield Bank and Trust Co.	Lamont Cranston and Gloria Reeve	Release	May 2, 1995

ANSWER KEY

Matching

1. f **2.** d **3.** b **4.** h **5.** c **6.** i **7.** j **8.** a
9. e **10.** g

True or False

1. **True.** Public records are just that—records that are open to the public—which means that anyone interested in a particular property can review the records to learn about the documents, claims, and other details that affect its ownership. p. 211

2. **False.** Any written document that affects any estate, right, title, or interest in land must be recorded in the county or, in some states, town in which the *property is located.* p. 211

3. **False.** To be eligible for recording, a document pertaining to real estate must be drawn and executed in accordance with the requirements of the *recording acts of the state in which the property is located.* p. 211

4. **False.** *Actual notice* means that not only is the information about property available, but someone has been given access to that information. p. 212

5. **False.** A search of the public records will disclose all *recorded* liens that exist against a property. p. 212

6. **True.** The chain of title is the record of a property's ownership, beginning with the earliest owner. p. 213

7. **False.** In a typical title search, the chain of title is examined beginning with the *present owner and tracing backwards to the earliest records of ownership or a definite period of years, depending on state statute.* p. 213

8. **True.** Extended coverage as provide by an American Land Title Association (ALTA) policy includes the protections of a standard policy plus additional protections. p. 215

9. **True.** A marketable title should disclose no serious defects, should not depend on doubtful questions of law, and should convince a reasonably well-informed and prudent purchaser, acting on business principles and principles and with full knowledge of the significant facts, that the property could be resold or mortgaged at a later time. p. 214

10. **False.** A certificate of title is evidence but not a guarantee of ownership. A certificate of title is a statement of opinion of the title's status on the date the certificate is issued. p. 214

Multiple Choice

1. **a.** A recorded deed is nothing more than that. Other verifications of thorough examinations of recorded documents can affect the title. p. 214

2. **b.** Because land is immobile, it makes sense to record all information about title to the property in the county where it is located. Some owners frequently relocate, and they would be hard to find. p. 211

3. **b.** Because the woman was a partner, she knew that the lien was filed. Constructive notice is not given, because the lien was not filed in the county where the property is located, which is where it would be expected to be filed. p. 212

4. **d.** Professionals should look at the evidence of ownership before closing. There is more leverage to get problems corrected before closing than after closing. p. 213

5. **a.** The recorder's office is a central place to deposit and discover information. If it is recorded, researchers cannot claim ignorance; they would have known if they had researched the records. p. 212

6. **d.** The title insurance policy lists coverage and exceptions to the policy. Unrecorded documents have not been examined. The chain of title traces ownership. The abstract is the most complete documentation of recorded liens and encumbrances. p. 213

7. **b.** The abstractor searches all of the public records, and then summarizes the various events that affected the title throughout its history. p. 213

8. **c.** Title insurance does not protect against claims of parties in possession, because the grantee should have visited the property; nor does it cover unrecorded liens. Easements and restrictive covenants are found in the deed and should be known to the grantee. p. 215

9. **b.** The mortgagee is the lender. The mortgagee's policy is transferable. p. 216

10. **c.** The law extinguishes certain interests and cures certain defects arising before the root of the title. p. 213

Fill-in-the-Blank

1. To protect the buyer, in some states, a *preliminary title search* is conducted as soon as an offer to purchase has been accepted.

2. The type of notice that means the information is not only available, but that someone has been given the information and is aware of it, is called *actual notice*.

3. If a title has no serious defects, does not expose a purchaser to litigation, and does not cause the property to have a poor likelihood of resale, it is called *marketable title*.

4. Rather than a certificate of title, in some parts of the country, an *attorney's opinion of title* is used as evidence of title.

5. The premium for a title insurance policy is paid *once, at closing*.

6. Uninsurable losses, such as zoning ordinances, named in a title insurance policy are called *exclusions*.

7. A summary report of what a title search found in the public record is called an *abstract of title*.

8. The standard coverage title policy insures against hidden defects, such as *improperly delivered deeds*.

9. Registration in the *Torrens system* provides evidence of title without needing to make an additional search of public records.

10. The legal presumption that information about rights in a property may be obtained by a person through diligent questioning and research is called *constructive notice*.

Activity: Tracing the Chain of Title

In November 1958, Peter and Mary Parker conveyed title as grantors, but there is no indication that they ever received title as grantees from Anton Feldspar.

Grantor	Grantee	By Instrument	Conveyance Date
Ferris-Bumper Builders, Inc.	Barton Doyle and Jane Doyle	Warranty Deed	January 19, 1909
Barton Doyle and Jane Doyle	Market Title & Trust Company	Trust Deed	January 20, 1909
Market Title & Trust Company	Barton Doyle and Jane Doyle	Reconveyance Deed	June 10, 1935
Barton Doyle and Jane Doyle	Anton Feldspar	Bargain and Sale Deed	March 7, 1940
Peter Parker and Mary Parker	Lamont Cranston and Gloria Reeve	Warranty Deed	November 16, 1958
Lamont Cranston and Gloria Reeve	Brookfield Bank and Trust Company	Mortgage	November 8, 1958
Lamont Cranston and Gloria Reeve	Gerald Carlos and Lydia Carlos	Warranty Deed	September 4, 1979
Brookfield Bank and Trust Co.	Lamont Cranston and Gloria Reeve	Release	May 2, 1995

CHAPTER 14

Real Estate Financing: Principles

■ **LEARNING OBJECTIVES**   *Before you answer these questions, you should be able to*

- **identify** the basic provisions of security and debt instruments: promissory notes, mortgage documents, deeds of trust, and land contracts;

- **describe** the effect of discount points on yield;

- **explain** the procedures involved in a foreclosure;

- **distinguish** between lien and title theories;

- **explain** the three methods of foreclosure; and

- **define** the following *key terms:*

acceleration clause	foreclosure	owner financing
alienation clause	hypothecation	prepayment penalty
assume	interest	promissory note
beneficiary	lien theory	release deed
deed in lieu of foreclosure	loan origination fee	satisfaction
deed of trust	mortgage	statutory right of
defeasance clause	mortgagee	redemption
deficiency judgment	mortgagor	"subject to"
discount points	negotiable instrument	title theory
equitable right of	note	trustor
redemption	novation	usury

MATCHING A *Write the letter of the matching term on the appropriate line.*

a. *acceleration clause*

b. *hypothecation*

c. *discount points*

d. *executing*

e. *deed of trust*

f. *mortgagor*

g. *mortgagee*

h. *usury*

i. *interest*

j. *promissory note*

1. ___ The borrower in a mortgage loan clause

2. ___ The lender in a mortgage loan

3. ___ The act of signing a loan instrument

4. ___ A borrower's personal pledge to repay a debt according to agreed-upon terms

5. ___ The pledging of a property as security for payment of a loan without actually surrendering the property itself

6. ___ A financing instrument that conveys bare legal title on behalf of a beneficiary, but no right of possession

7. ___ A charge for the use of money

8. ___ The act of charging interest in excess of the maximum legal rate

9. ___ A charge imposed by lenders to adjust for the difference between a loan's interest rate and the yield an investor demands

10. ___ The part of a financing agreement that gives the lender the right to declare the entire debt due and payable immediately on default

MATCHING B   *Write the letter of the matching term on the appropriate line.*

a. *alienation clause*

b. *deed in lieu of foreclosure*

c. *loan origination fee*

d. *deficiency judgment*

e. *equitable right of redemption*

f. *foreclosure*

g. *lien theory*

h. *defeasance clause*

i. *statutory right of redemption*

j. *subordination agreement*

k. *prepayment penalty*

l. *title theory*

m. *beneficiary*

n. *trustee*

o. *trustor*

1. ___ Percentage of the loan amount charged to a borrower for the costs of generating a loan

2. ___ The part of a financing agreement that requires the lender to execute a satisfaction or release when the note has been paid in full

3. ___ A provision in a financing agreement that permits the lender to declare the entire debt due immediately in the event the property is sold

4. ___ A device by which one lender agrees to change the priority of its loan relative to another lender

5. ___ A legal procedure in which property pledged as security is taken from the borrower to satisfy the debt

6. ___ A document by which property is transferred to the lender by mutual agreement rather than by lawsuit

7. ___ A borrower's option of reinstating a defaulted debt prior to the foreclosure sale by paying the amount due

8. ___ A right established by state law that permits a defaulted borrower to recover property within a limited time after a foreclosure sale

9. ___ A procedure for obtaining the unpaid balance of a debt where the foreclosure sale does not generate sufficient funds

10. ___ Idea that a mortgage is purely a lien on real property

11. ___ Concept that the borrower actually gives legal title to the lender (or other party) and retains equitable title

12. ___ The borrower's legal status on a deed of trust

13. ___ Fee that a borrower pays on any payment made ahead of schedule (if allowed)

14. ___ The lender's legal status on a deed of trust

15. ___ On a deed of trust, a third party who holds the deed as security for the loan

TRUE OR FALSE   *Circle the correct answer.*

1. T   F   A mortgage is classified as an involuntary lien on real estate.

2. T   F   A *mortgage* is a security instrument in which a mortgagee pledges real property to the mortgagor as security for the debt.

3. T   F   In title theory states, the mortgagor actually gives legal title to the mortgagee, while retaining equitable title.

4. T   F   When a property is mortgaged, the owner must execute both a promissory note and a security instrument.

5. T   F   *Subordination* is the pledging of property as security for payment of a loan while retaining possession of the property.

6. T   F   In a typical deed of trust, the mortgagee is the beneficiary, and the borrower is the trustor.

7. T   F   A point is 1 percent of the purchase price of the property being offered as security for the loan.

8. T   F   In the event of a borrower's default, a subordination clause makes foreclosure easier by giving a lender the right to declare the entire debt due and payable.

9. T   F   In most mortgage documents, the defeasance clause requires the mortgagee to execute a satisfaction when the note has been fully paid, returning to the mortgagor all interest in the real estate.

10. T   F   When a real estate loan secured by a deed of trust has been repaid in full, the beneficiary executes a discharge that releases the property back to the trustor.

11. T   F   A buyer who purchases real property and assumes the seller's debt becomes personally obligated for the repayment of the entire debt.

12. T   F   To give constructive notice of the lien, a mortgage or deed of trust must be recorded in the recorder's office of the county in which the real estate is located.

13. T   F   In states that permit strict foreclosure, the court simply awards full legal title to the lender and no sale of the property takes place.

14. T   F   The statutory right of redemption is the right of a defaulted borrower to redeem the real estate after default, but before the foreclosure sale.

15. T   F   *Usury* is defined as the act of charging interest in excess of the maximum legal rate.

16. T   F   After the redemption period (if applicable), the successful bidder at a foreclosure sale receives a deed that conveys whatever title the borrower had, with no warranties.

17. T   F   Lenders are allowed to charge prepayment penalties on mortgage loans insured or guaranteed by the federal government.

18. T   F   If the lender must obtain insurance on property because the borrower let it lapse, the lender can add the premium cost to the unpaid debt.

19. T   F   An assignment of mortgage occurs when the borrower pays off the loan.

20. T   F   When a mortgage lender finds that a borrower has not made necessary repairs to the property, the lender usually immediately proceeds to foreclosure.

MULTIPLE CHOICE   *Circle the correct answer.*

1. States that recognize the lender as the *owner* of the mortgaged property are known as
   a. subordination theory states.
   b. recordation theory states.
   c. title theory states.
   d. lien theory states.

2. A document that indicates that a loan has been made is referred to as a
   a. promissory note.   c. deed of trust.
   b. mortgage deed.   d. satisfaction.

3. A woman defaults on her mortgage, and the lender forecloses. The lender's foreclosure suit is filed on March 15, and the sale is to be held on May 10. If the woman attempts to redeem the property on May 1, which of the following statements applies?
   a. The woman is exercising her statutory right of redemption.
   b. The woman is exercising her equitable right of redemption.
   c. The woman's attempt to redeem the property is too early; by statute, she must wait until after the sale.
   d. The woman cannot redeem the property after a foreclosure suit is filed.

4. A house is listed for $250,000. A man buys it for $230,000, with a 20 percent down payment. He borrows the balance on a fixed-rate mortgage at 6 percent. The lender charges four points. If there are no other closing costs involved, how much money does the man need at closing?
   a. $7,360   c. $46,000
   b. $26,000   d. $53,360

5. One afternoon, a client calls a real estate broker. "My lender just told me that my note and mortgage is a negotiable instrument," says the client. "What does that mean?" Which of the following would be the broker's *BEST* response?
   a. "That's great! It means the lender is willing to negotiate on the interest rate."
   b. "Oh no! That means the mortgage can't be assumed by the next person you sell to."
   c. "Don't worry. That means the mortgage can be sold by the lender, but you're not affected."
   d. "Uh-oh! That means we have to go back to the sellers and ask them to pay the points."

6. A deed of trust involves all of the following terminology *EXCEPT*
   a. lender.   c. trustee.
   b. borrower.   d. mortgagor.

7. One state is a lien theory state. A buyer purchases property from a seller and gives him a mortgage as part of the purchase price. Therefore, the buyer is the borrower, and the seller is the lender. All of the following statements are correct *EXCEPT*
   a. the buyer retains equitable title to the property.
   b. if the buyer defaults on the loan, the seller must undergo a formal foreclosure proceeding to recover the security.
   c. the buyer has given legal title to the seller.
   d. the seller has only a lien interest in the property.

8. Where a trust deed is used, the lender is the
   a. trustee.   c. trustor.
   b. beneficiary.   d. maker.

9. A mortgage company charges borrowers a 1.5 percent loan origination fee. A man buys a house for $210,000 and pays $50,000 in cash. He applies for a mortgage to cover the balance. What will the mortgage company charge as a fee if the asking price of the house was $235,000?
   a. $2,400   c. $3,525
   b. $3,150   d. $3,750

MULTIPLE CHOICE *(Continued)*

10. A mortgage document contains the following clause: "In the event of Borrower's default under the terms of this Agreement, Lender may declare the entire unpaid balance of the debt due and payable immediately." This clause is referred to as a(n)

    a. hypothecation clause.
    b. acceleration clause.
    c. defeasance clause.
    d. release clause.

11. This month, a man made the last payment on a mortgage loan secured by a woman. The man's lender must execute a

    a. release deed.
    b. promissory note.
    c. possessory note.
    d. satisfaction of mortgage.

12. A woman took out a 30-year mortgage on a parcel of property in 1992. On April 1, 2010, her lender discovered that the property lies in a flood hazard area as defined by the National Flood Insurance Reform Act of 1994. The lender informed the woman of the situation on April 15. Based on these facts, which of the following statements is correct?

    a. The National Flood Insurance Reform Act of 1994 does not apply to the woman's property.
    b. The woman has until May 15 to purchase flood insurance.
    c. The woman has until May 30 to purchase flood insurance.
    d. If the woman refuses to purchase flood insurance, the lender must do so; however, the lender may not charge the cost of the additional insurance to the woman.

13. A buyer purchases property from a seller for $45,000 in cash and assumes the seller's outstanding mortgage balance of $98,500. The lender executes a release for the seller. The buyer fails to make any mortgage payments, and the lender forecloses. At the foreclosure sale, the property is sold for $75,000. Based on these facts, who is liable and for what amount?

    a. The seller is solely liable for $23,500.
    b. The buyer is solely liable for $23,500.
    c. The buyer and the seller are equally liable for $23,500.
    d. The buyer is solely liable for $30,000.

14. All of the following statements are characteristic of a typical land contract *EXCEPT*

    a. at the end of the loan term, the seller will deliver clear title.
    b. the buyer is granted equitable title and possession.
    c. the vendee holds legal title during the contract term.
    d. in the event of a default, the vendor may retain any money already paid.

15. The borrower defaulted on his mortgage loan, leaving an unpaid balance of $95,000. After receiving only $85,000 from the sale of the property, the lender filed for a

    a. lis pendens.
    b. release deed.
    c. satisfaction piece.
    d. deficiency judgment.

MULTIPLE CHOICE   *(Continued)*

16. A woman was the owner of a parcel of property. When she defaulted on her loan, the trustee immediately sold the property to recover the debt. The trustee acted under the terms of the security instrument. Based on these facts, which of the following statements is *TRUE*?

    a. The exercise of this power of sale clause is an example of strict foreclosure.

    b. The trustee's sale of the property was illegal unless the woman's state permits a so-called *friendly foreclosure*.

    c. The exercise of this power of sale clause is an example of nonjudicial foreclosure.

    d. The woman could have exercised her statutory right of redemption at any time prior to the trustee's sale of the property.

17. The woman could have exercised her statutory right of redemption at any time prior to the trustee's sale of the property. The difference between the interest rate that the lender charges and what the investor demands can be made up by charging

    a. discount points.

    b. loan origination fees.

    c. satisfaction fees.

    d. underwriting fees.

18. What is the term that refers to a lender charging an interest rate that is higher than that permitted by law?

    a. Alienation   c. Hypothecation

    b. Usury   d. Defeasance

19. Parties to lending agreements are referred to by different terms. Which of the following refers to the same party?

    a. Borrower = Beneficiary

    b. Borrower = Mortgagor

    c. Trustee = Borrower

    d. Trustor = Mortgagee

20. If the lender wants to call the entire note due and payable if the borrower stops making payments, the security instrument must include a(n)

    a. acceleration clause.

    b. defeasance clause.

    c. alienation clause.

    d. prepayment clause.

21. When a deed of trust is the security instrument, which party usually chooses the trustee?

    a. The borrower

    b. The lender

    c. The devisee

    d. The county government

22. What is the purpose of usury laws?

    a. To maximize a lender's yield from real estate loans

    b. To set limits on the loan origination fees lenders can charge

    c. To protect consumers from lenders charging excessively high rates

    d. To set limits on discount points investors can demand from lenders

23. How does an acceleration clause help lenders?

    a. Without the acceleration clause, lenders would have to sue the borrower for every overdue payment.

    b. Lenders would rather foreclose on property than hold a long-term loan.

    c. It results in a deed in lieu of foreclosure rather than the default process.

    d. It sets out the provisions for the impound account.

MULTIPLE CHOICE *(Continued)*

25. What is a major disadvantage to lenders of accepting a deed in lieu of foreclosure?
    a. The lender takes the real estate subject to all junior liens.
    b. The lender gains rights to private mortgage insurance.
    c. The process is lengthy and involves a lawsuit.
    d. It is an adverse element in the borrower's credit history.

ACTIVITY: Redemption Rights Timeline

Write "Equitable" or "Statutory" in the appropriate "Right of Redemption" boxes.

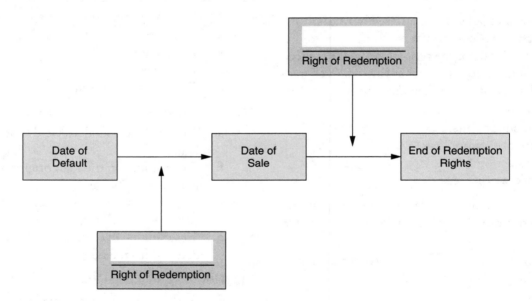

ANSWER KEY

Matching A

1. f **2.** g **3.** d **4.** j **5.** b **6.** e **7.** i **8.** h
9. c **10.** a

Matching B

1. c **2.** h **3.** a **4.** j **5.** f **6.** b **7.** e **8.** i
9. d **10.** g **11.** l **12.** o **13.** k **14.** m **15.** n

True or False

1. **False.** A mortgage is classified as a voluntary lien on real estate. p. 223

2. **False.** A *mortgage* is a financing agreement in which a *mortgagor* pledges real property to the *mortgagee* as security for the debt. p. 223

3. **True.** In title theory states, the mortgage give actual title to the mortgagor, and legal title is returned to the mortgagor only when the debt is repaid in full (or some other obligation is fulfilled). p. 223

4. **True.** The borrower signs a promissory note pledging to repay the debt and gives the lender a mortgage, which is security for the property. p. 223

5. **False.** *Hypothecation* is the pledging of property as security for payment of a loan while retaining possession of the property. p. 224

6. **True.** There are three parties to a deed of trust: the trustee holds the deed of trust on behalf of the lender, who is known as the beneficiary, the holder of the note. The borrower is the trustor. p. 227

7. **False.** A *point* is 1 percent of the *amount being borrowed*. For borrowers, one discount point equals 1 percent of the loan amount and is charged as prepaid interest at the closing. p. 226

8. **False.** In the event of a borrower's default, an *acceleration clause* makes foreclosure easier by giving a lender the right to declare the entire debt due and payable. p. 228

9. **True.** By the defeasance clause, the lender is required to execute a satisfaction when the note has been fully paid. The lender is then divested of all interest in the property. p. 229

10. **False.** After a real estate loan that is secured by a deed of trust has been repaid in full, the *trustee* executes a release deed that releases the property back to the trustor. p. 229

11. **True.** Unlike buying *subject* to the mortgage, a buyer who purchases a property and assumes the seller's debt becomes personally obligated for the payment of the entire debt. The only way to avoid this is if the lender executes a novation, making the buyer responsible for the debt. p. 230

12. **True.** Both a mortgage and a deed of trust must be recorded to provide constructive notice that the property has been pledged as security. When the debt is repaid in full, the release is then recorded. p. 229

13. **True.** After appropriate notice is made to the delinquent borrower, in some states, the lender may acquire mortgaged property through strict foreclosure. The court awards full legal title to the lender, and no sale takes place. p. 232

14. **False.** The *equitable right of redemption* is the right of a defaulted borrower to redeem real estate after default, but before the foreclosure sale. p. 233

15. **True.** Usury is the practice of charging interest at a higher rate than the maximum rate established by state law. p. 225

16. **True.** After the redemption period, if the delinquent borrower does not repay the loan, an official, such as a sheriff, executes a deed to the person who paid the debts. The deed conveys whatever title the borrower had prior to the redemption period. p. 233

17. **False.** Mortgage lenders also cannot charge prepayment penalties on loans that have been sold to Fannie Mae or Freddie Mac. p. 226

18. **True.** If the lender purchases insurance on behalf of the borrower, the cost of the insurance may be charged back to the borrower. p. 230

19. **False.** An assignment of mortgage occurs when the lender sells the loan to an investor or other mortgage company. p. 225

20. **False.** The loan documents may provide for a grace period, such as 30 days, within which the borrower can meet the obligation and cure the default. p. 228

Multiple Choice

1. **c.** In lien theory states, a mortgage is simply a lien on the property, whereas title theory states interpret a mortgage to mean that the lender is the owner of the mortgaged property. p. 223

2. **a.** The evidence that a loan has been made is found in the promissory note. A mortgage or deed of trust provides security for the loan. A satisfaction or release indicates that the loan has been repaid in full. p. 224

3. **b.** The woman has an equity interest in the property until the foreclosure sale is complete; thus, she is exercising her equitable right of redemption. In some states, she may retain a statutory right of redemption for a period of time after the foreclosure sale. p. 233

4. **d.** The man needs $53,360 at closing. Three steps:

    (1) Calculate down payment: $230,000 × 20% = $46,000.

    (2) Determine points charge: $230,000 × 80% × 4% = $7,360.

    (3) Total the two amounts: $46,000 + $7,360 = $53,360.

5. **c.** Negotiable instruments are transferable. A note and mortgage will often be sold on the secondary market. p. 225

6. **d.** A mortgagor is the borrower in a mortgage. In a deed of trust, the borrower is the trustor, and the trustee holds naked title in trust for the beneficiary (lender). p. 227

7. **c.** In a lien theory state, a borrower who gives a mortgage, even in the seller financing situation described in this question, retains both equitable and legal title to the property serving as security. p. 223

8. **b.** The trustor (borrower) conveys naked or bare title to the trustee who holds it in trust for the beneficiary (lender). p. 227

9. **a.** The man's loan origination fee is $2,400: $210,000 – $50,000 × 1.5% = $2,400. The asking price is not relevant to this problem. p. 228

10. **b.** *Hypothecation* is the act of offering the property as security without giving up possession. The *defeasance clause* in a mortgage defeats the granting clause. A *release* indicates that the loan has been repaid in full. p. 224

11. **d.** The *promissory note* shows that a loan was made. The *satisfaction* indicates that the loan was fully repaid. Satisfaction of mortgage is also sometimes called a *release*, but not a release deed. p. 229

12. **c.** If the lender discovers that a secured property is in a flood hazard area, the borrower must be notified. The borrower has 45 days to purchase flood insurance. If the borrower does not buy the insurance, the lender must purchase the insurance and charge back the cost of the insurance to the borrower. p. 230

13. **b.** Because the lender released the original borrower, the second borrower is fully responsible for the deficiency. p. 230

14. **c.** The *vendor* retains legal title during the contract term in this form of seller financing. p. 231

15. **d.** A *deficiency* results when the foreclosed property does not bring enough money to fully repay the loan; the mortgagor may be entitled to a personal judgment against the borrower for the unpaid balance. *Lis pendens* gives notice that the property is the subject of legal action. A *satisfaction* indicates that the loan was fully repaid. p. 234

16. **c.** Strict foreclosure and friendly foreclosure do not involve a sale. The statutory right of redemption applies only after the sale. A nonjudicial foreclosure does not involve the courts. p. 232

17. **a.** Loan origination fees are charged to cover the cost of making the loan. The satisfaction indicates that the loan has been fully repaid. p. 226

18. **b.** *Hypothecation* is giving property as security without giving up possession. p. 224

19. **b.** The person who makes the payments to repay the loan is called the borrower. The person who gave the property as security is called the mortgagor. Both are the same person. p. 223

20. **a.** The acceleration clause permits the lender to declare the entire note due upon default by the borrower. The alienation clause is also known as the *due on sale* clause, permitting the lender to declare the entire note due if the property is sold, and thus preventing a loan assumption. p. 228

21. **b.** The lender usually also reserves the right to substitute trustees in the event of death or dismissal. p. 227

22. **c.** Usury laws limit the interest rates lenders can charge so that consumers are protected from unscrupulous lenders. p. 225

23. **a.** A lender's purpose is to make long-term loans, not foreclose. The impound account is set up under a different provision of the loan. p. 228

24. **d.** The proceeds from the sale are used to pay off the mortgage and junior lienholders. If the proceeds are insufficient, these creditors can seek a deficiency judgment against the original owner for the remaining debt. The purchaser is not involved unless the purchaser is a mortgage or lienholder. p. 232

25. **a.** The lender loses rights to FHA or private mortgage insurance or VA guarantees. The process is called *friendly foreclosure*, because a lawsuit is not involved. It is an adverse element for the borrower, but that does not affect the lender. p. 233

Activity: Redemption Rights Timeline

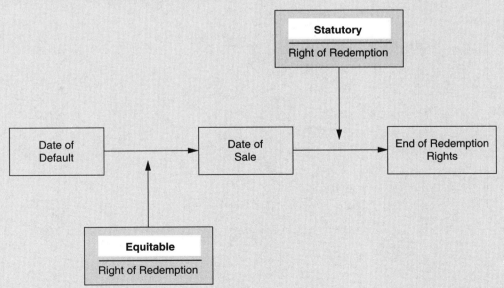

CHAPTER 15

Real Estate Financing: Practice

■ **LEARNING OBJECTIVES**   *Before you answer these questions, you should be able to*

■ **identify** the types of institutions in the primary and secondary mortgage markets;

■ **describe** the various types of financing techniques available to real estate purchasers and the role of government financing regulations;

■ **explain** the requirements and qualifications for conventional, FHA, and VA loan programs;

■ **distinguish** among the different types of creative financing techniques that address borrowers' different needs; and

■ **define** the following *key terms:*

adjustable-rate mortgage (ARM)
amortized loan
balloon payment
blanket loan
buydown
certificate of reasonable value (CRV)
Community Reinvestment Act of 1977 (CRA)
computerized loan origination (CLO)
construction loan
conventional loan
Equal Credit Opportunity Act (ECOA)
Fannie Mae

Federal Deposit Insurance Corporation (FDIC)
Federal Reserve System (Fed)
FHA loan
Freddie Mac
Ginnie Mae
growing-equity mortgage
home equity loan
index
interest-only mortgage
loan-to-value ratios (LTV)
margin
mortgage insurance premium (MIP)
open-end loan
package loan

primary mortgage market
private mortgage insurance (PMI)
purchase-money mortgage (PMM)
Real Estate Settlement Procedures Act (RESPA)
Regulation Z
reverse mortgage
sale-and-leaseback
secondary mortgage market
straight loan
trigger terms
Truth in Lending Act
VA loan
wraparound loan

MATCHING A   *Write the letter of the matching term on the appropriate line.*

a. Federal Reserve

b. amortized loan

c. fiduciary lenders

d. private mortgage insurance

e. Ginnie Mae

f. mortgage brokers

g. secondary mortgage market

h. reverse mortgage

i. primary mortgage market

j. straight loan

1. ___ A national system of banking districts designed to maintain sound credit conditions and a favorable economic climate

2. ___ Type of loan in which payments are made to the borrower by the lender and is usually repaid from the sale of the property

3. ___ Lenders who originate loans by making money available to borrow

4. ___ Thrifts, savings associations, and commercial banks

5. ___ Intermediaries who bring borrowers and lenders together

6. ___ Investors who buy and sell loans after the loan is funded

7. ___ A method of providing a lender with part of a conventional loan balance in the event that a borrower defaults on the loan

8. ___ A wholly governmental agency organized as a non-stock corporation that administers special assistance programs and guarantees mortgage-backed securities using FHA and VA loans

9. ___ A type of loan in which the borrower makes periodic interest payments, followed by the payment of the principal in full at the end of the term

10. ___ A loan in which both principal and interest are paid off gradually, over time

MATCHING B   *Write the letter of the matching term on the appropriate line.*

a. blanket loan

b. adjustable-rate mortgage

c. buydown

d. certificate of eligibility

e. Equal Credit Opportunity Act

f. package loan

g. growing equity mortgage

h. purchase-money mortgage

i. Truth in Lending Act

j. Real Estate Settlement Procedures Act

1. ___ A form of loan in which the interest rate fluctuates depending on the change in an objective economic index

2. ___ A fixed interest-rate mortgage in which monthly payments of principal are increased over the life of the loan according to an index or schedule; each such increase enlarging the regular monthly payment

3. ___ The document that determines the maximum VA loan guarantee to which a veteran is entitled

4. ___ A form of seller financing whereby the buyer gives the seller a note and mortgage

5. ___ A loan that finances the purchase of both real and personal property

6. ___ A method of financing the purchase of property that temporarily (or permanently) lowers the interest rate through the payment of a lump sum of cash to the lender

7. ___ Lending law prohibiting discrimination based on marital status or sex

8. ___ Type of mortgage used by developers, securing the loan with several parcels

9. ___ Law that is designed to ensure that buyer and seller are both fully informed of all closing costs

10. ___ Law that requires lenders to reveal the true cost of borrowing money

TRUE OR FALSE   *Circle the correct answer.*

1. T F   The Federal Reserve System is comprised of the lenders who originate loans.

2. T F   Income from a loan is generated by up-front finance charges collected at closing, plus interest collected during the loan term.

3. T F   The primary mortgage market includes savings associations, insurance companies, and mortgage bankers.

4. T F   Fannie Mae is a privately owned corporation.

5. T F   At first, an *amortized loan* applies monthly payments toward the total interest owed over the life of the loan. Once the total interest is paid off, the monthly payments are applied to the principal amount.

6. T F   In an adjustable-rate mortgage, the interest rate is usually based on an objective economic indicator, plus an additional premium, called a *margin.*

7. T F   In an adjustable-rate mortgage, the conversion option establishes how often the rate may be changed.

8. T F   In a 20-year straight loan of $92,500 at 6.8 percent interest, the borrower's final monthly payment will be $93,024.17.

9. T F   The *value* portion of a property's loan-to-value (LTV) ratio is the higher of the sale price or the appraised value.

10. T F   The FHA is not a mortgage lender.

11. T F   A home equity loan takes first lien priority over the original mortgage loan.

12. T F   A *wraparound loan* covers more than one parcel or lot and is usually used to finance subdivision developments.

13. T F   In an *open-end loan* the interest rate on the initial amount borrowed is fixed, but the rate on future advances is linked to future market rates.

14. T F   Under the Truth in Lending Act, consumers must be fully informed of all finance charges and of the true interest rate prior to the completion of a transaction.

15. T F   Under Regulation Z, a residential purchase-money borrower has three days in which to rescind a transaction by notifying the lender of intent to rescind.

16. T F   Under the Community Reinvestment Act, the findings of the government agency review of an institution's reinvestment activities are strictly confidential.

17. T F   A computerized loan origination system allows a real estate broker to select a lender and apply for a loan on a buyer's behalf.

18. T F   A VA appraisal is referred to as a *certificate of reasonable value* (CRV).

19. T F   Under the Truth in Lending Act, a phrase, such as *no money down*, triggers certain disclosures.

20. T F   FHA loans are attractive to lenders, because the loans have insurance against loss due to borrower default.

21. T F   The VA limits the amount of principal in a VA loan.

22. T F   The Community Reinvestment Act requires financial institutions to help meet their communities' needs for low-income and moderate-income housing.

23. T F   When a loan is sold in the secondary mortgage market, the purchasing investor always assumes the servicing of the loan.

MULTIPLE CHOICE   *Circle the correct answer.*

1. All of the following are roles of the Federal Reserve System *EXCEPT*
    a. help counteract inflationary trends.
    b. create a favorable economic climate.
    c. maintain sound credit conditions.
    d. make direct loans to buyers.

2. A lender who collects payments, processes them, and follows up on loan delinquencies is said to
    a. increase the yield to the lender.
    b. service the loan.
    c. insure loan payments.
    d. underwrite the loans.

3. The primary mortgage market lenders that have most recently branched out into making mortgage loans are
    a. credit unions.
    b. endowment funds.
    c. insurance companies.
    d. savings associations.

4. What is the kind of real estate loan in which the interest rate is tied to the movement of an objective economic indicator?
    a. Buydown
    b. Graduated mortgage payment
    c. Adjustable-rate mortgage
    d. Straight loan

5. The loan in which equal payments reduce the full amount of principal and interest to zero is a(n)
    a. hypothecation.   c. amortized loan.
    b. straight loan.   d. buydown.

6. The borrower who chooses an adjustable-rate mortgage can depend on the margin to
    a. remain constant for the life of the loan.
    b. fluctuate according to some economic index.
    c. only change according to an agreed-upon amount.
    d. decrease over the life of the loan.

7. To qualify for most conventional loans, the borrower's monthly housing expenses and total other monthly obligations cannot exceed what percent of the total gross monthly income?
    a. 28 percent   c. 41 percent
    b. 36 percent   d. 45 percent

8. What does private mortgage insurance cover?
    a. Pays the lender if the borrower dies
    b. Reimburses the cosigner if the borrower defaults
    c. Protects the top 20 to 30 percent of the loan against borrower default
    d. Pays the borrower if the borrower loses the house to a title claim

9. Regulation Z generally applies to
    a. a credit transaction secured by a residence.
    b. business loans.
    c. commercial loans.
    d. agricultural loans of more than $25,000.

10. Who is responsible for paying the broker or the broker's salesperson when one of them uses a computerized loan origination system to take the loan application from a borrower?
    a. The lender
    b. The borrower
    c. The seller
    d. It is split between the lender and borrower

11. A man's monthly mortgage payment is $665.50. The interest rate on the amortized loan is 6 percent, and the outstanding balance is $111,000. When the man makes this month's payment, what amount of the total payment will be applied to interest, and what amount to principal?
    a. $555 interest; $110.50 principal
    b. $503.50 interest; $162 principal
    c. $497 interest; $168.50 principal
    d. $450 interest; $215.50 principal

12. All of the following are lenders in the primary mortgage market *EXCEPT*
    a. endowment funds.
    b. mortgage brokers.
    c. insurance companies.
    d. credit unions.

MULTIPLE CHOICE   *(Continued)*

13. On loans originated after July 1999, when must a lender automatically terminate private mortgage insurance?
    a. When a new appraisal shows that the property's value has increased by at least 10 percent
    b. When the borrower has accumulated at least 22 percent equity and is current on payments
    c. After borrower's equity reaches at least 28 percent
    d. After loan payments have been paid for at least five years without delinquency

14. A house had a sale price of $240,000. The buyer obtained a loan for $220,000. If the lender charges three points, how much will the buyer pay in points?
    a. $5,335   c. $6,950
    b. $6,600   d. $7,540

15. On which type of loan can the borrower prepay without penalty?
    a. Loans sold to Fannie Mae and Freddie Mac
    b. FHA loans
    c. VA loans
    d. All of the above

16. Under the terms of a man's adjustable-rate mortgage, the interest rate he must pay is (1) the U.S. Treasury bill rate as of June 1 of each year, not to exceed 8.95 percent for any period; plus (2) 1.5 percent. What is the term used to describe (2)?
    a. Rate cap   c. Margin
    b. Index   d. Payment cap

17. A woman bought a home. The asking price for the home was $585,000; the woman offered $565,000 and the seller accepted. The appraised value of the home is $560,000. The woman plans to pay $94,600 in cash and take out a mortgage for the remainder. What is the LTV ratio for this property?
    a. 82 percent   c. 84 percent
    b. 83 percent   d. 85 percent

18. A buyer is purchasing property from a seller. The seller bought the property on December 20, 1989, with an FHA loan and has lived there ever since. Because of its favorable terms, the buyer would like to assume the seller's mortgage. Is this possible?
    a. Yes, there are no restrictions on the assumption of this mortgage.
    b. Yes, but the buyer will have to undergo the complete buyer qualification process.
    c. Yes, but the buyer will have to undergo a creditworthiness review only.
    d. No, this FHA loan is not assumable.

19. In 1967, a man served for six months on active duty in Vietnam. In 1998, he was killed in a skiing accident. His widow wishes to use the man's life insurance money to make a down payment on a condominium and believes she is entitled to a VA-guaranteed loan. Is she correct?
    a. Yes, the unremarried spouse of a qualified veteran is entitled to a VA-guaranteed loan.
    b. Yes, whether or not she remarries, the man's widow is entitled to the same VA benefits as he was during his lifetime.
    c. No, the man's death was not service-related.
    d. No, the man did not meet the time-in-service criteria for qualified veterans.

20. Which of the following makes direct loans to qualified borrowers?
    a. VA   c. Fannie Mae
    b. FSA   d. FHA

21. A woman is purchasing a fully furnished condominium unit. In this situation, the woman would be MOST likely to use a
    a. package loan.   c. wraparound loan.
    b. blanket loan.   d. buydown.

MULTIPLE CHOICE (Continued)

22. A real estate broker has a CLO terminal in her office. Because there are more than a dozen lending institutions in the city, the broker has found that the CLO greatly streamlines the application process for her clients. She sits down at the terminal with a homebuyer and the following three events take place:

    1. The broker explains that there is a fee for using the terminal of one-half point, based on the loan amount, and that the homebuyer may choose to finance the fee.

    2. The broker explains only the different kinds of services offered by the two local lenders who pay her a monthly *screen fee* to be included on the CLO system.

    3. The broker helps the homeowner answer the on-screen qualification questions.

    Which of these events is an improper use of a CLO system?

    a. 1 only
    b. 2 only
    c. 2 and 3
    d. 1 and 3

23. The Equal Credit Opportunity Act prohibits lenders from discriminating against credit applicants on the basis of all of the following factors *EXCEPT*

    a. religion.
    b. past credit history.
    c. income from public assistance.
    d. marital status.

24. Lenders that make conventional loans to sell in the secondary mortgage market follow the standardized forms and guidelines issued by Fannie Mae and

    a. the FSA.
    b. the FHA.
    c. Ginnie Mae.
    d. Freddie Mac.

25. Because some of the principal is still owed at the end of the term, a balloon payment loan is a(n)

    a. negatively amortized loan.
    b. interest-only loan.
    c. automatically-extended loan.
    d. partially amortized loan.

26. A feature of an adjustable-rate mortgage that limits the amount the interest rate may increase at any one time is a

    a. periodic rate cap.
    b. payment cap.
    c. margin cap.
    d. life-of-the-loan rate cap.

27. What is a type of loan in which payments are made by the lender to the borrower and is usually repaid from the sale of the property?

    a. Buydown
    b. Wraparound loan
    c. Reverse mortgage
    d. Home equity loan

28. What helps lenders reduce the risk on a conventional mortgage loan with a high LTV?

    a. Private mortgage insurance
    b. Flood insurance
    c. Sale-and-leaseback arrangement
    d. Home equity

MATH PRACTICE

Use the following loan table to solve the following five problems.

Annual Interest Rate (%)	Amortized Loans Life of Loan (in Years) (Monthly Payments per $1,000 of Loan Principal)							
	5	**10**	**15**	**20**	**25**	**30**	**35**	**40**
5.00	$18.87	$10.61	$7.91	$6.60	$5.85	$5.37	$5.05	$4.82
5.50	19.10	10.85	8.17	6.88	6.14	5.68	5.37	5.16
6.00	19.33	11.10	8.44	7.16	6.44	6.00	5.70	5.50
6.50	19.57	11.35	8.71	7.46	6.75	6.32	6.04	5.85
7.00	19.80	11.61	8.99	7.75	7.07	6.65	6.39	6.21
7.50	20.04	11.87	9.27	8.06	7.39	6.99	6.74	6.58
8.00	20.28	12.13	9.56	8.36	7.72	7.34	7.10	6.95
8.50	20.52	12.40	9.85	8.68	8.05	7.69	7.47	7.33
9.00	20.76	12.67	10.14	9.00	8.39	8.05	7.84	7.71
9.50	21.00	12.94	10.40	9.32	8.74	8.41	8.22	8.10
10.00	21.25	13.22	10.75	9.65	9.09	8.78	8.60	8.49
10.50	21.49	13.49	11.05	9.98	9.44	9.15	8.98	8.89
11.0	21.74	13.78	11.37	10.32	9.80	9.52	9.37	9.28

1. A man wants to borrow $125,000 for 20 years. He will pay 8.5 percent interest.
    a. What will be his monthly payments?
    b. What will be the cost of interest over the life of the loan?

2. A woman wants to borrow $200,000 to buy a house. If she must pay 6.5 percent annual interest and can afford a monthly payment of $1,350 (principal and interest), what is the lowest number of years she can borrow the money?

3. A couple plans to borrow $75,000 to buy a condominium. If they obtain mortgage money at 6 percent instead of 7.5 percent for a 30-year loan, how much lower will their monthly principal and interest payments be?

4. A man can afford $1,175 per month for a payment that includes principal, interest, taxes, and insurance. Annual property taxes are $840, and insurance will cost $480 per year. If current interest rates are at 7 percent and the man wants a 30-year loan, how much can he afford to borrow?

5. A borrower wants a 15-year mortgage instead of the typical 30-year mortgage. He will be borrowing $300,000 at 6.5 percent.
    a. How much more will this cost each month compared to a 30-year mortgage?
    b. How much will he save in interest payments over the life of the loan?

Answers:

1. a. _____

    b. _____

2. _____

3. _____

4. _____

5. a. _____

    b. _____

ANSWER KEY

Matching A

1. a **2.** h **3.** i **4.** c **5.** f **6.** g **7.** d **8.** e
9. j **10.** b

Matching B

1. b **2.** g **3.** d **4.** h **5.** f **6.** c **7.** e **8.** a
9. j **10.** i

True or False

1. **False.** The *primary mortgage market* consists of the lenders who originate loans—those who make loans directly to borrowers. p. 239

2. **True.** Up-front fees (origination fees and discount points) collected at the time of closing as well as interest collected over the term of the loan generate income. p. 239–240

3. **True.** Some of the major lenders in the primary market include thrifts, savings associations, commercial banks, insurance companies, credit unions, pension funds, endowment funds, mortgage brokers, mortgage banking companies, and other investors. p. 240–241

4. **False.** In September 2008, Fannie Mae became a government-owned enterprise; prior to that time, it was organized as a completely privately owned corporation that issued its own stock. p. 241

5. **False.** An *amortized loan* applies each payment first toward the interest owed on the loan; the remainder of each payment is then applied toward paying off the principal amount. p. 243

6. **True.** In an adjustable-rate loan, the interest rate consists of the index rate plus a margin that represents the lender's cost of doing business. p. 244

7. **False.** In an adjustable rate mortgage, the *adjustment period* establishes how often the rate may be changed. p. 244

8. **True.** The principal plus the last month's interest is due at the end of the term:

   $92,500 \times 0.068 = $6,290

   $6,290 \div 12 = $524.17

   $92,500 + $524.17 = $93,024.17. p. 246

9. **False.** The *value* portion of a property's LTV is the *lower* of the sale price or the appraised value. p. 247

10. **True.** The FHA insures loans; it does not make loans, and it does not hold loans. p. 249

11. **False.** A home equity loan has a junior lien priority to a first mortgage lien. p. 255

12. **False.** A *blanket loan* covers more than one parcel or lot and is usually used to finance sub-division developments. p. 253

13. **True.** An open-end loan is often less-costly than a home improvement loan; the initial interest rate is fixed, but interest on future advances may be charged at the market rate in effect. p. 254

14. **True.** The Truth in Lending Act and Regulation Z requires that credit institutions inform borrower of the true cost of obtaining credit. p. 256

15. **False.** Under Regulation Z, a borrower *other than* a residential purchase-money or first mortgage borrower, has three days in which to rescind a transaction by notifying the lender of intent to rescind. p. 256

16. **False.** Under the Community Reinvestment Act, the findings of the government agency review of an institution's community reinvestment activities *must be made public*. p. 258

17. **False.** A computerized loan origination system allows a real estate broker to *assist a buyer* in *selecting a lender and applying for a loan*. p. 258

18. **True.** The VA's certificate of reasonable value states the property's current market value based on a VA-approved appraisal. p. 252

19. **True.** Under the Truth in Lending Act, certain credit terms, such as down payment or monthly payment, are referred to as trigger terms and may not be advertised unless the advertisement includes additional information. p. 257

20. **True.** As with private mortgage insurance, the FAH insures lenders against loss from borrower default. p. 245

21. **False.** The VA limits the amount of the loan it will *guarantee*. Lenders determine the amount of the loan and qualification of the borrower. p. 251

22. **True.** Under the Community Reinvestment Act of 1977 (CRA), financial institutions are responsible for meeting the deposit and credit needs of the communities in which they are located. p. 258

23. **False.** The original lender may continue to service the loan and collect payments. The investor is then charged a fee for servicing the loan. p. 240

Multiple Choice

1. **d.** The Federal Reserve helps counteract inflationary trends, creates a favorable economic climate, maintains sound credit conditions, but it does not make direct loans to consumers. p. 239

2. **b.** In addition to the income directly related to loans, some lenders derive income from servicing loans for other mortgage lenders or investors who have purchased the loans. p. 240

3. **a.** Credit unions were known for short-term consumer loans but have more recently branched out into originating mortgage loans. p. 240

4. **c.** Adjustable-rate mortgage loans generally originate at one rate of interest and then fluctuate up or down during the loan term, based on an objective economic indicator. p. 244.

5. **c.** Unlike a straight loan payment, the payment in an amortized loan partially pays off both principal and interest. Each payment is first credited to the interest owed, and the remainder is applied to reduce the principal. p. 243

6. **a.** The margin remains constant during the life of the loan; the interest rate tied to the index fluctuates as the index fluctuates. p. 244

7. **b.** To be considered a conforming loan that can be sold in the secondary market, the borrower's monthly housing expenses and total other monthly obligations must not exceed 36 percent of total monthly gross income.

8. **c.** Private mortgage insurance, usually required for loans more than 80 percent of value, provides security to the lender if the borrower defaults. p. 249

9. **a.** The truth-in-lending law, implemented by Regulation Z, generally applies to a credit transaction secured by a residence, but it does not apply to commercial, business, or agricultural loans of more than $25,000. p. 256

10. **b.** The borrower who uses a computerized loan originator must pay the fee to the broker or salesperson who takes the application. p. 259

11. **a.** $111,000 × 6% ÷ 12 = $555 monthly interest. $665.50 − $555 = $110.50 principal. p. 246

12. **b.** Mortgage brokers do not loan their own money; they are intermediaries who bring borrowers and lenders together. p. 241

13. **b.** On loans originating after July 1999, federal law requires that PMI automatically terminate if a borrower has accumulated at least 22 percent equity in the home and is current on mortgage payments; the 22 percent of equity is based on the purchase price of the home. p. 249

14. **b.** The buyer will pay $6,600: $220,000 × 3% = $6,600. Points are charged on the loan amount, not the sale price. p. 251

15. **d.** Prepayment penalties are fairly unusual in today's market. p. 252

16. **c.** The rate set by the U.S. Treasury bill rate is the index in the adjustable rate mortgage. The cost of doing business is the margin that remains constant during the life of the loan and is added to the Treasury bill rate. p. 244

17. **c.** The LTV on the loan amount is 84%. LTV = Loan Amount ÷ Appraised Value or Sale Price (whichever is lower), thus: $565,000 − $94,600 = $470,400; $470,400 ÷ $560,000 = 84%. p. 247

18. **b.** Because the loan was made after December 15, 1989, assumptions are not permitted without complete buyer qualification. p. 250

19. **c.** The widow of a serviceman whose death is service-related may use his entitlements. In this situation, she is not entitled. p. 251

20. **b.** The Farm Service Agency will guarantee loans made and serviced by private lenders and guaranteed for a specific percentage; the FSA will also make loans directly to the borrower. p. 252

21. **a.** A loan secured by a fully furnished condominium unit is secured by both real and personal property. A blanket loan is secured by several properties. p. 253

22. **b.** Consumers must be informed of the availability of other lenders. p. 259

23. **b.** Lenders may deny a loan request because of the borrower's previous credit history. Otherwise, lenders may not discriminate on the basis of race, color, religion, national origin, sex, receipt of public assistance, age, or marital status. p. 257

24. **d.** Freddie Mac and Fannie Mae are the dominant participants in the secondary mortgage market. p. 241–242

25. **d.** When the periodic payments are not enough to fully amortize the loan by the time the final payment is due, the final payment is larger than the others. This final payment is called a balloon payment. p. 243

26. **a.** A life-of-the-loan rate cap limits the amount the rate may increase over the entire life of the loan. A payment cap sets a maximum amount for payment increases. p. 244

27. **c.** A *reverse mortgage loan* allows people 62 or older to borrow money against the equity they have built in the home; reverse mortgages are the opposite of conventional mortgages in that the homeowner's equity diminishes as the loan amount increases. p. 247

28. **a.** *Private mortgage insurance* provides lenders with funds in case of borrower default and encourages lenders to make higher LTV loans. p. 248–249

Math Practice

1. **a.** The monthly payment will be $1,085:

    $125,000 ÷ 1,000 × 8.68 = $1,085 monthly

    b. Interest over the life of the loan is $135,400:

    $1,085 × 240 = $260,400; $260,400 − $125,000 = $135,400 interest over the life of the loan.

2. Lowest number of years she can borrow the money is 25: $200,000 ÷ 1,000 = 200.

    $1,350 ÷ 200 = 6.75, which is the factor for 6.5 percent at 25 years

3. The couple's payment will be $74.25 lower each month:

    At 7.5%: 75 × 6.99 = $524.25

    At 6%: 75 × 6.00 = $450.00

    $524.25 − $450 = $74.25 lower each month

4. The maximum loan amount is $160,150:

    $840 ÷ 12 = $70 tax per month

    $480 ÷ 12 = $40 insurance per month

    $1,175 − $70 − $40 = $1,065; $1,065 ÷ 6.65 × 1,000 = $160,150 (maximum loan amount)

5. **a.** The borrower will have to pay $717 more each month with the 15-year loan:

    15-year: 300 × 8.71 = $2,613

    30-year: 300 × 6.32 = $1,896

    $2,613 - $1,896 = $717

    b. The borrower will save $212,220 in interest over the life of the loan with the 15-year loan:

    15-year: $2,613 × 15 × 12 = $470,340

    30-year: $1,896 × 30 × 12 = $682,560

    In actuality, lenders usually offer a lower interest rate on 15-year loans as opposed to 30-year loans. Therefore, the borrower is likely to have a lower monthly payment than the one projected for the 15-year loan term and will save even more in total interest.

CHAPTER 16

Leases

- **identify** the four types of leasehold estates;

- **describe** the requirements and general conditions of a valid lease and how a lease may be discharged;

- **explain** the rights of landlords and tenants in an eviction proceeding and the effect of protenant legislation and civil rights laws on the landlord-tenant relationship;

- **distinguish** the various types of leases; and

- **define** the following *key terms:*

actual eviction	ground lease	percentage lease
assignment	holdover tenancy	purchase option
constructive eviction	lease	renewal option
estate at sufferance	leasehold estate	reversionary right
estate at will	lease purchase	right of first refusal
estate for years	lessee lessor	sale-and-leaseback
estate from period to period	month-to-month tenancy	security deposit
gross lease	net lease	sublease
	nondisturbance clause	

MATCHING   *Write the letter of the matching term on the appropriate line.*

a. *actual eviction*

b. *constructive eviction*

c. *tenancy at will*

d. *option*

e. *periodic tenancy*

f. *reversionary right*

g. *sublease*

h. *lease*

i. *tenancy for years*

j. *tenancy at sufferance*

1. ___ A contract between a real estate owner and a tenant

2. ___ A landlord's right to possession of the premises after the expiration of the lease term

3. ___ A leasehold estate that has a specific beginning and a definite end

4. ___ The estate created when a landlord and tenant enter into a lease agreement that automatically renews

5. ___ A leasehold estate with an indefinite term that may be terminated by the death of either the landlord or tenant

6. ___ The leasehold estate created when a tenant, who was in lawful possession of real property, continues in possession without the landlord's consent

7. ___ The transfer of some of a tenant's interest, but no tenant obligations

8. ___ A lessee's privilege of renewing a lease

9. ___ The legal process by which a landlord regains possession of leased premises following a tenant's breach

10. ___ The action by which a tenant may properly abandon premises that have become unusable due to the landlord's conscious neglect

TRUE OR FALSE   *Circle the correct answer.*

1. T F In a lease agreement, the landlord is the lessee and the tenant is the lessor.

2. T F Unlike a freehold estate, a leasehold estate is considered personal property.

3. T F The primary difference between a tenancy at will and a tenancy at sufferance is the landlord's consent.

4. T F Although an extension of a tenancy for years requires a new contract, the lease may be terminated prior to the expiration date by either party at any time.

5. T F Periodic tenancies are characterized by continuity because they are automatically renewable.

6. T F The elements of a valid lease are (1) offer and acceptance, (2) capacity of the parties, (3) consideration, and (4) legal objective.

7. T F The *covenant of quiet enjoyment* is a guarantee by the landlord that the tenant is entitled to a quiet building without interference from noisy neighbors.

8. T F A tenant who is leasing only a part of a building is not required to continue paying rent if the lease premises are destroyed.

9. T F When a tenant transfers all leasehold interests to another person, the tenant has assigned the lease.

10. T F Under a *net lease agreement*, the landlord pays all of the operating expenses of the property, while the tenant pays only a fixed rental.

11. T F Ground leases are generally short-term net leases.

12. T F The death of either party terminates a tenancy at will.

13. T F To be entitled to constructive eviction, the tenant must show only that the premises have become unusable for the purpose stated in the lease.

14. T F The Fair Housing Amendments Act of 1988 requires that, in leased housing, the same criteria must be applied to tenants with children as are applied to adults.

15. T F All leases must require a security deposit as part of the consideration.

MULTIPLE CHOICE   *Circle the correct answer.*

1. A tenant pays for his own utilities and makes one payment each month to the landlord who pays the taxes, insurance on the building, and maintenance. What type of lease arrangement is this?
   a. Net
   b. Gross
   c. Percentage
   d. Graduated

2. Some tenants want to buy the house they are renting. However, they do not have enough money for the down payment. The landlord agreed to put part of the tenants' rent toward the purchase price. The landlord and tenants have agreed to a(n)
   a. lease purchase.
   b. sale leaseback.
   c. ground lease.
   d. option.

3. The expiration date of a one-year lease is September 30. On July 1, the house is sold to a family that wants to live in the rental property. Assuming the lease does not include a sale clause, how soon can they move in?
   a. July 1, present year
   b. July 1, next year
   c. October 1, present year
   d. December 31, present year

4. A woman rents an apartment from a man under a one-year written lease. The expiration date of the lease is May 1. How much notice must the man give the woman to recover possession when the lease expires?
   a. 30 days
   b. 60 days
   c. One week
   d. No notice required

5. Two years ago, a woman rented a parcel of property to a man. The agreement stated only that the man agreed to pay the woman $500 per month. What type of tenancy does the man have?
   a. Holdover
   b. At sufferance
   c. For years
   d. Periodic

6. A man rents an apartment under a two-year written lease from a landlord. Three months after signing the lease, the man is transferred to another country for a year. During this period, he leases the apartment to a woman. The woman mails monthly rent checks to the man, who continues to make monthly rental payments to the landlord. In this situation, the woman has a
   a. lease.
   b. tenancy at will.
   c. sublease.
   d. periodic tenancy.

7. A tenant lives in an apartment building owned by a landlord. Vandals break into the building and destroy the central air-conditioning system. The tenant's apartment becomes uncomfortably warm. The next day, the tenant sues the landlord for constructive eviction. Under these facts, will the tenant win?
   a. Yes, if the tenant's lease promises that the apartment will be air conditioned.
   b. Yes, to claim constructive eviction, it is not necessary that the condition be the result of the landlord's personal actions.
   c. No, to claim constructive eviction, the tenant must prove that the premises are uninhabitable.
   d. No, the premises are not unusable, the condition was not due to the landlord's conscious neglect, and the tenant has not abandoned the apartment.

MULTIPLE CHOICE   *(Continued)*

8. In August, a tenant signs a one-year lease in an apartment complex. Rent payments are due on the 15th of each month. On December 12, the apartment complex is sold to a new owner. On March 14, the building burns. Which of the following statements accurately describes the tenant's obligations?

   a. The tenant is not required to continue paying rent after March 14, because the premises have been destroyed.

   b. The tenant is not required to continue paying rent after December 12, because the sale voids the preexisting lease.

   c. The tenant is required to continue paying rent for the full lease term, because a tenancy for years cannot be terminated by the destruction of the premises.

   d. The tenant is required to continue paying rent, but the residential lease is converted by law into a ground lease.

9. A woman signs a lease to rent an apartment. Her lease runs from October 1 until November 1 of the following year. A man signs a two-year lease to rent an apartment in a new building that will be ready for occupancy in 15 months. Which of these leases must be in writing to satisfy the statute of frauds?

   a. The woman's only

   b. The man's only

   c. Both the man's and the woman's

   d. Neither the man's nor the woman's

10. A tenant signed a one-year lease with a landlord on April 10. On the following March 1, the landlord asked the tenant whether the lease would be renewed. The tenant did not respond but was still in the apartment on April 11. What can the landlord do?

    a. The landlord must initiate eviction proceedings within the first one-month rental period.

    b. The landlord cannot evict the tenant; because the tenant remained in possession of the premises, the lease has been automatically renewed for an additional year.

    c. If the tenant offers a rent check, the landlord must accept it and the tenant is entitled to a renewal of the one-year lease.

    d. The landlord may either evict the holdover tenant or accept a rent check, creating a holdover or periodic tenancy.

11. If a tenant remains in possession of leased property after the expiration of the lease term, without paying rent and without the landlord's consent, what is the tenant's status?

    a. Tenant at will

    b. Trespasser

    c. Periodic tenant

    d. Freehold tenant

12. A woman wanted to rent an apartment from a man. Because of a physical disability, it would be necessary for the woman to have all the doorknobs replaced with lever-type handles. In this case, which of the following statements is *TRUE*?

    a. The Fair Housing Act requires that the man make the accommodation for the woman at the man's expense; no additional rent may be charged for the woman's modified unit.

    b. The man is legally obligated to permit the modifications to be made at the woman's expense.

    c. Because the modifications demanded by the woman are not reasonable, the man is not legally required to permit them.

    d. Because the proposed modifications would interfere with a future tenant's use of the premises, the woman may refuse to permit them.

MULTIPLE CHOICE (Continued)

13. A man operates a small store in a shopping center. Under the terms of the lease, the landlord pays all operating expenses. The man pays a base rent of $1,000 per month, plus 15 percent of monthly gross profits over $10,000. The man has a

    a. gross lease.
    b. percentage lease.
    c. net lease.
    d. variable lease.

14. When a landowner leases unimproved land to a tenant, who agrees to erect a building on the land, the lease is usually referred to as a(n)

    a. lease purchase.
    b. gross lease.
    c. ground lease.
    d. improvement lease.

15. A man rented a house from a landlord. During the lease term, the man moved out of the state without telling the landlord. The man assigned the lease to a woman, who failed to make any rental payments. In this situation, which of the following statements is *TRUE*?

    a. The man has no obligation to the landlord, because the lease was assigned, not sublet.
    b. The woman has no obligation to the landlord, because her lease agreement is with the man.
    c. The man is still liable to the landlord for the outstanding rent, because the landlord did not release the man when the lease was assigned to the woman.
    d. The man is still liable to the landlord because his arrangement with the woman as described is a sublease, not an assignment.

16. What is the purpose of a security deposit held by a landlord?

    a. It compensates the landlord in the event of rent default or premises damage
    b. It functions as the last month's rent on the lease
    c. It acts as an investment option for the tenant
    d. All of these

17. Who owns the building that is erected on land that has a ground lease?

    a. Testator
    b. Lessor
    c. Lessee
    d. Trustee

18. What *must* a landlord do before commencing a lawsuit for actual eviction?

    a. Notify the sheriff
    b. Contract with a company to forcibly remove the tenant and possessions
    c. Obtain a judgment from the court
    d. Serve notice on the tenant

19. A tenant has a lease on a top-floor apartment in a building owned by a landlord. The building is old, and the landlord has been planning to replace the roof. However, she has not yet replaced it. In spring, a heavy rainstorm created a roof leak that badly damaged the tenant's apartment. The landlord laid a tarp on the roof to prevent more water coming in. However, after two months, the landlord had still not repaired the damage to the apartment. The tenant moves out and claims construction eviction. Can she win this case?

    a. No, because the apartment was not uninhabitable.
    b. No, because the time period was not long enough.
    c. Yes, because the landlord was negligent in not repairing the damage.
    d. Yes, because placing the tarp was an admission of responsibility by the landlord.

20. A lease that provides for specified rent increases at set future dates is called a(n)

    a. adjustable lease.
    b. graduated lease.
    c. percentage lease.
    d. interval lease.

FILL-IN-THE-BLANK   *Select the word or words that best complete the following statements:*

actual eviction

actual notice

consideration

estate at sufferance

estate at will

estate for years

Fair Housing Amendments Act of 1988

gross

lessee

lessor

nondisturbance

reversionary right

right of first refusal

sale and leaseback

sublease

net

Uniform Residential Landlord and Tenant Act

1. A type of leasehold estate that gives the right of possession with the landlord's consent for an unspecified term is called a(n) _____.

2. Although rent is the usual _____ given for the right to occupy leased premises, labor could also serve this function.

3. Recording a lease is usually considered unnecessary, because anyone who inspects the property receives _____.

4. If the lease allows the tenant the opportunity to buy the property before the owner accepts an offer from another party, the tenant has the _____.

5. If the tenant pays basic rent plus all or most property charges, the tenant has a(n) _____ lease.

6. In a lease agreement, the tenant is called the _____ and the landlord is called the _____.

7. A leasehold estate that continues for a definite period of time is the _____.

8. A mortgage clause that states the lender agrees not to terminate the tenancies of rent-paying tenants in the event the lender forecloses on the building is the _____ clause.

9. The arrangement when an owner of property sells the property and then obtains a lease from the new owner is called _____.

10. A model law that addresses obligations in leases, such as the landlord's right of entry, premises maintenance, and protection of the tenants from retaliation by the landlord in the event of complaints is the _____.

ACTIVITY: Types of Commercial Leases

Based on the following information, write the type of lease and current month's rental beneath each store.

A few years ago, a developer purchased a historic downtown block in the exclusive suburban community of West Flightpath. The developer combined the storefronts into a shopping mall. Currently, the mall is completely leased to three tenants.

Acrylic Acres pays a base rent of $1,500 per month and 15 percent of the shopping mall's property charges, limited to utilities and taxes. Blue Buttons Boutique pays a base rent of $2,000 per month and no property charges. Custom Custards pays a base rent of $1,850 per month and no property charges, but pays 12 percent of its monthly gross sales over $4,000 to the landlord.

Acrylic Acres earned $10,000 in gross profits and netted $4,850. Blue Buttons Boutique grossed $6,500 and earned a net profit of $3,000. Custom Custards had gross sales of $9,542, with profits after expenses of $7,370 for the month.

This month, the shopping mall had to pay $6,790 in utility bills and $495 in regular repairs and maintenance. The month's prorated share of local property taxes was $2,560, and the prorated insurance fee was $900.

Lease Type: _____   Lease Type: _____   Lease Type: _____

Rent: _____   Rent: _____   Rent: _____

ANSWER KEY

Matching

1. h **2.** f **3.** i **4.** e **5.** c **6.** j **7.** g **8.** d
9. a **10.** b

True or False

1. **False.** In a lease agreement, the landlord is the *lessor* and the tenant is the *lessee*. p. 268

2. **True.** A tenant's right to possess real estate for the term of the lease is called a leasehold, less-than-freehold, estate and is generally considered personal property. p. 268

3. **True.** An estate at will is an indefinite term, and possession is with the landlord's consent, while an estate at sufferance is the result of the tenant's previously lawful possession continued with the landlord's consent. p. 270

4. **False.** Although an extension of a tenancy for years requires a new contract, the lease may be terminated prior to the expiration date *only if both parties agree, or if one party has breached the agreement*. p. 269

5. **True.** Periodic tenancies are characterized by continuity, because it is automatically renewable under the original terms of the agreement until one of the parties gives notice to terminate. p. 269

6. **True.** As a contract between the lessor and the lessee, a valid lease must have the same requirements as any other contract: offer and acceptance, capacity of the parties, consideration, and legal objective. p. 271

7. **False.** The covenant of quiet enjoyment is a guarantee by the landlord that the tenant is entitled to *possession of the premises without interference from the landlord*. p. 276

8. **True.** Generally, tenants who are leasing only part of a building, such as offices or commercial space, are not required to continue to pay rent after the leased premises are destroyed. p. 277

9. **True.** When a tenant transfers all leasehold interests to another person, the lease has been assigned; when a tenant transfers less than all the leasehold interests by leasing them to a new tenant, the original tenant has subleased the property. p. 278

10. **False.** Under a *gross lease agreement*, the landlord pays all the operating expenses of the property, while the tenant pays only a fixed rental. p. 279

11. **False.** Ground leases are generally *long-term net leases and are often recorded*. p. 280

12. **True.** An estate at will is a tenancy of indefinite duration and is automatically terminated by the death of either party. p. 270

13. **False.** To be entitled to constructive eviction, the tenant must show only that the premises have become unusable for the purpose stated in the lease *due to the landlord's conscious neglect*. p. 282

14. **True.** All persons must have access to housing of their choice without any differentiation in the terms and conditions because of their race, color, religion, national origin, sex, disability, or familial status. p. 282

15. **False.** Consideration in a lease consists of the landlord promising possession and the tenant promising rents. A requirement for a security deposit *may* be a part of the agreement. It is available for unpaid rent and/or damages to the property. p. 276

Multiple Choice

1. **b.** The one-lump sum every month to the landlord is a *gross lease*. In a *net lease*, the tenant is responsible for paying all or most of the property charges. *Percentage leases* are generally used by retail establishments and are based on gross sales. p. 279

2. **a.** The tenant typically pays a higher *rent* with a portion being applied to the subsequent purchase of the property. It differs from a sale leaseback, whereby the owner of the property wants to obtain equity from the building. The owner sells the building and agrees to rent it back. p. 280

3. **c.** The tenants have the right to possess the property until the end of their lease. The new owners will have to wait to move in. p. 269

4. **d.** This lease will be terminated May 1, an estate for years. By definition, no notice is required. If the landlord wants notice, the landlord must add a paragraph to override this fact. p. 269

5. **d.** Any lease that automatically renews itself is a *periodic tenancy*. It will continue until either party gives proper notice requesting a change. p. 269

6. **c.** The woman holds a *sublease* because the tenant has given up possession for some of the portions of the lease. Giving up all of the remaining rights would be an *assignment*. In either situation, the lessee is still responsible for the rental obligation. p. 278

7. **d.** *Constructive eviction* is a result of the landlord not providing essential services, such as the place is unsafe or uninhabitable, conditions that are not met in this situation. p. 282

8. **a.** Typically, if a residential rental unit is destroyed, the lease is terminated. This is not the case with agricultural land or ground leases. p. 277

9. **c.** Both leases are covered by the statute of frauds, because they are both more than one year in length. p. 271

10. **d.** The original lease was an *estate for years and no notice was required to terminate*. If the tenant does not pay rent, it will become a *tenancy at sufferance*. If the tenant pays rent and the landlord accepts it, it will be a *holdover* or *periodic tenancy*, which could be changed into an *estate for years* if they enter into yet another year-long lease. p. 270–271

11. **b.** The landlord can treat the tenant as a trespasser and proceed with eviction and damages action. However, the landlord must comply with *notice to quit* requirements. p. 281

12. **b.** These modifications would appear to be within the scope of *reasonable* modifications. They also would not interfere with a future tenant's use of the property. p. 282

13. **b.** Many retail shopping centers use percentage leases. Part of the tenant's success is due to location. Landlords will help with promotional events to draw in customers knowing that the more successful the tenant, the more rent for the landlord. p. 279

14. **c.** A tenant who intends to construct a building on leased land generally does so under a *ground lease*, often for up to 50 years. The tenant will often record the lease to serve constructive notice of their long-term interest. p. 280

15. **c.** While rights to possession may be assigned or sublet, the obligation to pay rent may not be assigned to another party unless the landlord agrees to the plan. p. 278

16. **a.** Security deposits are often required to be used if the tenant defaults on payment of rent or destroys the premises; they cannot usually be applied to the final month's rental. This would be an advance rental, and the landlord must treat it as income for tax purposes. p. 276

17. **c.** Ground leases typically involve separate ownership of the land and the buildings, so the lessor owns the land, and the lessee owns the building. p. 280

18. **d.** To regain possession through a legal process known as actual eviction, the landlord must serve notice on the tenant before commencing the lawsuit. p. 281

19. **a.** The premises must have become unusable because of the conscious neglect of the landlord. The fact that the tenant stayed two more months indicates that the property actually was inhabitable. p. 282

20. **b.** A form of variable lease is the graduated lease that provides for specified rent increases at set future dates. p. 280

Fill-in-the-Blank

1. A type of leasehold estate that gives the right of possession with the landlord's consent for an unspecified term is called an *estate at will*.

2. Although rent is the usual *consideration* given for the right to occupy leased premises, labor could also serve this function.

3. Recording a lease is usually considered unnecessary, because anyone who inspects the property receives *actual notice*.

4. If the lease allows the tenant the opportunity to buy the property before the owner accepts an offer from another party, the tenant has the *right of first refusal*.

5. If the tenant pays basic rent plus all or most property charges, the tenant has a *net* lease.

6. In a lease agreement, the tenant is called the *lessee*, and the landlord is called the *lessor*.

7. A leasehold estate that continues for a definite period of time is the *estate for years*.

8. A mortgage clause that states the lender agrees not to terminate the tenancies of rent-paying tenants in the event the lender forecloses on the building is the *nondisturbance* clause.

9. The arrangement when an owner of property sells the property and then obtains a lease from the new owner is called *sale-and-leaseback*.

10. A model law that addresses obligations in leases, such as the landlord's right of entry, premises maintenance, and protection of the tenants from retaliation by the landlord in the event of complaints is the *Uniform Residential Landlord and Tenant Act*.

Activity: Types of Commercial Leases

Acrylic Acres has a net lease, with $2,902.50 rent for the current month, calculated as follows:

$$\$6{,}790 \text{ Utilities} + \$2{,}560 \text{ Taxes} \times 15\% = \quad \$1{,}402.50$$

$$\text{Base Rent} = \quad \underline{1{,}500.00}$$

$$\text{Total Rent} = \quad \$2{,}902.50$$

Blue Buttons Boutique has a gross lease, with $2,000 rent for the current month. With a gross lease, no calculations are required. The tenant pays the rent; the landlord takes care of all expenses.

Custom Custards has a percentage lease, with $2,515 rent for the current month calculated as follows:

$$\$9{,}542 \text{ Gross Sales} - \$4{,}000 \text{ Forgiven Sales} = \quad \$5{,}542.00$$

$$\$5{,}542.00 \text{ Qualifying Sales} \times 12\% = \quad 665.04$$

$$\text{Base Rent} = \quad \underline{1{,}850.00}$$

$$\text{Total Rent} = \quad \$2{,}515.04$$

CHAPTER 17

Property Management

■ **LEARNING OBJECTIVES**   *Before you answer these questions, you should be able to*

- ■ **identify** the basic elements of a management agreement;

- ■ **describe** a property manager's functions;

- ■ **explain** the role of environmental regulations and the Americans with Disabilities Act in the property manager's job;

- ■ **distinguish** the various types of risk management; and

- ■ **define** the following *key terms*:

budget comparison statement	multiperil policies	routine maintenance
cash flow report	operating budget	surety bonds
corrective maintenance	preventive maintenance	tenant improvements
management agreement	profit and loss statement	workers' compensation acts
management plan	property manager	
	risk management	

MATCHING *Write the letter of the matching term on the appropriate line.*

a. *management agreement*

b. *consequential loss*

c. *multiperil*

d. *preventive maintenance*

e. *asset management*

f. *risk management*

g. *casualty*

h. *audit*

i. *tenant improvements*

j. *surety bond*

1. ___ The document that creates the agency relationship between an owner and property manager

2. ___ A type of property management specialty that helps owners decide which properties to purchase and when to sell

3. ___ Performance of regularly scheduled activities, such as painting and servicing appliances and systems

4. ___ Major alterations to a building's interior to meet a tenant's particular needs

5. ___ Evaluating perils of any risk in terms of options

6. ___ An owner's protection against financial losses due to an employee's criminal acts

7. ___ Insurance policies that offer a package of standard coverages

8. ___ Insurance policies that provide coverage against theft, burglary, and vandalism; specific, not all-inclusive

9. ___ Insurance that covers the revenue a business loses due to a disaster

10. ___ An investigation to determine the need for insurance and types of insurance required

TRUE OR FALSE   *Circle the correct answer.*

1. T F One of the key responsibilities of a property manager is to preserve or increase the value of the property.

2. T F The *management agreement* creates a general agency relationship between an owner and the property manager.

3. T F Unlike real estate brokers' commissions, property management fees may be standardized by local associations.

4. T F Rental rates are influenced primarily by supply and demand.

5. T F An example of a readily achievable modification under the ADA is installing a ramp at a building entrance.

6. T F The manager of a residential building should carefully consider a prospective tenant's compatibility with existing tenants.

7. T F A high tenant turnover rate results in higher profits for the owner.

8. T F The three types of maintenance necessary to keep a property in good condition are preventive, rehabilitation, and tenant relations.

9. T F *Corrective maintenance* helps prevent problems and expenses before they arise.

10. T F Tenant improvements are major alterations to the interior of commercial or industrial property, to accommodate the tenant.

11. T F Under Title I of the ADA, all existing barriers must be removed from both residential and commercial properties.

12. T F The ADA requirements for new construction are stricter than those for buildings existing before the law was implemented.

13. T F The four alternative risk management techniques are transfer, control, avoid, and retain.

14. T F In a commercial property, the risk of a shopper suffering a slip-and-fall injury would be covered by casualty insurance.

15. T F A *depreciated value policy* insures a building for what it would cost to rebuild it.

16. T F A cash flow report is the most important financial report, because it provides a picture of current financial status of a property.

17. T F Property managers have a responsibility to properly manage hazardous environmental problems, such as asbestos.

18. T F Courts have always held that tenants, rather than property owners and their agents, are responsible for protecting against physical harm inflicted by intruders.

19. T F A critical maintenance objective is to protect the physical condition of the property over the long term.

20. T F Examples of variable expenses of property management are employee wages and utilities.

MULTIPLE CHOICE   *Circle the correct answer.*

1. A property manager's first responsibility to the owner should be to
   a. keep the building's occupancy rate at 100 percent.
   b. report all day-to-day financial and operating decisions to the owner on a regular basis.
   c. realize the highest return possible consistent with the owner's instructions.
   d. ensure that the rental rates are below market average.

2. The property manager's relationship with the owner is most similar to that of a
   a. tenant with a landlord.
   b. cashier with the owner of a store.
   c. stockholder with the board of directors of a corporation.
   d. salesperson with his or her broker.

3. All of the following should be included in a written management agreement *EXCEPT*
   a. a list of the manager's duties and responsibilities.
   b. a statement of the owner's purpose.
   c. a statement identifying the manager's creditors.
   d. an allocation of costs.

4. If an apartment rents for $750 per month and the manager receives a 12 percent commission on all new tenants, how much will the manager receive when renting an apartment, assuming that this commission is calculated in the usual way?
   a. $90
   b. $750
   c. $1,080
   d. $1,800

5. What would be the annual rent per square foot for a 30 ft × 40 ft property that rents for $2,950 per month?
   a. $1.20
   b. $2.46
   c. $24.65
   d. $29.50

6. Of the following, a high vacancy rate MOST likely indicates
   a. rental rates are too low.
   b. the property is attractive.
   c. building management is effective and responsive.
   d. an undesirable property.

7. Which of the following is an example of corrective maintenance?
   a. Seasonal recharge of refrigerant in an air conditioning unit
   b. Picking up litter in common areas
   c. Repairing a leaking water heater
   d. Moving a partition wall to make a larger office

8. How can tenants insure their personal belongings in apartments they rent?
   a. Pay an extra fee so they are added to their landlord's commercial insurance
   b. Obtain a surety bond
   c. Obtain HO-4 or renter's insurance
   d. Obtain errors and omissions (E&O) insurance

9. Under the ADA, existing barriers *must* be removed
   a. in all public buildings by the end of 2015.
   b. only on request from a person with a disability.
   c. even though reasonable alternative accommodation is more practical.
   d. when removal may be accomplished in a readily achievable manner.

10. A company was moving from one part of the city to another. During the move, a truck carrying equipment worth more than $250,000 accidentally ended up in a river, and the equipment was destroyed. Fortunately, the company was insured under several policies. The policy that would most likely cover the computer during the move from one facility to another is a
    a. consequential loss, use, and occupancy policy.
    b. casualty policy.
    c. contents and personal property policy.
    d. liability policy.

MULTIPLE CHOICE   *(Continued)*

11. All of the following are principal responsibilities of the property manager *EXCEPT*

    a. forcibly removing tenants for nonpayment of rent.

    b. generating income for the owners.

    c. preserving and/or increasing the value of the property.

    d. achieving the objectives of the owners.

12. What is the purpose of an operating budget for a property manager?

    a. It documents the month's actual income and expense.

    b. It is a guide for the property's financial performance in the future.

    c. It presents the current cash flows in a standardized format.

    d. It lists the assets, liabilities, and equity of the investment property.

13. What type of plan does a property manager implement to manage renters who do *NOT* pay their rent in a timely way?

    a. Eviction plan   c. Foreclosure plan

    b. Collection plan   d. Cash flow plan

14. One way that property managers meet the goals of ECOA is by

    a. disqualifying tenant applicants on the basis of receiving welfare payments.

    b. not evaluating certain tenant applicants through the use of credit reports.

    c. establishing that certain buildings do not allow children as residents.

    d. making sure to use the same lease application for every applicant.

15. According to the Fair Housing Act, what is *steering*?

    a. Channeling of protected class members to certain buildings or neighborhoods

    b. Encouraging people to rent or sell by claiming that certain protected classes of people will have a negative impact on property values

    c. An appropriate method to manage risks associated with rental property ownership

    d. A method of providing reasonable accommodation for people with disabilities.

ACTIVITY: Types of Maintenance

In the following floor plan illustration, identify each maintenance item listed as Preventive, Corrective, or Routine. Mark the approximate location of each item on the floor plan.

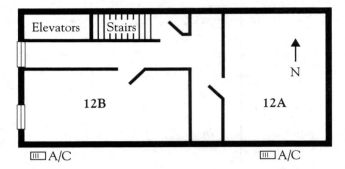

1. Wash wall mirror across from elevators _____

2. Fix air conditioner in 12B: blows hot _____

3. Repaint exterior brick on west side _____

4. Replace torn carpet on stair landing _____

5. Repair crakced window, hallway-south _____

6. Annual elevator inspection and repair _____

7. Clean off cobweb above doorway to Apartment 12A _____

_____

ANSWER KEY

Matching

1. a   **2.** e   **3.** d   **4.** i   **5.** f   **6.** j   **7.** c   **8.** g
9. b   **10.** h

True or False

1. **True.** The role of the property manager is to achieve the objectives of the property owners, generate income for the owners, and preserve and/or increase the value of the investment property. p. 292

2. **True.** The management agreement creates an agency relationship between the owner and the property manager; the manager is generally considered a general agent empowered to make many decisions on behalf of the owner. p. 295

3. **False.** Like real estate brokers commissions, property management fees may *not* be standardized by local associations but must be negotiated between the parties. p. 296

4. **True.** Because rental rates are influenced primarily by supply and demand, the property manager should be aware of the advantages and disadvantages of competing space. p. 298

5. **True.** Existing barriers must be removed when this can be accomplished in a readily achievable manner with little difficulty and at low cost. One example is ramping or removing an obstacle from an otherwise accessible entrance. p. 304

6. **False.** The manager of a *commercial* building should carefully consider a prospective tenant's compatibility with existing tenants, such as traffic counts, noise, etc. p. 299

7. **False.** A high tenant turnover rate results in lower profits for the owner. p. 301

8. **False.** The three types of maintenance necessary to keep a property in good condition are *preventive*, *corrective*, and *routine*. p. 302

9. **False.** *Preventive maintenance* helps prevent problems and expenses before they arise. Corrective maintenance involves the actual repairs that keep the building's equipment, utilities, and amenities functioning. p. 302

10. **True.** Tenant improvements, or build-outs, are construction alterations to the interior of the building to meet a tenant's particular space needs. p. 302

11. **False.** Under Title III of the ADA, existing barriers must be removed from commercial properties *when this can be accomplished in a readily achievable manner.* p. 304

12. **True.** New construction and remodeling commercial properties must meet higher standards of accessibility and usability, because it costs less to incorporate accessible features in the design than to retrofit. p. 304

13. **True.** Risk management involves answering the question: What happens if something goes wrong? The four alternative risk management techniques include avoidance, control, transfer, or retention. p. 306

14. **False.** In a commercial property, insurance against the risk of a shopper suffering a slip-and-fall injury would be covered by *liability* insurance. p. 307

15. **False.** A building is insured for what it would cost to rebuild it in a *current replacement cost* policy. p. 307

16. **True.** A cash flow report is a monthly statement that details the financial status of the property; as such, it is the most important financial report, because it provides a picture of the current financial status of the property. p. 297

17. **True.** The property manager is not expected to be an expert in all of the disciplines necessary to operate a property; they are expected to be knowledgeable in many diverse subjects, including environmental concerns, such as asbestos, radon, indoor air quality, etc. p. 308

18. **False.** Court decisions have held owners and their agents responsible for physical harm that was inflicted on tenants by intruders. p. 305

19. **True.** One of the most important functions of a property manager is the supervision of property maintenance, balancing the services provided with their costs. That is, to satisfy tenants' needs while minimizing operating expenses. p. 301

20. **False.** Employee wages and utilities are fixed expenses. Variable expenses may be recurring or nonrecurring, and can include capital improvements, building repairs, and landscaping. p. 297

Multiple Choice

1. **c.** The role of the property manager is to achieve the objectives of the property owners, generate income for the owners, and preserve and/or increase the value of the investment property. p. 292

2. **d.** A property manager is hired as a general agent with broad authority for a specific activity and for a long time. A salesperson is usually a general agent for the broker. p. 292

3. **c.** A management agreement establishes owner and manager responsibilities, determining who pays for what, all in keeping with the owner's purpose. It does not include a statement identifying the manager's creditors. p. 295

4. **c.** The manager will receive $1,080:

   $750 per month × 12 months × 12% = $1,080. p. 296

5. **d.** The annual rent is $29.50 per square foot: 30 × 40 = 1,200 square feet; $2,950 × 12 = $35,400; $35,400 ÷ 1,200 = $29.50. p. 300

6. **d.** An elevated level of vacancy may indicate poor management, a defective or undesirable property, or rental rates that are too high for the market or the property. p. 298

7. **c.** Repairing a leaking water heater is an example of *corrective maintenance*, which is fixing what is broken. Seasonal servicing is *preventive*; picking up litter is *routine*; moving a partition wall is *construction*. p. 302

8. **c.** A surety bond covers an owner against financial losses resulting from an employee's criminal acts or negligence. p. 307

9. **d.** Existing barriers must be removed when this can be can be accomplished in a readily achievable manner with little difficulty and at low cost. One example is ramping or removing an obstacle from an otherwise accessible entrance. p. 304

10. **c.** *Contents and personal property insurance* covers building contents and personal property during periods when they are not actually located on the business premises. *Consequential loss* is also known as *loss of rent* or *business interruption; casualty* covers theft, vandalism, machinery damage; *liability* covers injuries sustained on the premises. p. 307

11. **a.** The property manager may start eviction proceedings but does not carry out the proceedings, which must be carried out by an officer of the court. p. 301

12. **b.** The *budget* is a forward-looking plan that guides and provides expectations. The *cash flow report* is a monthly statement that details the financial status of the property. The *profit and loss statement* documents the actual income and expense. p. 297

13. **b.** Property managers must implement methods to collect rent before resorting to legal action that is costly and time-consuming. p. 300–301

14. **d.** Equality is the key. It is acceptable to use credit reports; however, managers need to require them on all applicants. ECOA prohibits discrimination on the basis of receipt of public assistance, such as welfare. p. 300

15. **a.** *Steering* is prohibited under the Fair Housing Act. *Blockbusting* is encouraging people to rent or sell by claiming that the entry of certain protected classes of people in an area will have a negative impact on property values. p. 305

Activity: Types of Maintenance

Types of Maintenance

1. routine
2. corrective
3. preventive
4. corrective
5. corrective
6. preventive
7. routine

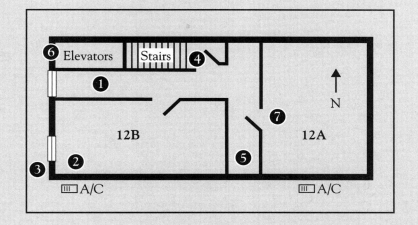

CHAPTER 18

Real Estate Appraisal

■ **LEARNING OBJECTIVES**   *Before you answer these questions, you should be able to*

■ **identify** the different types and basic principles of value;

■ **describe** the three basic valuation approaches used by appraisers;

■ **explain** the steps in the appraisal process;

■ **distinguish** the four methods of determining reproduction or replacement cost; and

■ **define** the following *key terms:*

accrued depreciation	external obsolescence	plottage
anticipation	functional obsolescence	progression
appraisal	gross income multiplier (GIM)	reconciliation
assemblage		regression
broker's price opinion	gross rent multiplier (GRM)	replacement cost new
capitalization rate	highest and best use	reproduction cost
change	income approach	sales comparison approach
competitive market analysis (CMA)	law of diminishing returns	sales price
competition	law of increasing returns	substitution
conformity	market data approach	supply and demand
contribution	market value	Uniform Standards of Professional Appraisal Practice (USPAP)
cost approach	net operating income (NOI)	
depreciation		value
economic life	physical deterioration	

MATCHING A   *Write the letter of the matching term on the appropriate line.*

a. anticipation

b. appraisal

c. appraiser

d. assemblage

e. change

f. conformity

g. contribution

h. highest and best use

i. income approach

j. market value

1. ___ An estimate or opinion of value based on supportable evidence and approved methods

2. ___ An independent professional who is trained to provide an unbiased estimate of value

3. ___ A way to estimate value based on the present worth of the rights to future income

4. ___ The most probable price that a property should bring in a fair sale

5. ___ The principle that value is created by the expectation that certain events will occur

6. ___ The principle that no physical or economic condition remains constant

7. ___ The principle that value is created when a property is in harmony with its surroundings

8. ___ The principle that the value of any part of a property is measured by its effect on the value of the whole property

9. ___ The most profitable single use to which property may legally, physically, and financially be put

10. ___ The process of merging two separately owned lots under one owner

MATCHING B   *Write the letter of the matching term on the appropriate line.*

a. cost approach

b. depreciation

c. economic life

d. sales comparison

e. regression

f. replacement cost

g. reproduction cost

h. plottage

i. supply and demand

j. substitution

1. ___ The principle that merging or consolidating adjacent lots into a single one will produce a higher total value than the sum of the two sites valued separately

2. ___ The principle that the worth of a better-quality property is adversely affected by the presence of a nearby lesser-quality property

3. ___ The principle that the maximum value of a property tends to be set by how much it would cost to purchase an equally desirable property

4. ___ The economic principle that the value of a property depends on the number of similar properties available in the marketplace

5. ___ The approach that estimates value by comparing the subject property with recently sold similar properties

6. ___ An estimate of value made by determining the value of the land as if it were vacant, adding the current cost of constructing improvements, and deducting accrued depreciation

7. ___ The cost of constructing an exact duplicate of the subject property at current prices

8. ___ The current price of constructing a property similar to the subject property using current construction methods

9. ___ A loss in value due to any cause

10. ___ The period during which a property is expected to remain useful for its original intended purpose

TRUE OR FALSE   *Circle the correct answer.*

1. T F Title XI of FIRREA requires that all residential property be appraised by a federally licensed or certified appraiser.

2. T F A competitive market analysis should never be represented as an appraisal.

3. T F The *market value* of a property is what it actually sells for in an open market transaction.

4. T F Cost and market value are the same.

5. T F The value of a property may be affected by events that have not yet occurred.

6. T F The *law of diminishing returns* applies when, no matter how much money is spent on a property, its value will not keep pace with the expenditures.

7. T F According to the economic principle of *plottage*, combining two adjacent lots into a large one will produce a higher total land value than the sum of the value of the two sites if owned separately.

8. T F The economic principle of contribution holds that the maximum value of a property tends to be set by the cost of purchasing a similarly desirable property.

9. T F In the *sales comparison approach* to value, the value of a feature that is present in the subject property but is not present in a comparable property, is subtracted from the sale price of the comparable.

10. T F The square-foot method and the unit-in-place method are both techniques used in the cost approach to value.

11. T F Depreciation may be curable or incurable, depending on whether the expense required to correct it contributes to the property's value.

12. T F External obsolescence is always incurable.

13. T F The income approach to value is based on the future value of the rights to present income.

14. T F A GRM or GIM is often used as a substitute for an income capitalization rate.

15. T F *Reconciliation* involves averaging the results derived from the three approaches to value.

16. T F The first step in using the income approach to value is to add the debt service to the annual operating expenses.

17. T F The art of analyzing and weighing the findings from the three approaches to value in an appraisal is called *reconciliation*.

18. T F If a property improvement results in a higher value, the law of increasing returns applies.

19. T F To use the sales comparison approach, an appraiser must find a minimum of four properties comparable to the property being appraised.

20. T F An estimate of the rate of return (yield) that an investor would expect for investing in a piece of property is called the *anticipation rate*.

MULTIPLE CHOICE   *Circle the correct answer.*

1. A property is listed for sale at $235,000. A buyer's offer of $220,000 is rejected by the seller. Six months later, the seller reduces the price to $225,000. Another buyer offers $210,000, and the seller accepts because the seller has found another house to buy and needs to close quickly. The property is subsequently appraised at $215,000. Which of these figures MOST accurately represents the property's market value?

   a. $210,000
   b. $215,000
   c. $225,000
   d. $235,000

2. Which appraisal approach would be BEST to appraise a 25-year-old owner-occupied house in a 30-year-old neighborhood?

   a. Sales comparison
   b. Income approach
   c. Cost approach
   d. GRM

3. When appraising a new home in which no one has ever lived, the appraiser will likely use the

   a. sales comparison approach.
   b. income approach.
   c. cost approach.
   d. GRM.

4. Assuming that all of the following transactions are federally related, the properties would have to be appraised by a state licensed or certified appraiser EXCEPT

   a. the commercial property valued at $350,000.
   b. the condominium unit with a sale price of $67,850.
   c. the residential property valued at $262,500.
   d. the commercial property valued over $1 million in a refinance.

5. What is the role of an appraiser?

   a. Set price
   b. Average value
   c. Determine value
   d. Estimate value

6. The principle that maximum value is realized when land use is in harmony with surrounding standards is

   a. contribution.
   b. conformity.
   c. highest and best use.
   d. competition.

7. A woman plans to build a large house in a neighborhood of smaller homes, so she purchases three neighboring lots from their three owners. What is the term for the woman's activity?

   a. Substitution
   b. Plottage
   c. Progression
   d. Assemblage

8. A woman buys a small house in a desirable neighborhood and pays $390,000. A man buys a nearly identical house in a neighborhood of similar homes and pays $290,000. What economic principle BEST describes the reason why the woman paid more than the man?

   a. Plottage
   b. Substitution
   c. Regression
   d. Progression

9. It cost approximately $350,000 to build a house and its various improvements on a parcel of property. If the property was vacant, undeveloped land, it would be worth about $100,000. As it currently exists, the property's physical deterioration equals about $60,000. If an appraiser were to apply the cost approach, what would be the value of this property?

   a. $250,000
   b. $390,000
   c. $450,000
   d. $480,000

10. In which approach to value are the square-foot method, the unit-in-place method, and the quantity-survey method used?

   a. Sales comparison approach
   b. Cost approach
   c. Income approach
   d. Reconciliation approach

MULTIPLE CHOICE *(Continued)*

11. Air pollution from increased automobile traffic near a building with ornate exterior decoration has dissolved much of the intricate detail work. The cost of restoring the front of the building is roughly five times the building's present value. These facts describe which of the following?

    a. Curable external obsolescence
    b. Incurable functional obsolescence
    c. Incurable physical deterioration
    d. Curable external deterioration

12. The land on which a house was built is worth $50,000. The house was constructed in 1986 at a cost of $265,000 and was expected to last 50 years. Using the straight-line method, determine how much the house has depreciated by 2010.

    a. $28,600   c. $127,200
    b. $96,600   d. $145,200

13. Which of the following reports would a salesperson MOST likely research and deliver to a prospective seller?

    a. Competitive market analysis
    b. Appraisal
    c. Letter of intent
    d. Cost benefit analysis

14. What is the GRM for a residential duplex with a selling price of $234,000 if the monthly rent for each unit is $925?

    a. 1.054   c. 126.5
    b. 10.54   d. 252.9

15. Which of the following approaches is given the greatest weight in reconciling the appraised value of a two-bedroom, owner-occupied home?

    a. Income approach
    b. Sales comparison approach
    c. Cost approach
    d. Market value approach

16. An old, historical house has a leaking slate roof. A deed restriction requires that the new roof be made of slate. This is an example of

    a. reproduction.
    b. replacement.
    c. regression.
    d. substitution.

17. A house has been on the market for several months because most buyers do not want to walk through the master bedroom to reach another bedroom in the back. This floor plan is an example of

    a. regression.
    b. economic obsolescence.
    c. functional obsolescence.
    d. physical deterioration.

18. The owner is considering installing a below-ground swimming pool, which may cost many thousands of dollars to build. Before he starts, he should consider the concept of

    a. change.
    b. competition with the neighbors.
    c. conformity within the neighborhood.
    d. contribution.

19. All of the following formulas are correct for the income approach EXCEPT

    a. Income ÷ Value = Rate.
    b. Income ÷ Rate = Value.
    c. Value ÷ Rate = Income.
    d. Value × Rate = Income.

20. A house sits on the corner of a busy intersection. Two of the corners are occupied by gas stations, and directly across from the house is a fast food restaurant. The house's owners have been told that the property would be worth more if the lot were vacant. This is an example of

    a. progression.
    b. highest and best use.
    c. regression.
    d. conservation.

21. A two-unit apartment building is being appraised. In this neighborhood, the accepted gross rent multiplier is 144. The annual income on the building is $16,800 (both units rented). The monthly expenses are $300. Based on the income approach, what is the estimated market value of the apartment building?

    a. $201,600   c. $224,800
    b. $232,500   d. $258,600

MULTIPLE CHOICE   *(Continued)*

22. An apartment building has $65,000 in potential gross annual income. The vacancy rate is estimated at 5 percent. Total operating expenses are $29,000. The capitalization rate is 9 percent. Using the income approach, what is the value of the building?
    a. $324,773
    b. $363,889
    c. $372,895
    d. $392,367

23. Which of the following concepts applies to every appraisal?
    a. Diminishing returns
    b. Plottage
    c. Highest and best use
    d. Assemblage

24. The property being appraised is called the
    a. lot.
    b. parcel.
    c. subject property.
    d. comparable property.

25. An empty lot is located in a neighborhood of single-family homes. It is the only lot in this well-maintained neighborhood. A busy street with many stores is located three blocks away. An industrial area is about six blocks away. What is the probable highest and best use of this lot?
    a. A store
    b. A factory
    c. A parking lot
    d. A single-family home

26. What is the process for creating a broker's price opinion?
    a. Broker drives by property, takes picture, and fills out BPO form
    b. Broker engages a certified appraiser to perform an appraisal
    c. Broker prepares a report compiled from research of comparable properties
    d. Attorney engages broker to perform a competitive market analysis

27. All of the following are essential assumptions in determining market value *EXCEPT*
    a. that the buyer and seller must be unrelated.
    b. that the payment must be in cash or its equivalent.
    c. that the buyer and seller must be acting without excessive pressure.
    d. that the property must be on the market for at least three months.

28. The principle of value that is the interaction of supply and demand is called
    a. anticipation.
    b. competition.
    c. conformity.
    d. contribution.

29. The most common and easiest method of cost estimation is the
    a. unit-in-place method.
    b. quantity-survey method.
    c. index method.
    d. the square-foot method.

30. Touching-up peeling paint is an example of curing
    a. physical deterioration.
    b. functional obsolescence.
    c. external obsolescence.
    d. straight-line depreciation.

ACTIVITY: Pennytree Lane Appraisals

Complete the following appraisal problems based on the five homes on the 1200 block of Pennytree Lane depicted in the photos.

    1230   1231   1232   1233   1234

1. 1230 Pennytree Lane was just sold. Which house is the best comparable property? _____
   _____

2. The principle of regression is best illustrated by which property?_____

3. The principle of progression is best illustrated by which property? _____

4. Pennytree Lane is near an increasingly fashionable and upscale part of town. Incomes in the area are rising rapidly. If 1233 is a newly constructed home, it is an example of which principle of value?_____
   _____

5. When a garage was added to 1231 and 1233 was built, what likely happened to the values of 1230 and 1232? Why? _____

6. House number 1233 violates which principle of value? _____

7. When the kitchen in 1232 was remodeled, which principle of value describes its effect?_____
   _____

ANSWER KEY

Matching A

1. b   **2.** c   **3.** i   **4.** j   **5.** a   **6.** e   **7.** f   **8.** g
9. h   **10.** d

Matching B

1. h   **2.** e   **3.** j   **4.** i   **5.** d   **6.** a   **7.** g   **8.** f
9. b   **10.** c

True or False

1. **False.** Title XI of FIRREA requires that residential property valued at $250,000 or more in a federally related transaction be appraised by a state licensed or certified appraiser. p. 315

2. **True.** Licensees prepare Competitive Market Analysis (CMAs) for their sellers and buyers. The CMA is *NOT* an appraisal, but rather a tool to assist the clients in determining an appropriate asking or offering price. p. 315–316

3. **False.** The *market price* of a property is what it actually sells for in an open market transaction. p. 324

4. **False.** Cost and market value may be, but are not necessarily, the same. When the improvements on a property are new, cost and value are likely to be equal. p. 325

5. **True.** According to the concept of anticipation, value is created by the expectation that certain events will occur; this concept is the foundation on which the income approach to value is based. p. 325

6. **True.** The *law of diminishing returns* applies when, no matter how much money is spent on a property, its value will not keep pace with the expenditures. For example, adding restaurant-quality appliances and gold faucets to a modest home are costs that the owner probably would not be able to recover. p. 326

7. **True.** Plottage is the principle that the individual value of two adjacent properties may be greater if they are combined than if each is sold separately. p. 326

8. **False.** The economic principle of *substitution* holds that the maximum value of a property tends to be set by the cost of purchasing a similarly desirable property. Under the principle of contribution, the value of any part of a property is measured by its effect on the value of the whole parcel. p. 325

9. **False.** In the sales approach to value, the value of a feature that is present in the subject property but not present in a comparable property is *added to* the sales price of the comparable. Remember, CBS is "comp better, subtract" and CPA "comp poorer, add." p. 328

10. **True.** The cost approach is based on the principle of substitution; the cost of improvements, less depreciation, is added to the cost of the land. p. 327–328

11. **True.** In real estate, depreciation is the loss in value for any reason; land never depreciates. Depreciation is the result of a negative condition that affects real property. p. 329

12. **True.** If caused by negative factors not on the subject property, such as environmental, social, or economic force, the depreciation is always incurable, because the cure is outside the efforts of the owner. p. 330

13. **False.** The income approach to value is based on the *present* value of the rights to *future* income. p. 331

14. **True.** A GRM or GIM is often used to value a single-family residence used to produce rental incomes. These are unlikely to be used when valuing commercial and industrial properties, because they usually generate income for many other sources. p. 333

15. **False.** *Reconciliation* involves a detailed and professional analysis and application of the three approaches to value, not simply an average of the different values. p. 333–334

16. **False.** Debt service (mortgage payments) are not considered expenses, so they are not included in annual operating expenses. p. 331

17. **True.** Reconciliation is the act of analyzing and effectively weighing the findings from three appraisal approaches. p. 333

18. **True.** As long as money spent on improvements produces an increase in income or value, the law of increasing returns applies. p. 326

19. **False.** The usual standard is three comparable properties. Most appraisals for residential properties include a minimum of three comparable sales that are reflective of the subject property. p. 327

20. **False.** An estimate of the rate of return (yield) that an investor would expect for investing in a piece of property is called the *capitalization* or *"cap" rate*. p. 331

Multiple Choice

1. **b.** The property's market price is $210,000, while its appraised value (and most probable market value) is $215,000. The seller accepted the lower price because of the pressure to close on the new house. p. 324

2. **a.** The most appropriate method to appraise an older home in an established neighborhood is the sales comparison approach. p. 327

3. **c.** A newly constructed house may be appraised using the cost approach and omitting depreciation. p. 329

4. **b.** Appraisals of residential property and commercial property valued at $250,000 or less in federally related transactions are exempt and need not be performed by licensed or certified appraisers. p. 315

5. **d.** An *appraiser* is an independent professional trained to provide an unbiased estimate of value in an impartial and objective manner, according to the appraisal process. p. 315

6. **b.** *Contribution* is the principle that evaluates the cost of adding an improvement against the value of the property as a whole. *Competition* is the interaction of supply and demand, while *highest and best use* is the most profitable single use to which the property may be used. p. 325

7. **d.** The process of merging separately owned lots under one owner is called *assemblage*. *Plottage* holds that merging these lots together into a single larger one produces a greater total land value than the sum of the individual lots valued separately. p. 326

8. **d.** The woman's house benefits from being a smaller one alongside larger, more prestigious ones, i.e., progression. The man's house is appropriately valued for its neighborhood. p. 326

9. **b.** The *cost approach* subtracts the depreciation from the cost of today's improvements and then adds on the value of the land as if it were vacant: $350,000 − $60,000 + $100,000 = $390,000. p. 327–328

10. **b.** The cost approach uses the square-foot method, the unit-in-place method, and the quantity-survey method .The *sales approach* compares values of comparable properties; the *income approach* places a value on acquiring future income. p. 327–328

11. **c.** Air pollution has damaged the old design, and the cost of correcting the defect is not financially feasible. This is an example of incurable physical deterioration. p. 330

12. **c.** The value of the land is not relevant to this problem. The cost of the building is divided by the number of years of its useful life and multiplied to determine the depreciation after 24 years:

    $265,000 ÷ 50 = $5,300; $5,300 × 24 = $127,200. p. 331

13. **a.** A real estate salesperson often prepares a *competitive market analysis* (CMA), a comparison of the prices of recently sold homes that are similar to a listing seller's home in terms of location, style, and amenities. The CMA helps the owner set an appropriate asking price for the property. p. 315

14. **c.** Because GRM for one-unit and two-unit residential properties is based on gross monthly rent, GRM = Sales Price ÷ Gross Rent: $234,000 ÷ (2 × $925) = 126.5 GRM. p. 333

15. **b.** Most owner-occupied residences are best appraised by comparing them to similar properties; that is, by using the sales comparison approach. p. 334

16. **a.** Construction cost at current prices of an exact duplicate of the subject improvement is called *reproduction*, e.g., slate for slate. The roof could be replaced with a modern material at a lower cost and be just as effective at keeping the rain out of the house. p. 329

17. **c.** There is nothing physically wrong with the house, but the design is outdated (functionally obsolescent). Perhaps buyers would be more interested if the room were changed to a home office use. p. 330

18. **d.** Before embarking on installing the pool, the owner should consider its overall contribution to the value of the property, especially alongside his neighbors. Sometimes, the improvement does not add value equal to its cost. p. 326

19. **c.** As the capitalization rate goes down, the value increases. p. 331–332

20. **b.** Under the principle of highest and best use, the single most profitable use for this property is not a residential mansion; more likely, it would be better suited to another commercial use. p. 326

21. **a.** The monthly rental income is $1,400: ($16,800 ÷ 12 = $1,400) Rental Income × GRM = Estimated Market Value. ($1,400 × 144 = $201,600) The monthly expenses are not included in the calculation. p. 333

22. **b.** Gross Income – Vacancy and Rent Losses – Operating Expenses = Net Operating Income: $65,000 × 5% = $3,250; $65,000 – $3,250 – $29,000 = $32,750.

    Net Operating Income ÷ Capitalization Rate = Value: $32,750 ÷ 9% = $363,889. p. 332

23. **c.** The principal of *highest and best use* is the most profitable single use to which a property supports the highest present value. Or, it is the use that is most likely to be in demand in the near future, and is applied to every appraisal. p. 326

24. **c.** The subject property is the one being appraised. *Comparable properties* are properties similar to the subject property. Each comparable property is analyzed for differences and similarities between it and the subject property. p. 327

25. **d.** The *highest and best use* is the most profitable or the most likely to be in demand soon. In this neighborhood, the demand is most likely to be for another single-family home. A parking lot is not needed. A store or factory would not be in conformity with the area and might not even be allowed. p. 326

26. **a.** The broker's price opinion (BPO) is a less-expensive alternative of valuating properties often used by lenders working with home equity lines, refinancing, etc. Most are simply *drive-bys* that verify the existence of the property along with a listing of comparable sales. p. 316

27. **d.** Market value is the most probable price that a property should bring at a fair sale. The property must be on the market for a *reasonable time*, but no specific time period must be met. p. 324

28. **b.** *Anticipation* is the expectation that certain events will occur. *Conformity* states that value is created when a property is in harmony with its surroundings. *Contribution* means that the value of any part of a property is measured by its effect on the value of the entire property. p. 325

29. **d.** The square foot method of cost estimation is the most common and easiest method of cost estimation. With the *unit-in-place method*, the replacement cost of a building is estimated based on the construction cost per unit of measure of individual building components, such as labor. The *quantity-survey method* is so detailed that it is usually used only when appraising historical structures, but it is the most accurate for new construction. The *index method* is useful only as a check of the estimate reached by one of the other methods. p. 329

30. **a.** Touching up peeling paint is an example of curing physical deterioration. External obsolescence is always incurable. Functional obsolescence is a loss in value from the *market's response* to the item. p. 330

Activity: Pennytree Lane Appraisals

1. The best comparable appears to be 1232 because it is in the same style and condition as the subject property.

2. Regression is illustrated by 1233 because its value is lowered because of the lesser quality of neighboring properties.

3. Progression is illustrated by 1234 because its value is increased because of the larger, fancier quality of neighboring properties.

4. The new home at 1233 exemplifies the principle of anticipation.

5. The values of 1230 and 1232 increased due to progression.

6. The house at 1233 violates the principle of conformity.

7. Remodeling the kitchen at 1232 illustrates the principle of contribution.

CHAPTER 19

Land-Use Controls and Property Development

■ **LEARNING OBJECTIVES** *Before you answer these questions, you should be able to*

- ■ **identify** the various types of public and private land-use controls;

- ■ **describe** how a comprehensive plan influences local real estate development;

- ■ **explain** the various issues involved in subdivision;

- ■ **distinguish** the function and characteristics of building codes and zoning ordinances; and

- ■ **define** the following *key terms*:

buffer zone	density zoning	planned unit development (PUD)
building code	developer	
certificate of occupancy	enabling acts	plat
comprehensive plan	inverse condemnation	restrictive covenants
conditional-use permit	Interstate Land Sales Full Disclosure Act	subdivider
covenants, conditions, and restrictions (CC&Rs)	nonconforming use	subdivision
		variance
		zoning ordinances

MATCHING A *Write the letter of the matching term on the appropriate line.*

a. *buffer zones*

b. *bulk zoning*

c. *comprehensive plan*

d. *conditional-use permit*

e. *enabling acts*

f. *certificate of occupancy*

g. *nonconforming use*

h. *taking*

i. *variance*

j. *zoning ordinances*

1. ___ The device by which local governments establish development goals

2. ___ Document issued by a building inspector after a newly constructed building is found satisfactory

3. ___ Local laws that implement a comprehensive plan and regulate the control of land and structures within districts

4. ___ The legal means by which states confer zoning powers on local government

5. ___ Areas such as parks used to screen residential from nonresidential areas

6. ___ A special type of zoning used to control density by imposing restrictions, such as setbacks or limiting new construction

7. ___ The seizure of land through the government's power of eminent domain or condemnation

8. ___ A lot or improvement that is not in harmony with current zoning, because it existed prior to the enactment or amendment of the zoning

9. ___ The device by which a daycare center might be permitted to operate in a residential neighborhood

10. ___ A form of permitted use, despite being prohibited by zoning, that is granted to an owner because of unique hardship caused by the regulation

MATCHING B *Write the letter of the matching term on the appropriate line.*

a. *building codes*

b. *Interstate Land Sales Full Disclosure Act*

c. *Planned Unit Development (PUD)*

d. *density zoning*

e. *developer*

f. *subdivider*

g. *building permit*

h. *plat*

i. *police power*

j. *restrictive covenants*

1. ___ An item that a property owner must obtain from municipal officials before constructing a new building

2. ___ A person who buys undeveloped acreage and divides it into smaller lots for sale to others

3. ___ An individual who constructs improvements and sells them

4. ___ A detailed map that illustrates the geographic boundaries of individual lots in a subdivision

5. ___ Ordinances that restrict the average maximum number of houses per acre

6. ___ Standards for building style, setbacks, and use that are included in a deed for property in a subdivision

7. ___ Ordinances that specify construction and safety standards for construction

8. ___ A development where land is set aside for mixed-use purposes, such as residential, commercial, and public areas

9. ___ Law that requires developers to file statements with HUD before the developer can market unimproved lots interstate

10. ___ State's authority to make rules needed to protect the public health, safety, and welfare

TRUE OR FALSE   *Circle the correct answer.*

1. T F *Zoning ordinances* create the broad, general framework for a community; the comprehensive plan defines the details and implements the ordinances.

2. T F *Bulk zoning* ensures that certain types of uses are incorporated into developments.

3. T F Property owners are protected against the unreasonable or arbitrary taking of their land by the seizure clause of the Fifteenth Amendment to the United States Constitution.

4. T F The government's payment to a landowner for seizure of the landowner's property is referred to as *just compensation.*

5. T F A *conditional-use permit* allows a landowner to use property in a way that is not ordinarily permitted by zoning, due to unusual hardship or deprivation of reasonable use by the regulation.

6. T F Zoning permits are usually required before building permits can be issued.

7. T F A *subdivider* is a person who buys undeveloped acreage and divides it into smaller lots for sale to individuals or developers.

8. T F A plan is a detailed map that illustrates the geographic boundaries of individual lots in a subdivision.

9. T F Zoning is a state and local issue; there is no national zoning ordinance.

10. T F The average number of residential units per acre in a development is referred to as the development's *gross density.*

11. T F A restrictive covenant is considered a reasonable, legal restraint if it protects property values or restricts the free transfer of property.

12. T F The Interstate Land Sales Full Disclosure Act requires developers of any property to file a disclosure statement with HUD.

13. T F If a local zoning ordinance requires a 30-foot setback on property and a restrictive covenant for the subdivision calls for a 40-foot setback, the 30-foot setback takes precedence because it is less restrictive.

14. T F One of the basic elements of the comprehensive plan of a municipality can be energy conservation to reduce energy consumption, and to promote the use of renewable energy sources.

15. T F Through powers conferred by state enabling acts, local governments exercise their authority based on the state's obligation to protect public health, safety, and welfare.

MULTIPLE CHOICE   *Circle the correct answer.*

1. A subdivision built in 1974 includes covenants, conditions, and restrictions (CC&Rs) in the deeds for all properties. One covenant bans "all outdoor structures designed for the storage of equipment or as habitations for any animals for 32 years from the date recorded on the original plat of subdivision." In 2010, a resident built a tool shed and a doghouse. Do the neighbors have any recourse?

    a. Yes, they can go to court and sue for monetary damages for violating the covenant.

    b. Yes, they can go to court and be awarded injunctive relief.

    c. No, the covenant is no longer operative unless the subdivision's property owners have agreed to its extension.

    d. No, covenants such as this are usually considered to be unenforceable restrictions on the free transfer of property.

2. A state delegates zoning powers to a municipality through

    a. its police power.

    b. eminent domain.

    c. a comprehensive plan.

    d. an enabling act.

3. All of the following could be included in a zoning ordinance EXCEPT

    a. objectives for future development of the area.

    b. permissible height and style of new construction.

    c. style and appearance of structures.

    d. the maximum allowable ratio of land area to structural area.

4. Which of the following protects property owners against being deprived of their property by the government without just compensation?

    a. The Preamble to the U.S. Constitution

    b. The *takings clause* of the Fifth Amendment to the U.S. Constitution

    c. The *due process clause* of the Fourteenth Amendment to the U.S. Constitution

    d. The *compensation clause* of Article VII of the Bill of Rights

5. A city has passed a new zoning ordinance that prohibits all commercial structures over 30 feet high. A man wants to build an office building that will be 45 feet high. Given these facts, what are the man's options to obtain permission for the building?

    a. Apply for a nonconforming use permit

    b. Apply for a zoning permit

    c. Apply for a conditional-use permit

    d. Apply for a variance or zoning change

6. A woman would like to operate a business in her home, but she lives in an area zoned for residential use only. What should she do?

    a. Request that the zoning board declare her home to be a nonconforming use

    b. Ask a court to grant an injunction against the zoning board

    c. Seek a conditional-use permit from the zoning board, if it is defined as allowable

    d. Apply to the zoning board for a variance

7. A man goes all over the country buying large tracts of vacant land, splitting them into smaller parcels, and building identical communities of single-family ranch-style homes surrounding a central shopping center. He sells the homes to residents and leases space in the shopping center to merchants. The man is a(n)

    a. developer only.

    b. subdivider only.

    c. developer and subdivider.

    d. assembler.

8. Which of the following BEST defines density zoning?

    a. The mandatory use of clustering

    b. The average number of units in a development

    c. A restriction on the average number of houses per acre

    d. A restriction on the average number of acres per parcel

MULTIPLE CHOICE   (Continued)

9. Before granting a zoning variance, a zoning board of appeals must
   a. hold a public hearing where neighbors of a proposed use may voice their opinions.
   b. conduct a door-to-door opinion survey of property owners adjacent to the proposed use.
   c. check whether the landowner has been granted previous variances.
   d. determine whether the proposed use will result in higher property taxes.

10. All of the following are common tests of a valid zoning ordinance EXCEPT
    a. clear and specific provisions.
    b. anticipation of future housing needs.
    c. a nondiscriminatory effect.
    d. all property owners being affected in a similar manner.

11. A man owns a 2,000-acre tract of undeveloped woodland surrounding a scenic lake. He has divided the tract into 106 individual lots, ranging in size from 15 acres to 100 acres. He has also hired telemarketers to sell the lots to residents of the state and the three states with which it shares a common border. Based on these facts, how does the Interstate Land Sales Full Disclosure Act apply to the project?
    a. The man must file a disclosure statement with HUD.
    b. Because the man's project is not fraudulent, it is exempt from the requirements of the law.
    c. This development project is exempt from the law because of the lot size exemption.
    d. The man's project is exempt from the law because it is not being marketed outside a contiguous multistate region.

12. Zoning ordinances affect all of the following EXCEPT
    a. lot sizes.
    b. building heights.
    c. style and appearance of buildings.
    d. racial composition of neighborhood.

13. A developer has included a playground and running trails between the commercial properties facing a busy street and the houses further back in the subdivision. The recreational area is considered
    a. aesthetic zoning.
    b. a buffer zone.
    c. a taking.
    d. a nonconforming use.

14. When an area was rezoned as residential, a store was grandfathered in and allowed to continue business. This is an example of
    a. a variance.
    b. nonconforming use.
    c. a conditional-use permit.
    d. an amendment.

15. A new structure has been completed to the satisfaction of the inspecting city engineer. What documentation must be issued before anyone can move in?
    a. Appraisal report
    b. Certificate of occupancy
    c. Certificate of reasonable value
    d. Conditional-use permit

FILL-IN-THE-BLANK   *Select the word or words that best complete the following statements:*

aesthetic zoning
   ordinances

before-and-after method

bulk zoning ordinances

covenants, conditions,
   and restrictions
   (CC&Rs)

environmental impact
   report

Fair Housing Act

gross density

incentive zoning
   ordinances

Interstate Land Sales Full
   Disclosure Act

inverse condemnation

subdivision

straight-line-depreciation

zones

zoning classifications

1. The coding system that outlines how the land may be used
    (C = commercial, R = residential, etc.) divides the land into

    _____.

2. Zoning laws that specify certain types of architecture for all new construc-
    tion are called _____.

3. Along with an application for subdivision approval, a developer often
    must submit a(n) _____ to explain what effect
    the proposed development will have on the surrounding area.

4. Private rules established by a developer for all parcels within the defined
    subdivision are called _____ .

5. The federal government passed the _____ to help
    prevent fraudulent marketing schemes when land is sold without being
    seen by purchasers.

6. When a woman's home lost value because a new airport was constructed
    next to it, she filed a(n) _____ action to be
    compensated for the loss in property value.

7. A developer must keep the average number of units in the develop-
    ment at or below the maximum number per acre, which is also called the

    _____.

8. A useful method to determine just compensation to a property owner
    when a portion of the owner's land is seized for public use is the

    _____.

9. Taking previously undeveloped acreage and splitting it into smaller lots for
    sale is called _____ .

10. Zoning laws that control overcrowding by requiring setbacks or limiting
    building heights are called _____.

ACTIVITY: City Zoning

Answer the following questions based on the following city zoning map.

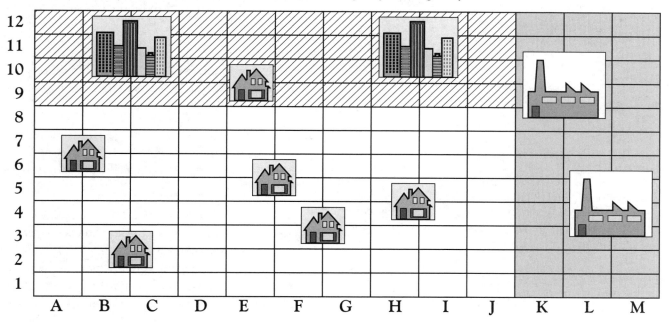

1. What would be necessary before a daycare center could be legally operated in area D5? _____
    _____
    _____

2. Where do you think it would be most beneficial for the city to locate a new park as a buffer zone? Why?
    _____
    _____

3. The city rezones blocks G8 and H8 as a historic district with restrictions on the type of architecture for
    new buildings. What type of zoning is this? _____
    _____

4. The house at E9 was built prior to the city's zoning ordinance. Why is it permitted to continue being a
    residence? _____
    _____

5. The city has asked you where to place a new retail and professional services zone, which will take up to
    six square units on the map. Where would you locate this new zone, and why? _____
    _____

ANSWER KEY

Matching A

1. c **2.** f **3.** j **4.** e **5.** a **6.** b **7.** h **8.** g
9. d **10.** i

Matching B

1. g **2.** f **3.** e **4.** h **5.** d **6.** j **7.** a **8.** c
9. b **10.** i

True or False

1. **False.** A *comprehensive plan* creates the broad, general framework for a community; *zoning ordinances* define the details and implement the plan. p. 339–340

2. **False.** *Incentive zoning* ensures that certain types of uses are incorporated into developments. p. 341

3. **False.** Property owners are protected against the unreasonable or arbitrary taking of their land by the *takings clause* of the *Fifth Amendment* to the United States Constitution. p. 342

4. **True.** The *Fifth Amendment* of the U.S. Constitutions reads " nor shall private property be taken for public use, without just compensation." p. 342

5. **False.** This is a *variance*, not a conditional-use permit. A variance provides relief if zoning regulations deprive an owner of the reasonable use of the property. p. 343

6. **True.** Typically, a zoning permit is required before building permits are issued; the building permit allows municipal officials to be aware of new construction or alterations and can verify compliance with building codes and zoning ordinances. p. 344

7. **True.** A subdivider is a person who buys undeveloped acreage and divides it into smaller lots for sale to individuals or developers or for the subdivider's own use. A developer improves the land, constructs homes or other buildings on the lots, and then sells them. p. 345

8. **False.** A detailed map that illustrates the geographic boundaries of individual lots in a subdivision is called a *plat*. p. 345

9. **True.** Although no nationwide or statewide zoning ordinances exist, the state's enabling acts confer zoning powers to local municipal governments. p. 340

10. **True.** Density zoning ordinances restrict the average maximum number of houses per acre that may be built within a particular subdivision. p. 346

11. **False.** A *restrictive covenant* is considered a reasonable, legal restraint if it protects property values and *does not* restrict the free transfer of property. Restrictive covenants may not be used for illegal purposes, such as for the exclusion of members of certain races, nationalities, or religions. p. 347

12. **False.** The Interstate Land Sales Full Disclosure Act requires developers of any *unimproved property offered in interstate commerce by telephone or through the mail* to file a disclosure statement with HUD. p. 347–348

13. **False.** Because the more restrictive requirement takes precedence, the 40-foot setback would be required. Private land-use controls may be more restrictive of an owner's use than the local zoning ordinances. The rule is that the more restrictive of the two takes precedence. p. 347

14. **True.** A comprehensive plan includes plans for orderly growth, including energy conservation to reduce energy consumption and to promote the use of renewable energy sources. p. 340

15. **True.** Although no nationwide or statewide zoning ordinances exist, the state's enabling acts confer zoning powers to local municipal governments. p. 340

Multiple Choice

1. **c.** The deed restriction will not be considered unreasonable, but this is not a municipality issue. If the neighbors were concerned, they needed to rally support and gain consent to an extension of the restrictive covenant. p. 347

2. **d.** *Enabling acts* permit the state to delegate authority to local officials to enact rules to protect the public's health and safety. This *police power* includes creating a comprehensive plan and acquiring private property for public use through the right of eminent domain. p. 340

3. **a.** A zoning ordinance might include restrictions for permissible height and style of new construction, style, and appearance of structures, and the maximum allowable ratio of land area to structural area, while objectives for future development of the area might be found in a comprehensive plan. p. 340

4. **b.** The takings clause of the Fifth Amendment to the U. S. Constitution protects property owners against being deprived of their property by the government without just compensation. p. 342

5. **d.** Because the man's building does not yet exist, it does not qualify for *nonconforming use*; a *conditional-use permit* is issued for a special use that meets certain standards. A *variance*, if granted, will permit the landowner to use the property in a manner that is otherwise prohibited by the existing zoning. p. 343

6. **c.** A conditional-use permit might be granted in this situation if the intended use would not greatly impact the residential nature of the neighborhood. p. 343–344

7. **c.** *Subdividers* buy undeveloped acreage and divide it into smaller lots. A *developer* improves the land, constructs homes, or other buildings, and sells them. Developing is usually more complex than subdividing. p. 345

8. **c.** *Density zoning* ordinances restrict the average maximum number of houses per acre that may be built within a particular subdivision. p. 346

9. **a.** Both variances and conditional-use permits can only be issued after public hearings. p. 344

10. **b.** The comprehensive plan would seek to anticipate future housing needs. p. 340, 343

11. **a.** The man must file the disclosure statement: His project is being marketed over state lines, it consists of more than 25 lots, and some lots are smaller than 25 acres. p. 347–348

12. **d.** Zoning may not affect the racial composition of the neighborhood; they must apply in a non-discriminatory way. p. 341

13. **b.** A *buffer zone* is a strip of land, such as a park, separating land dedicated to one use (commercial) from land dedicated to another use (residential). p. 341

14. **b.** Because the store had been there legally before the zoning ordinance, it is permitted to continue operating, usually until its use changes or the building is destroyed. p. 343

15. **b.** Once the completed building has been inspected and found to comply with the building codes, the municipal inspector issues a *certificate of occupancy* or *occupancy permit*. p. 344

Fill-in-the-Blank

1. The coding system that outlines how the land may be used (C = commercial, R = residential, etc.) divides the land into *zones*.

2. Zoning laws that specify certain types of architecture for all new construction are called *aesthetic ordinances*.

3. Along with an application for subdivision approval, a developer often must submit an *environmental impact report* to explain what effect the proposed development will have on the surrounding area.

4. Private rules set up by a developer for all parcels within the defined subdivision are called *covenants, conditions, and restrictions (CC&Rs)*.

5. The federal government passed the *Interstate Land Sales Full Disclosure Act* to help prevent fraudulent marketing schemes when land is sold without being seen by purchasers.

6. When the woman's home lost value because a new airport was constructed next to it, she filed an *inverse condemnation* action to be compensated for the loss in property value.

7. A developer must keep the average number of units in the development at or below the maximum number per acre, which is also called the *gross density*.

8. A useful method to determine just compensation to a property owner when a portion of the owner's land is seized for public use is the *before-and-after method*.

9. Taking previously undeveloped acreage and splitting it into smaller lots for sale is called *subdivision*.

10. Zoning laws that control overcrowding by requiring setbacks or limiting building heights are called *bulk zoning ordinances*.

Activity: City Zoning

1. The daycare center needs a conditional-use permit to legally operate in D5.

2. The most beneficial spot would be J-1 through J-8: A park would serve the residential neighborhoods and provide a buffer between the residential and industrial zones.

3. Rezoning as an historic district is *aesthetic zoning*.

4. The house is a nonconforming use. It was most likely grandfathered in.

5. One possible location would be the square bounded by J-6, I-6, I-8, and J-8. This location would provide retail services near the residential neighborhood and professional services near the commercial zone, and it would not be disruptive to the industrial zone. Other possibilities include A-8 through F-8, or six units between J-1 and J-8 as a buffer. It would probably not be wise to place the new zone in the center of the residential area (due to traffic and noise) or in the industrial zone (it could present hazards to shoppers).

CHAPTER 20

Fair Housing and Ethical Practices

■ **LEARNING OBJECTIVES**   *Before you answer these questions, you should be able to*

■ **identify** the classes of people who are protected against discrimination in housing by various federal laws;

■ **describe** how the Fair Housing Act is enforced;

■ **list** the exemptions allowed in the Fair Housing Act;

■ **explain** how fair housing laws address a variety of discriminatory practices and regulate real estate advertising;

■ **distinguish** the protections offered by the Fair Housing Act, the Housing and Community Development Act, the Fair Housing Amendments Act, the Equal Credit Opportunity Act, and the Americans with Disabilities Act; and

■ **define** the following *key terms:*

Americans with
  Disabilities Act (ADA)
blockbusting
Civil Rights Act of 1866
code of ethics

Department of
  Housing and Urban
  Development (HUD)
Equal Credit Opportunity
  Act (ECOA)
ethics
Fair Housing Act

Fair Housing
  Amendments Act
redlining
steering
Title VIII of the Civil Rights
  Act of 1968

MATCHING   *Write the letter of the matching term on the appropriate line.*

a. *familial status*

b. *Equal Credit Opportunity Act*

c. *Civil Rights Act of 1968*

d. *disability*

e. *blockbusting*

f. *Fair Housing Act*

g. *ADA*

h. *HUD*

i. *steering*

j. *Jones v. Mayer*

1. ___ A law that prohibits discrimination in housing based on race, color, religion, and national origin

2. ___ The Civil Rights Act of 1968, the Housing and Community Development Act of 1974, and the Fair Housing Amendments Act of 1988, collectively

3. ___ The agency that administers the federal fair housing laws

4. ___ The presence of one or more persons who are under the age of 18, living with a parent or adult guardian

5. ___ A physical or mental impairment

6. ___ A U.S. Supreme Court decision that prohibits all racial discrimination in housing

7. ___ A law that prohibits discrimination against protected classes in evaluating loan applications (includes nonhousing-related loans)

8. ___ A law that requires accessibility to employment, goods, and services for individuals with disabilities

9. ___ Encouraging the sale or renting of property by claiming a protected class of people are moving into the area and will have a negative impact on property values

10. ___ Encouraging home seekers to limit their search to particular neighborhoods based on noneconomic factors such as race or religion

TRUE OR FALSE   *Circle the correct answer.*

1. T F The purpose of the civil rights laws that affect the real estate industry are to make everyone equal.

2. T F Failing to comply with state and federal fair housing laws may subject a licensee to both fines and disciplinary action.

3. T F The Civil Rights Act of 1968 applies only to race.

4. T F Under HUD regulations, a *dwelling* is limited to single-family houses, condominiums, and cooperatives.

5. T F The fair housing laws under the *disabled persons* classification protect persons with AIDS.

6. T F There are no exemptions under the federal Fair Housing Act.

7. T F The protections under the Equal Credit Opportunity Act are broader than those under the Fair Housing Act.

8. T F The *Accessibility Guidelines* contain ADA's specific requirements for curb ramps, elevators, and other measures to make spaces accessible for people with disabilities.

9. T F *Redlining* is the act of encouraging people to sell or rent their homes on the basis that the entry of members of a protected class into the neighborhood will reduce property values.

10. T F Channeling home seekers to particular neighborhoods based on noneconomic factors is an illegal practice known as *steering*.

11. T F There are no exceptions to HUD's rules regarding statements of preference or limitations in advertising regarding race.

12. T F While not valid considerations for the underlying real estate transaction, the following factors may be considered by an appraiser in evaluating a property: race, color, religion, national origin, sex, disability, and familial status.

13. T F Individuals who believe they are the victim of illegal discrimination in a real estate transaction may file a complaint with HUD within three years of the alleged act.

14. T F Failure to prominently display the Equal Housing Opportunity poster can be considered evidence of discriminatory practices.

15. T F The National Association of REALTORS® Code of Ethics establishes professional standards of behavior that guide all real estate brokerage licensees throughout the United States.

16. T F If a tenant has a visual disability and needs an assistance dog, the landlord can require a higher security deposit than for other tenants.

17. T F A church violates the Fair Housing Act if it owns and operates rental housing only for its member employees and others who belong to the religion.

18. T F One reason that real estate licensees need to be concerned about meeting requirements of the ADA is because their offices are public spaces.

19. T F If a real estate licensee says to a potential seller that the neighborhood is "changing" and "isn't what it used to be," that message is considered *blockbusting*.

20. T F The Fair Housing Act prohibits landlords from asking potential tenants for citizenship or immigration documents during the screening process.

MULTIPLE CHOICE   *Circle the correct answer.*

1. Which of the following laws extended housing discrimination protections to families with children and persons with disabilities?
   a. Civil Rights Act of 1866
   b. Fair Housing Amendments Act of 1988
   c. Housing and Community Development Act of 1974
   d. Civil Rights Act of 1968

2. The Fair Housing Act is administered by the
   a. Office of Equal Opportunity.
   b. Department of Housing and Urban Development.
   c. Justice Department.
   d. Federal court system.

3. The Fair Housing Act prohibits discrimination on the basis of all the following factors *EXCEPT*
   a. familial status.
   b. national origin.
   c. religious preference.
   d. sexual preference.

4. The Equal Credit Opportunity Act prohibits discrimination on the basis of all of the following factors *EXCEPT*
   a. amount of income.
   b. source of income.
   c. marital status.
   d. age.

5. Real estate licensees may have a legal obligation to comply with the ADA because they
   a. often have clients with disabilities.
   b. frequently own their own homes.
   c. may be employers.
   d. may need to require *reasonable accommodation* in a home they have listed.

6. A real estate broker sends a bright yellow flier to all the homeowners in a neighborhood. The flier contains a reprinted article from a local newspaper describing the future relocation plans of various employers in the region and the following statement, printed in bold red letters: "Warning! The failure to sell your property within the next six months could cost you a bundle!" At the bottom of the page was printed the broker's name, photo, office address, and phone number. Based on these facts, the broker
   a. is guilty of steering.
   b. is guilty of blockbusting.
   c. has committed no offense.
   d. has violated the HUD advertising guidelines.

7. In the past six months, a local bank has been forced to foreclose on several mortgages in a mostly Asian suburb. The bank's board of directors tells the loan department to make no further loans on properties located in the suburb. Based on these facts, which of the following statements is *TRUE*?
   a. The bank is guilty of redlining.
   b. The bank is in violation of the Home Mortgage Disclosure Act.
   c. The bank's action falls under the *reasonable purpose* exception to the Fair Housing Act.
   d. The bank is guilty of discrimination on the basis of race.

8. Under what conditions can someone refuse to rent to an African-American on the basis of race?
   a. Never
   b. If the owner is also living in one of the apartments of a small apartment building
   c. If the owner is handling the leasing without the aid of a real estate agent
   d. If the owner is a small investor and is selling one of the three houses

MULTIPLE CHOICE   *(Continued)*

9. Under the Fair Housing Act, what is HUD's first action on receiving a complaint of illegal discrimination?

    a. Investigates for reasonable cause to bring a charge
    b. Holds an administrative hearing
    c. Issues an injunction against the offender
    d. Files a civil action in federal district court

10. One of the provisions of the Fair Housing Amendments Act of 1988 is

    a. a repeal of the facilities and services requirements designed to help older persons with physical and social needs.
    b. the addition of sex to the list of protected classes.
    c. a change that made the penalties for violations more severe, and it also added additional damages.
    d. the addition of religion to the list of protected classes.

11. Under the Civil Rights Act of 1968, what is the time limit to file a housing discrimination complaint with HUD?

    a. 100 days
    b. 1 year
    c. 2 years
    d. The same as the statute of limitations for torts committed in the state in which the alleged discriminatory act occurred

12. Complaints of discriminatory housing practices filed with HUD will be referred to a local enforcement agency if

    a. the federal law is substantially more inclusive than the state or municipal law.
    b. HUD determines that an administrative law judge should decide the case.
    c. the state or municipal law is substantially equivalent to the federal law.
    d. the complaint involves a licensee who is the victim of a threat or act of violence because the licensee has complied with the fair housing laws.

13. The term *professional ethics* refers to

    a. the system of professional standards adopted by the National Association of REALTORS® in 1913.
    b. the requirements of the Fair Housing Act as they apply to real estate professionals.
    c. a system of moral principles, rules, and standards of conduct that govern a professional's relations with consumers and colleagues.
    d. a standard of integrity and competence, established and enforced by HUD, which is expected of professionals and licensees in the real estate industry.

14. All of the following people are considered members of protected classes *EXCEPT*

    a. a member of Alcoholics Anonymous.
    b. a visually disabled person with a seeing-eye dog.
    c. an AIDs patient.
    d. a person convicted of the manufacture or distribution of illegal drugs.

15. A homeowner decides to rent a spare bedroom in her single-family house to a tenant for $50 per month. When a 24-year-old man asks to see the room, the homeowner refuses, telling him that she will only rent to women over the age of 50. The prospective tenant threatens to sue for a violation of the Fair Housing Act on the basis of age. Should the homeowner be concerned?

    a. Yes, the amount of rent being charged is immaterial for purposes of the Fair Housing Act.
    b. Yes; while the homeowner is permitted to exclude individuals on the basis of age or sex, she cannot exclude on the basis of both.
    c. No, the rental of rooms in an owner-occupied single-family home is exempt from the Fair Housing Act.
    d. No; because there was no real estate licensee involved in this transaction, the homeowner is free to discriminate on the basis of any of the normally protected classes.

MULTIPLE CHOICE   *(Continued)*

16. The seller told the agent "don't show my house to anybody not born in the United States." In this circumstance, the agent
    a. must show the house to anyone who wants to see it.
    b. must decline to take the listing with this requirement.
    c. may take the listing and ignore the instruction.
    d. may take the listing and hope that no foreigners ask to see the property.

17. A neighborhood has a large number of Asians living there. When a Chinese couple came to a broker to look for a home to buy, he suggested they look at listings only in this neighborhood. The broker has violated the Fair Housing Act, because his actions constitute
    a. stereotyping.   c. redlining.
    b. blockbusting.   d. steering.

18. A woman has made an appointment with a landlord to see a two bedroom apartment. She has two children and is also pregnant. The landlord tells her that the rules of the building allow only two children per two-bedroom apartment, and therefore, he cannot rent to her. Is this a violation of the Fair Housing Act?
    a. No, rental standards can include a restriction on the number of occupants in an apartment.
    b. No, the Fair Housing Act allows property owners to limit the number of children in a development.
    c. Yes, indicating a preference for a certain number of children as occupants is illegal discrimination on the basis of familial status.
    d. Yes, until the third child is born, the woman meets the standards for the number of children in the family.

19. A landlord rented an apartment to a person with a wheelchair. He allowed the tenant to install bath rails and replace the bathroom sink vanity with a pedestal sink with lever faucet handles. However, the landlord required the tenant to sign a restoration agreement that the accommodations would be restored to the former condition at the end of the lease, because the vanity provided desirable storage space in the bathroom. In addition, he required the tenant to pay sufficient funds (over a period of time) into an escrow account to restore the bathroom. Has the landlord violated the Fair Housing Act?
    a. No, the landlord can require a restoration agreement and the escrow account.
    b. No, the landlord does not have to allow the tenant to make any of these modifications.
    c. Yes, the landlord cannot require restoration of the modifications.
    d. Yes, the landlord cannot require the escrow account.

20. An occupancy requirement is exempt from familial status protection under the Fair Housing Act if the housing is intended to be occupied by
    a. at least one person in each unit who is 50 years of age or older.
    b. persons 62 years of age or older.
    c. persons 55 years of age or older.
    d. at least one person age 60 or older in 80 percent of the units.

21. For fair housing purposes, what is the definition of *disability*?
    a. An impairment of mobility that prevents a person from using stairs
    b. A physical impairment that requires a caregiver's assistance
    c. An impairment that prevents a person from holding a job
    d. An impairment that substantially limits one or more of an individual's major life activities

MULTIPLE CHOICE   *(Continued)*

22. How does Megan's law affect real estate licensees?
    a. It adds the protected class of disability to the Fair Housing Act requirements.
    b. It requires education of licensees about how to avoid steering potential buyers to certain neighborhoods.
    c. It may require licensees to disclose information about a released sex offender residing in a particular area.
    d. It establishes a Code of Ethics that licensees can voluntarily adopt.

23. The provisions of the ADA apply to any employer with
    a. at least five or more employees.
    b. at least ten or more employees.
    c. at least 12 or more employees.
    d. at least 15 or more employees.

24. What is one negative result of redlining?
    a. Appraisers have a difficult time evaluating properties in the area.
    b. It is often a major contributor to the deterioration of older neighborhoods.
    c. The effects test must be applied to determine whether to file a lawsuit.
    d. Licensees are not able to advertise in local newspapers.

25. The resolution of a fair housing complaint by obtaining assurance that the respondent will remedy the violation is called
    a. conciliation.
    b. administrative proceedings.
    c. civil action.
    d. a judgment.

ANSWER KEY

Matching

1. c **2.** f **3.** h **4.** a **5.** d **6.** j **7.** b **8.** g
9. e **10.** i

True or False

1. **False.** The purpose of the civil rights laws that affect real estate is to create a marketplace in which all persons of similar financial means have a similar range of housing choices. p. 345

2. **True.** Real estate licensees cannot allow their own prejudices to interfere with the ethical and legal conduct of their profession; nor can they allow discriminatory attitudes of property owners or property seeks to affect compliance with fair housing laws. p. 354

3. **False.** The Civil Rights Act of 1968 applies to housing discrimination based on race, color, religion, and national origin. p. 355

4. **False.** Under HUD regulations, a *dwelling* includes single-family houses, condominiums, cooperatives, mobile homes, and vacant land on which any of these structures will be built. p. 357

5. **True.** A disability is a physical or mental impairment; persons with AIDS are protected by the fair housing laws under this classification. p. 357

6. **False.** The Civil Rights Act of 1866, as interpreted by *Jones v. Mayer*, does not allow any exemptions involving race. Under the federal Fair Housing Act of 1968, some exemptions exist for small investors and certain organizations. p. 354

7. **True.** The Equal Credit Opportunity Act (ECOA) requires that credit applications be considered only on the basis of income, net worth, job stability, and credit rating. The ECOA mentions eight protected classes. p. 360

8. **True**

9. **False.** *Blockbusting* is the act of encouraging people to sell or rent their homes on the basis that the entry of members of a protected class into the neighborhood will reduce property values. p. 362

10. **True.** Steering is the illegal channeling of *prospective home buyers* to particular neighborhoods, or by discouraging potential buyers from considering some areas based on the basis of a protected class. p. 362

11. **True.** The Civil Rights Act of 1866, as interpreted by *Jones v. Mayer*, does not allow any exemptions involving race. Under the federal Fair Housing Act of 1968, some exemptions exist for small investors and certain organizations. p. 354

12. **False.** Race, color, religion, national origin, sex, disability, and familial status may not be considered in any formal or informal appraisal or evaluation of a property. p. 364

13. **False.** Individuals who believe they are the victim of illegal discrimination in a real estate transaction may file a complaint with HUD within one year of the alleged act. p. 365

14. **True.** Failure to display the Equal Housing Opportunity poster can be considered prima facie evidence of discriminatory practices. p. 355

15. **False.** The National Association of REALTORS® Code of Ethics guides only members of that organization. All licensees are governed by *the states that license them*. p. 367

16. **False.** A landlord cannot increase the customary security deposit only for tenants with disabilities. p. 357–358

17. **False.** A religious organization may restrict occupancy of dwelling units that it owns to members of the organization. However, membership in the religion must not be restricted on the basis of race, color, or national origin. p. 359

18. **True.** The Americans with Disabilities Act (ADA) is important, because real estate brokers are often employers, and their offices are public spaces. p. 360

19. **True.** Blockbusting is the act of encouraging people to sell or rent their homes by claiming that the entry of a protected class of people into the neighborhood will have some sort of negative impact on property values. p. 362

20. **False.** However, HUD provides a specific procedure for collecting and verifying citizenship papers. p. 364

Multiple Choice

1. **b.** Choice b, the Fair Housing Amendments Act of 1988, added disability and familial status. The Housing and Community Development Act of 1974 added sex to the list of protected classes, which is found in Title VIII of the Civil Rights Act of 1968. The Civil Rights Act of 1866, prohibits discrimination based on race. p. 354–355, 357

2. **b.** The Department of Housing and Urban Development (HUD) handles fair housing complaints on the national level. Most states have enacted *substantially* similar laws; so often, it is the state agency that is involved. p. 365–366

3. **d.** Sexual preference is not a protected class under the federal law, but it has been added to many city and state fair housing laws. p. 355

4. **a.** The ECOA prohibits discrimination in lending for eight protected classes; however, people still must have an adequate source of income to qualify for a loan. p. 360

5. **c.** Many real estate licensees are brokers who own an office, and the real estate office should be accessible to the public, including a person with a disability. p. 360

6. **c.** Although perhaps in poor taste, the broker is simply distributing a published newspaper article to which anyone has access. He is also not making any statements about a protected class of people moving into the neighborhood. p. 362–363

7. **a.** The bank is refusing to make mortgage loans in a specific area for reasons other than the economic qualifications of the applicants. p. 364

8. **a.** Under the Civil Rights Act of 1866, as reinforced by the *Jones v. Mayer* Supreme Court decision, there are no exemptions that permit someone to discriminate in housing simply because of someone's race. p. 358

9. **a.** Within 100 days of the filing of the complaint, HUD either determines that reasonable cause exists to bring a charge of illegal discrimination or dismisses the complaint. p. 365

10. **c.** The Fair Housing Amendments Act of 1988, expanded federal civil rights protections to familial status and disability. The Act also changed the penalties by making them more severe and by adding additional damages. p. 355

11. **b.** Persons who wish to file a complaint with HUD under Title VIII of the Civil Rights Act of 1968 must do so within one year of the alleged violation. p. 365

12. **c.** If a state or local law is substantially equivalent to the federal law, all complaints filed with HUD are referred to the local enforcement agencies. p. 366

13. **c.** A code of ethics is a written system of principles for ethical conduct, containing statements designed to advise, guide, and regulate behavior. p. 367

14. **d.** Persons convicted of manufacturing or distributing illegal drugs do not enjoy any protections under the Fair Housing Laws, although disability is a protected class. Individuals who are participating in addiction recovery programs are in a protected class of disability. p. 357

15. **c.** The woman is exempt from the law, because she will be renting a single room in her home. p. 359

16. **b.** An instruction to not show the home to someone who was not born in the United States violates the Fair Housing Act. The agent should not take the listing with this requirement. The agent cannot simply ignore the instructions or pretend they do not exist. p. 355

17. **d.** Channeling home seekers toward or away from particular neighborhoods based on national origin, or any of the other protected classifications, is called *steering*. p. 362

18. **c.** Occupancy standards must be based on objective factors, such as sanitation or safety, not number of children. p. 357

19. **a.** The landlord must permit these reasonable modifications; however, he can require the restoration agreement and escrow account. p. 358

20. **b.** Housing is exempt from the familial status protections if it is intended for occupancy only by persons 62 years of age, or for occupancy in 80 percent of its units by at least one person 55 years of age or older. Strict rules for ongoing verification and reporting are imposed on this second alternative. p. 359

21. **d.** The definition of *disability* is very broad and focuses on impairments that prevent or restrict a person from performing tasks that are of central importance to most people's lives. p. 357

22. **c.** Licensees may provide information about how their clients and customers can obtain information about the sex offender registry. p. 360

23. **d.** Employers must make reasonable accommodations that enable an individual with a disability to perform essential job functions. p. 361

24. **b.** Redlining is a prohibited practice by lenders and insurance companies. It frequently leads to the deterioration of older neighborhoods, because loans are not made based on racial grounds as opposed to any real objection to an applicant's creditworthiness. p. 364

25. **a.** *Conciliation* attempts to resolve the complaint without further legal action, such as an administrative proceeding. However, a conciliation agreement can be enforced through civil action. p. 365

CHAPTER 21

Environmental Issues and the Real Estate Transaction

■ **LEARNING OBJECTIVES** *Before you answer these questions, you should be able to*

■ **identify** the basic environmental hazards an agent should be aware of in order to protect the client's interests;

■ **describe** the warning signs, characteristics, causes, and solutions for the various environmental hazards most commonly found in real estate transactions;

■ **explain** the fundamental liability issues arising under environmental protection laws;

■ **distinguish** lead-based paint issues from other environmental issues; and

■ **define** the following *key terms*:

asbestos	encapsulation	radon
brownfields	environmental impact statement (EIS)	Small Business Liability Relief and Brownfields Revitalization Act
carbon monoxide (CO)		
chlorofluorocarbons (CFCs)	environmental site assessments (ESA)	Superfund Amendments and Reauthorization Act (SARA)
Comprehensive Environmental Response, Compensation, and Liability Act (CERCLA)	formaldehyde	
	groundwater	underground storage tanks (USTs)
	lead	
	mold	urea-formaldehyde foam insulation (UFFI)
electromagnetic fields (EMFs)	polychlorinated biphenyls (PCBs)	
		water table

MATCHING   *Write the letter of the matching term on the appropriate line.*

a. urea formaldehyde

b. electromagnetic field

c. encapsulation

d. capping

e. landfill

f. Superfund

g. radon

h. lead

i. asbestos

j. water table

1. ___ A highly friable mineral commonly used as insulation prior to being banned from use in construction in 1978

2. ___ The process of sealing off disintegrating asbestos and chipped or peeling lead-based paint without removing it

3. ___ A material once used in paint that can cause serious brain and nervous system damage

4. ___ A radioactive gas produced by the natural decay of other radioactive substances

5. ___ Chemical used in foam insulation and certain wood products that can release harmful gases

6. ___ An effect of electrical currents suspected of posing a health risk

7. ___ The natural level at which the ground is saturated

8. ___ A site for the burial of waste

9. ___ The process of covering a solid waste site with topsoil and plants

10. ___ Money set aside by the Comprehensive Environmental Response, Compensation, and Liability Act to pay for the cleanup of uncontrolled hazardous waste sites and spills

TRUE OR FALSE   *Circle the correct answer.*

1. T F The Environmental Protection Agency estimates that approximately 40 percent of commercial and public buildings contain asbestos insulation.

2. T F Asbestos removal is a relatively simple, inexpensive process that can be performed by any reasonably intelligent person.

3. T F Under the 1996 regulations published by the Environmental Protection Agency and the Department of Housing and Urban Development, owners of homes built prior to 1978 are required to test their properties for the presence of lead-based paint.

4. T F Radon is a naturally occurring substance that is suspected of being a cause of lung cancer.

5. T F Urea-formaldehyde foam insulation can release harmful gases.

6. T F The movement of electricity through high-tension power lines, secondary distribution lines, electrical transformers, and appliances creates electromagnetic fields.

7. T F Groundwater is water that lies on the earth's surface.

8. T F Federal regulations on underground storage tanks do not apply to tanks used to collect storm water or wastewater.

9. T F The process of laying two to four feet of soil over the top of a landfill site, and then planting foliage to prevent erosion, is referred to as *layering*.

10. T F Liability under Superfund is strict, joint and several, and retroactive.

11. T F Asbestos is most harmful when it is disturbed or exposed.

12. T F Radon gas mitigation consists of installing a minimum of R16-rated insulation in walls and attic spaces.

13. T F In homes, the most-likely sources of formaldehyde emissions are pressed wood products, such as particleboard.

14. T F Homeowners with private wells have little worry about contamination, because well water is drawn from far beneath the ground.

15. T F Possible causes of mold problems can be roof leaks, unvented combustion appliances, and gutters that direct water to the building.

16. T F *Strict liability* under the Superfund means that the owner is responsible to the injured party without excuse.

17. T F Today, licensees can feel secure that seller-supplied disclosure forms result in accurate and complete disclosure of environmental issues.

18. T F Federal requirements for disclosure of mold contamination in homes are contained in the Home Mold Disclosure Act.

19. T F Because CFCs are nontoxic and nonflammable, they are easily and safely disposed of by homeowners.

20. T F To protect against liability due to mold contamination, real estate licensees should ask sellers about leaks, flooding, and prior damage.

MULTIPLE CHOICE   *Circle the correct answer.*

1. Individuals have suffered all of the following health problems due to exposure to formaldehyde *EXCEPT*

    a. asthma.
    b. eye irritations.
    c. mold infections.
    d. a burning sensation in the throat.

2. Lead is commonly found in all of the following *EXCEPT*

    a. soldered water pipes.
    b. alkyd oil-based paint.
    c. soil around industrial sites.
    d. insulating material.

3. A seller accepts an offer on her home, which was built in 1892. Based on these facts, all of the following statements about lead-based paint are correct *EXCEPT*

    a. the seller must attach a lead-based paint disclosure statement to the sales contract.
    b. if the seller is aware of any lead-based paint on the premises, she must disclose that fact to the buyer.
    c. if the buyer requests a lead-based paint inspection, the seller has ten days in which to obtain one at her own expense.
    d. the buyer is entitled to receive a pamphlet that describes the hazards posed by lead-based paint.

4. Where in the United States does radon occur?

    a. Mostly in the western states
    b. Mostly in the warm southern and southwestern regions
    c. In every state in the United States
    d. Only in large urban areas

5. All of the following have been proven to pose a health hazard *EXCEPT*

    a. asbestos.
    b. electromagnetic fields.
    c. lead-based paint.
    d. radon.

6. Harry stores toxic chemical waste in a large steel tank that has only 15 percent of its volume underground. Jena lives in the wilderness and has her own gas pump connected to a 1,500-gallon tank of gasoline buried ten feet underground near her garage. Lars keeps three large tanks filled with formaldehyde and battery acid in his basement. Which of these people are covered by federal regulations regarding USTs?

    a. Harry and Lars
    b. Harry and Jena only
    c. Lars only
    d. Jena only

7. Which of the following is responsible for administering Superfund?

    a. EPA   c. CERCLA
    b. PRP   d. HUD

8. Which of the following would disqualify someone from claiming innocent landowner immunity under the Superfund Amendments and Reauthorization Act (SARA)?

    a. Pollution was caused by a third party.
    b. A landowner exercised *due care* when the property was purchased.
    c. A landowner had only constructive knowledge of the damage.
    d. A landowner took reasonable precautions in the exercise of ownership rights.

9. If a potentially responsible party (PRP) refuses to pay the expenses of cleaning up a toxic site, the EPA may

    a. bring a criminal action and have the PRP jailed for up to ten years.
    b. bring a civil action and be awarded three times the actual cost of the cleanup.
    c. bring an administrative action and be awarded the actual cost of the cleanup, plus court costs.
    d. have no legal recourse.

10. Sealing off asbestos instead of removing it is called

    a. encapsulation.
    b. capping.
    c. irresponsible remediation.
    d. extended liability.

MULTIPLE CHOICE   *(Continued)*

11. Lead-based paint is found in about 75 percent of all private housing built before
    a. 1978.
    b. 1985.
    c. 1992.
    d. 1996.

12. Which of the following is the byproduct of fuel combustion that may result in death if such equipment is not properly vented?
    a. Radon
    b. Lead
    c. Urea-formaldehyde foam insulation
    d. Carbon monoxide

13. At least how much of a tank must be underground for it to be considered an underground storage tank?
    a. 10 percent
    b. 15 percent
    c. 25 percent
    d. 35 percent

14. How can property owners help avoid carbon monoxide exposure?
    a. Have fuel-burning heating systems checked and maintained annually
    b. Have their basements tested for carbon monoxide seeping in from the soil
    c. Encapsulate sources of carbon monoxide emissions
    d. Install attic vents

15. Which of the following is a source of polychlorinated biphenyls (PCBs)?
    a. Plywood and particle board
    b. Small home appliances, such as hair dryers or food processors
    c. Caulking compounds
    d. Computers

16. Why is mold a serious environmental problem in buildings?
    a. It causes stains and a fuzzy growth on walls.
    b. It destroys material it grows on and causes health problems for occupants.
    c. It has an unpleasant odor.
    d. It produces spores than can spoil food.

17. What is the purpose of the Brownfields Legislation that became law in 2002?
    a. It restores wilderness and agricultural areas damaged by toxic waste.
    b. It is specifically dedicated to cleaning up PCB spills and dumps.
    c. It establishes incinerators to destroy UFFI, DDT, and other persistent chemicals.
    d. It distributes funds to clean up polluted industrial sites so they can be restored to productive use.

18. What causes mold problems in buildings?
    a. Insects
    b. Chronic moisture problems
    c. Fiberglass building materials
    d. Air pollution

ANSWER KEY

Matching

1. i **2.** c **3.** h **4.** g **5.** a **6.** b **7.** j **8.** e
9. d **10.** f

True or False

1. **False.** The Environmental Protection Agency estimates that approximately *20 percent* of commercial and public buildings contain asbestos insulation. p. 376

2. **False.** Asbestos removal is a dangerous, expensive process that can be performed only by trained and licensed technicians under controlled conditions. p. 377

3. **False.** Under the 1996 regulations published by the Environmental Protection Agency and the Department of Housing and Urban Development, owners of homes built prior to 1978 are *not required* to test their properties for the presence of lead-based paint. However, they must complete a lead-based paint disclosure statement for potential buyers and renters. p. 377

4. **True.** Radon is a naturally occurring, colorless, odorless, tasteless, radioactive gas that has been classified as a Class A known human carcinogen. p. 380

5. **True.** When incorrectly mixed, urea-formaldehyde foam insulation (UFFI) never properly cures, resulting in strong emissions shortly after installation. p. 381

6. **True.** Electromagnetic fields (EMFs) are generated by the movement of electrical currents by any electrical appliance, as well as high-voltage lines. p. 384

7. **False.** *Groundwater* is water that lies *under* the earth's surface. p. 384

8. **True.** Tanks that are exempt from federal regulations include septic tanks and systems for collecting storm water and wastewater. p. 385

9. **False.** The process of laying two to four feet of soil over the top of a landfill site and then planting foliage to prevent erosion is referred to as *capping*. p. 386

10. **True.** Liability under Superfund is strict, joint and several, and retroactive. However, an *innocent landowner* immunity exits that in certain cases, a landowner in the chain of ownership was completely innocent of all wrongdoing, and therefore, should not be held liable. p. 388

11. **True.** Because intact asbestos is not harmful, encapsulation, or the sealing off of disintegrating asbestos, is an alternate method of asbestos control that may be preferable to removal, in certain circumstances. p. 377

12. **False.** Radon mitigation consists of a fan installed in a pipe running from the basement to the attic to draw the radon up and out of the building. p. 380

13. **True.** The largest source of formaldehyde in any building is likely to be the off-gassing from pressed-wood products made from using adhesives that contain urea-formaldehyde (UF) resins. p. 381

14. **False.** Groundwater can become contaminated when the earth's natural filtering systems may be inadequate to ensure clean water. Buyers of homes with private wells should have the water tested. p. 384

15. **True.** Mold can be found almost anywhere and can grow on almost any organic substance, so long as moisture, oxygen, and an organic food source are present. p. 382

16. **True.** *Strict liability* under the Superfund means that the owner is responsible to the injured party without excuse; joint and several liability means that each of the individual owners is personally responsible for the total damages. p. 388

17. **False.** Licensees should inform buyers of the need to ask and discover for themselves and not rely on disclosure forms as warranties or guarantees. Sellers also need to fully disclose problems of which they are aware. p. 390

18. **False.** Although the EPA has published guidelines for the remediation and/or cleanup of mold and moisture problems in schools and commercial buildings, there are no federal requirements for disclosure of mold contamination. p. 383

19. **False.** Because CFCs deplete the ozone layer of the earth, there is concern about their release. Consumers should be aware of the types of appliances, such as refrigerators and air conditioners, which may contain this chemical, so that they can be safely disposed. p. 382

20. **True.** Licensees may need to take extra steps to protect themselves from liability by asking many questions about leaks, floods, and prior damage. They may need to remind the sellers to honestly and truthfully disclose any insurance claims regarding mold and other water issues. p. 383

Multiple Choice

1. **c.** Although formaldehyde has been shown to cause cancer in animals and may cause it in humans, it is primarily responsible for triggering respiratory problems, such as shortness of breath, wheezing, chest tightness, and asthma, as well as eye and skin irritations. p. 381

2. **d.** Asbestos, not lead, was formerly used for insulating material. p. 376

3. **c.** No one is required to test for lead, but the federal law gives the prospective buyer ten days (or any time agreed to, or the buyer may waive the right) to have the home tested for lead at the buyer's expense. p. 377

4. **c.** Radon has been found in every state, although it's more likely to be found in some states than in others. The only way to know for sure if it is present is to have the home tested. p. 380

5. **b.** Most electrical appliances create an electromagnetic field (EMF), but there is conflicting opinion whether EMFs pose a health hazard. p. 384

6. **b.** Because Harry's tank is more than 10 percent underground, his storage of toxic chemical waste is covered by the law. Jena's tank is completely underground, so it is covered. Because Lars's tanks are in his basement, rather than underground, he is not covered. p. 385

7. **a.** Superfund is administered by the EPA. CERCLA is the law that established the Superfund. p. 387–388

8. **c.** Landowners cannot claim innocent landowner immunity if they had actual or constructive knowledge. p. 388

9. **b.** A PRP is a potentially responsible party. If the PRP does not clean up the site, the EPA bills the PRP for the cost. Then, if the PRP still refuses to pay, the EPA can seek damages in court for up to three times the actual cost of cleanup. p. 388

10. **a.** *Encapsulation* is the sealing off of disintegrating asbestos. *Capping* is covering over the top of a landfill with dirt and landscaping. p. 377

11. **a.** The federal government estimates that lead is present in about 75 percent of all private housing built before 1978, the year the Federal government banned the use of lead in interior paints. p. 377

12. **d.** *Carbon monoxide (CO)* is the colorless, odorless, and tasteless gas that is a byproduct of incomplete combustion. High concentrations of CO can lead to death. p. 381

13. **a.** The official definition of an underground storage tank is at least 10 percent of the tank is underground. p. 385

14. **a.** Heating systems are prime sources of carbon monoxide if they are poorly vented or poorly maintained. p. 381

15. **c.** Sources of PCBs include caulking compounds, electrical transformers, and hydraulic oil in older equipment. p. 382

16. **b.** Mold can trigger allergic reactions and asthma attacks. p. 383

17. **d.** *Brownfields* are defined as defunct, derelict, or abandoned commercial or industrial sites. Many have toxic wastes. p. 387

18. **b.** Moisture, oxygen, and a cellulosic food source feed mold growth. Mold can gradually destroy virtually anything on which it is growing. p. 383

CHAPTER 22

Closing the Real Estate Transaction

■ **LEARNING OBJECTIVES**   *Before you answer these questions, you should be able to*

■ **identify** the issues of particular interest to the buyer and the seller as a real estate transaction closes;

■ **describe** the steps involved in preparing a closing statement;

■ **explain** the general rules for prorating;

■ **distinguish** the procedures involved in face-to-face closings from those in escrow closings; and

■ **define** the following *key terms*:

accrued items	good faith estimate (GFE)	Real Estate Settlement
closing	impound accounts	Procedures Act
closing statement	Mortgage Disclosure	(RESPA)
credit	Improvement Act	survey
debit	(MDIA)	Uniform Settlement
escrow accounts	prepaid items	Statement (HUD-1)
escrow closing	prorations	

MATCHING   *Write the letter of the matching term on the appropriate line.*

a. *accrued items*	1. ___ The fulfillment of a real estate sales contract
b. *federally related loans*	2. ___ A method of closing in which a disinterested third party acts as the agent of both buyer and seller to coordinate the closing activities
c. *banking year*	3. ___ The type of loan in a real estate settlement governed by RESPA
d. *closing*	4. ___ A charge that a party owes and must pay at closing
e. *credit*	5. ___ An amount in a party's favor that has already been paid, that is being reimbursed, or that will be paid in the future
f. *debit*	6. ___ The division of financial responsibility for various items between the buyer and seller
g. *escrow*	7. ___ Expenses to be divided between the parties that are owed by the seller but later will be paid by the buyer
h. *kickback*	8. ___ Expenses that have been paid by and are credited to the seller
i. *prepaid items*	9. ___ A 360-day period used in calculating prorations
j. *proration*	10. ___ An unearned fee, paid as part of a real estate transaction, that is prohibited by RESPA

TRUE OR FALSE   *Circle the correct answer.*

1. T F At closing, the seller delivers marketable title to the property.

2. T F Shortly before the closing, the buyer will usually conduct a final inspection of the property, often called a *spot survey*.

3. T F While the particulars of closing in escrow vary from state to state, the escrow agent is always a licensed attorney.

4. T F When closing in escrow, the seller will deposit proof of a new hazard insurance policy with the escrow agent.

5. T F Under the Mortgage Disclosure Improvement Act, the timeliness of certain disclosures affects the date of closings.

6. T F RESPA applies to all federally related loans for purchase of real estate, except for those administered by HUD.

7. T F Real estate licensees are exempt from RESPA's rules governing controlled business arrangements and referrals.

8. T F A special HUD information booklet that provides information on settlement costs must be provided to all real estate loan applicants, if the loan is regulated by RESPA.

9. T F Borrowers have the right to inspect the completed HUD-1 form one business day before closing.

10. T F RESPA's rules prohibit paying or receiving kickbacks.

MULTIPLE CHOICE   *Circle the correct answer.*

NOTE: Some state licensing exams use a 360-day year and a 30-day month for proration calculations. Others use the actual number of days in the month and year. You may wish to concentrate your study on the questions that more closely apply to your state.

For questions 1 through 4, prorate using a 30-day month and a 360-day year; prorate the taxes as of the close of escrow. Split the escrow fee 50-50 between the parties. Closing is July 31. Use the following relevant facts:

- Purchase price: $25,000 Cash
- Earnest money: $1,000
- Commission rate: 7 percent, split 50-50
- Revenue stamps: $25
- Real estate taxes: $350 (paid in full for current tax year of Jan. 1 through Dec. 31)
- Water bill: $90 (six months paid to Sept. 15)
- Title insurance: $153.51
- Recording fee: $2
- Escrow fee: $168
- Loan balance: $9,450 (existing loan, including credit for the reserve account)

1. What amount is the buyer debited for the real estate taxes?
    a. $145.83
    b. $146.71
    c. $202.19
    d. $203.30

2. What amount is the seller debited for the broker's commission?
    a. $750
    b. $1,650
    c. $1,750
    d. $2,500

3. What amount of the escrow fee will the buyer pay?
    a. $56
    b. $84
    c. $160
    d. $168

4. What amount is the buyer debited for the water bill?
    a. $10
    b. $15
    c. $17.50
    d. $22.50

5. A sale is closing on August 31. Real estate taxes, calculated on a calendar year basis, have not been paid for the current year. The tax is estimated to be $1,800. What amount of proration will be credited to the buyer?
    a. $1,100
    b. $1,200
    c. $1,485
    d. $1,500

6. A seller would be responsible for providing all of the following items *EXCEPT*
    a. documents necessary to clear any clouds on the title.
    b. affidavits of title.
    c. the deed.
    d. preparation of mortgage and note.

7. What is the minimum time period a lender must retain a HUD-1 after the date of closing?
    a. Six months
    b. One year
    c. Two years
    d. Four years

8. A man owns a fully occupied rental apartment building. If he sells the apartment building to a woman, how will the tenants' security deposits be reflected on the closing statement?
    a. Credit man, debit woman
    b. Debit both man and woman
    c. Credit woman, debit man
    d. Security deposits are not reflected on a closing statement

MULTIPLE CHOICE *(Continued)*

9. A buyer is purchasing a house from a seller. The single-family home is subject to an existing 30-year mortgage of $286,500 at a fixed rate of 6 percent. Under the terms of the sales contract, the buyer will assume the seller's mortgage at 6 percent interest and pay the federally insured lender's assumption fee of $100. In addition, the seller will assist the buyer by taking back a purchase-money mortgage in the amount of $25,000 at 8 percent interest. Is this transaction subject to RESPA?

   a. No, because this transaction involves a purchase money mortgage taken back by the seller.

   b. No, because the terms of the assumed loan were not changed.

   c. Yes, because the seller is taking back a purchase money mortgage at an interest rate higher than that charged for the assumed loan.

   d. Yes, because the lender's fee on the assumed loan is more than $50.

10. Since 1994, a real estate broker has had an understanding with two of the five mortgage lenders in town. She recommends only those two lenders to her clients and does not tell clients about any other lenders. In return, the recommended lenders pay for the vacations the broker offers her salespeople as rewards for high performance. Based on these facts, which of the following statements is *TRUE*?

   a. The broker is not doing anything illegal.

   b. Because this arrangement has been in existence for more than 15 years, it is exempt from RESPA.

   c. This is a permissible controlled business arrangement under RESPA, because the broker is not paid a fee for the recommendations.

   d. The broker's arrangement with the lenders is an illegal kickback under RESPA.

11. All of the following items are usually prorated at closing *EXCEPT*

   a. prepaid general real estate taxes.

   b. interest on an assumed loan.

   c. appraisal fees.

   d. rents collected in advance.

For questions 12 through 14, prorate using the actual number of days in the month and year. Split the escrow fee 50-50. The seller will pay the revenue stamps, and the purchaser will pay title insurance and the recording fee. The purchaser assumes the existing mortgage balance of $127,042.42; the purchaser will pay cash at the closing in the amount of the difference between the purchase price and the loan balance; the present monthly payment on the loan is $1,01.40. Closing is October 15.

Following are other facts:

- Purchase price: $350,000
- Earnest money: $3,500
- Commission rate: 6 percent split 50-50
- Real estate taxes: $2,900 (paid in full for the current year Jan. 1 through Dec. 31)
- Escrow fee: $800
- Title insurance: $1,150
- Insurance policy: $758 (annual premium)
- Revenue stamps: $126.30
- Recording fee: $30
- Interest rate: 8.75 percent (paid in arrears, with the next payment due November 1)

12. What are the prorated real estate taxes to be charged to the buyer?

   a. $604.20   c. $690.67
   b. $611.78   d. $728.30

13. What will be the amount of commission paid to the cooperating broker?

   a. $8,750   c. $17,500
   b. $10,500   d. $21,000

14. What amount will the seller receive at the closing?

   a. $201,586.23   c. $217,749.28
   b. $205,572.33   d. $208,654.34

15. How is earnest money treated if the buyer does not default and shows up for closing?

   a. Credit seller   c. Credit buyer
   b. Debit buyer   d. Debit seller

FILL-IN-THE-BLANK   *Select the word or words that best complete the following statements:*

1099-S

affidavit of title

bring down

buyer

conventional loans

federally related loans

good-faith estimate

HUD-1

payoff statement

proration

seller

settlement and transfer

survey

1. The property map that indicates any encroachments and easements is called the _____.

2. The second title search, known as the _____, is done after the closing and usually is paid by the purchaser of the property.

3. Mortgage loans made by banks, savings associations, or other lenders whose deposits are insured by federal agencies, plus FHA and VA loans, are called _____ and are subject to the requirements of RESPA.

4. The form that itemizes all charges to be paid by a borrower and seller in connection with settlement is called the _____.

5. To ensure that an existing loan amount is paid in the correct amount on the date of closing, the lender provides a(n) _____ to the closing agent.

6. Another name for the closing is _____.

7. The closing agent or lender is usually responsible for filing Form _____ to report certain real estate sales to the IRS.

8. A sworn statement, or _____, is completed by the seller and assures the title insurance company (and the buyer) that there have been no judgments, bankruptcies, or divorce involving the seller since the date of the title examination.

9. One of the requirements of RESPA is that no later than three business days after receiving a loan application, the lender must provide the borrower with a(n) _____ of the settlement costs the borrower is likely to pay.

10. Usually, the _____ pays for recording charges, such as recording the deed, that are due to the actual transfer of title.

ACTIVITY: Closing Statement

Complete the following settlement statement worksheet based on the information provided. Carry out all computations to three decimal places until the final calculation. Prorate based on a 30-day month. The buyer's and seller's statements should be viewed separately, although many items will appear on both. The buyer's total debits and credits must balance, and the seller's total debits and credits must balance. However, their totals and cash due need not balance. The selling price for the property is $315,000; the earnest money deposit is $12,000.

Buyers:	Doug and Connie Cornwall	Loan origination:	$7,560 fee (3 points); paid by buyer
Seller:	Cordelia Lear		
Property address:	1604 North Albany	Transfer tax:	$.50 per $500; paid by seller
Closing date:	June 30 of the current year	Recording fees:	$10.00 per document (deed and new mortgage paid by buyer; release of mortgage paid by seller
Broker's fee:	7 percent commission	Attorney's fees:	$500 buyer; $600 seller
Property taxes:	$2,500/year; this year's taxes have not yet been paid	Title insurance:	owner's policy $700 (seller) mortgagee's policy $150 (buyer)
Loan payoff:	$43,000 balance of principal and accrued interest	Document prep:	$50; paid by buyer
Financing:	buyer is obtaining a new $252,000 first mortgage loan	Survey:	$300; paid by seller

CLOSING STATEMENT

PROPERTY: _____

SELLER(S): _____

BUYER(S): _____

SETTLEMENT DATE: _____

| SETTLEMENT ITEM | BUYER | | SELLER | |
	DEBIT	CREDIT	DEBIT	CREDIT
Purchase Price				
TOTALS				
Due from BUYER				
Due to SELLER				

ANSWER KEY

Matching

1. d   **2.** g   **3.** b   **4.** f   **5.** e   **6.** j   **7.** a   **8.** i
9. c   **10.** h

True or False

1. **True.** The seller delivers the deed to the property and the buyer accepts it. p. 402

2. **False.** Shortly before the closing, the buyer will usually conduct a final inspection of the property, often called a *walkthrough*. p. 398

3. **False.** While the particulars of closing in escrow vary from state to state, the escrow agent may be an attorney, title company, trust company, escrow company, or a lender's escrow department. p. 402

4. **False.** When closing in escrow, the *buyer* will deposit proof of new hazard insurance with the escrow agent. p. 403

5. **True.** Under the Mortgage Disclosure Improvement Act, the timeliness of certain disclosures affects the date of closings; if the annual percentage rate increases by more than a certain amount, then creditors must provide new disclosure with a revised annual percentage rate, and then wait an additional three business days before closing the loan. p. 405

6. **False.** RESPA applies to all federally related loans, *including* those administered by HUD. p. 405

7. **False.** Real estate licensees are *not* exempt from RESPA's rules governing controlled business arrangements and referrals. Licensees must clearly inform the consumer about the relationship among the service providers, that participation is not required, that other providers are available, and about the return on ownership interest or franchise relationship. p. 406

8. **True.** The Real Estate Settlement Procedures Act (RESPA) requires that a special information booklet be provided to borrowers who are applying for a federally related loan. p. 407

9. **True.** By law, borrowers have the right to inspect a completed HUD-1 form, to the extent that figures are available, one business day before closing. p. 411

10. **True.** RESPA prohibits the payment of kickbacks, or unearned fees, in any real estate settlement service; it prohibits referral fees *when no services are actually rendered*. p. 411

Multiple Choice

1. **a.** $350 ÷ 12 months × 5 months = $145.83. The seller is credited for five months of prepaid taxes, August through December. p. 415

2. **c.** The seller is debited $1,750 for the broker's commission: $25,000 × 7% = $1,750. p. 412

3. **b.** The buyer's escrow fee is $84: $168 ÷ 2 = $84. p. 412

4. **d.** The buyer is debited $22.50: For July 31 through September 15 = 1.5 months prepaid by seller $90 for 6 months = $15 for one month ($90 divided by 6) 1.5 months × $15 per month = $22.50 (debit buyer). p. 414, 417

5. **b.** The buyer's real estate tax proration is $1,200: $1,800 ÷ 12 months × 8 months = $1,200. p. 415

6. **d.** Documentation for the new loan—preparation of note and mortgage—is the responsibility of the buyer. The seller is responsible for documents necessary to clear any clouds on the title, affidavits of title and the deed. p. 402

7. **c.** Lenders must retain HUD-1 forms for two years after the dates of closing; additionally, state laws generally require that licensees retain all records of a transaction for a specific period. p. 411

8. **c.** The man must pay the security deposit to the woman, who will, as the new owner, be responsible for returning the money to the tenant at the end of the lease. p. 418

9. **d.** The transaction would not have been subject to RESPA if the assumption fee had been $50 or less. p. 406

10. **d.** By not telling her clients about the other lenders in town, the broker is limiting their ability to get the best possible financing. That, added to the fact that the lender pays for her salespeople's vacations, makes her behavior look very suspicious. p. 406–407

11. **c.** Appraisal fees and credit report fees are paid outside of closing (POC) by the buyer; they are not prorated. p. 413

12. **b.** The buyer's prorated real estate taxes are $611.78: $2,900 ÷ 365 × 77 = $611.78. The seller pays taxes on the day of closing. There are 16 days left in October, 30 in November, and 31 in December. Thus, the buyer owes the seller for 77 days. p. 415, 418

13. **b.** The cooperating broker's commission is $10,500: $350,000 × 6% ÷ 2 = $10,500. p. 412

14. **a.** Sales price $350,000 – Commission $21,000 + Credit for prepaid taxes $611.78 – Half of the escrow fee $400 – Assumed loan balance $127,042.42 – Revenue stamps $126.30 – Mortgage interest for first half of settlement month $456.83 = Amount to seller $201,586.23. (The seller owes accrued interest on the loan for the 15 days the money was used: $127,042.42 × 8.75% ÷ 365 × 15 = $456.83.) p. 412

15. **c.** The earnest money is brought to closing and credited to the buyer. p. 412

Fill-in-the-Blank

1. The property map that indicates any encroachments and easements is called the *survey*.

2. The second title search, known as the *bring down*, is done after the closing and usually is paid for by the purchaser of the property.

3. Mortgage loans made by banks, savings associations, or other lenders whose deposits are insured by federal agencies, plus FHA and VA loans, are called *federally related loans* and are subject to the requirements of RESPA.

4. The form that itemizes all charges to be paid by a borrower and seller in connection with settlement is called the *HUD-1*.

5. To ensure that an existing loan amount is paid in the correct amount on the date of closing, the lender provides a *payoff statement* to the closing agent.

6. Another name for the closing is *settlement and transfer*.

7. The closing agent or lender is usually responsible for filing Form *1099-S* to report certain real estate sales to the IRS.

8. A sworn statement, or *affidavit of title*, is completed by the seller and assures the title insurance company (and the buyer) that there have been no judgments, bankruptcies, or divorces involving the seller since the date of the title examination.

9. One of the requirements of RESPA is that no later than three business days after receiving a loan application, the lender must provide the borrower with a *good faith estimate* of the settlement costs the borrower is likely to pay.

10. Usually the *buyer* pays for recording charges, such as recording the deed, that are due to the actual transfer of title.

Activity: Closing Statement

SETTLEMENT DATE: JUNE 30, 20XX

Settlement Item	Buyer		Seller	
	Debit	Credit	Debit	Credit
Purchase Price	$315,000	—	—	$315,000
Earnest Money	—	12,000	—	—
Broker's Commission	—	—	22,050	—
Property Taxes	—	1,250	1,250	—
Payoff Existing Mortgage	—	—	43,000	—
New First Mortgage	—	252,000	—	—
Loan Originiation Fee	7,560	—	—	—
Transfer Tax	—	—	315	—
Recording Fees	20	—	10	—
Attorneys' Fees	500	—	600	—
Title Insurance	150	—	700	—
Document Preparation	50	—	—	—
Survey	—	—	300	—
	—	—	—	—
	—	—	—	—
Totals	$323,280	265,250	68,225	315,000
Due from buyer	—	58,030	—	—
Due to seller	—	—	246,775	—
	$323,280	$323,280	$315,000	$315,000

CHAPTER 23

Real Estate Investment

- **identify** the advantages and disadvantages of property investing;

- **describe** the difference between adjusted basis and capital gains;

- **explain** the concepts of pyramiding;

- **distinguish** between depreciation and appreciation; and

- **define** the following *key terms*:

adjusted basis	depreciation	liquidity
appreciation	equity buildup	pyramiding
basis	exchanges	real estate investment
boot	income property	trust (REIT)
capital gain	inflation	real estate mortgage
cash flow	intrinsic value	investment conduit
cost recovery	leverage	(REMIC)
		syndicate

MATCHING   *Write the letter of the matching term on the appropriate line.*

a. *syndicate*

b. *appreciation*

c. *inflation*

d. *cost recovery*

e. *pyramiding*

f. *basis*

g. *capital gain*

h. *leverage*

i. *income property*

j. *liquidity*

1. ___ How quickly an asset may be converted into cash

2. ___ The difference between the adjusted basis of property and its net selling price

3. ___ The process of using one property to drive the acquisition of additional properties

4. ___ An increase in the amount of money in circulation

5. ___ The investor's initial cost of the real estate

6. ___ A business venture in which people pool their resources to own or develop a particular piece of property

7. ___ Increasing value over time

8. ___ Property that is managed for appreciation or cash flow (income)

9. ___ The use of borrowed money to finance an investment

10. ___ Depreciation, or getting back the cost of an income-producing asset through tax deductions over the asset's useful life

TRUE OR FALSE   *Circle the correct answer.*

1. T F Investing in rental property has more risks than investing in unimproved land.

2. T F Under the rules of Section 1031 of the Internal Revenue Code, real estate investors can exchange property and defer taxation of capital gains.

3. T F *Intrinsic value* of a property is the result of a person's individual choices and preferences for a particular geographic area.

4. T F A high degree of leverage in real estate investing means lower risk for the investor and the lender.

5. T F Capital gain is the difference between the initial cost of the property and its net selling price.

6. T F In a real estate mortgage investment conduit (REMIC), the holders of regular interests receive interest or similar payments.

7. T F To receive high cash flow on investment property, investors try to keep operating expenses high.

8. T F Equity build-up in a property is realized as cash when the property is sold.

9. T F If a taxpayer sells real estate on an installment plan, the seller pays tax only on the principal portion of each payment received.

10. T F In pyramiding, the investor delays capital gains taxes by refinancing (rather than selling) the original property, and then using the cash generated to purchase additional properties.

MULTIPLE CHOICE   *Circle the correct answer.*

1. An investor adds the cost of any physical improvements to the initial cost of the property and then subtracts the amount of any depreciation claimed as a tax deduction. This is the method for calculating the
   a. basis.
   b. adjusted basis.
   c. leverage.
   d. cash flow.

2. Any additional capital or personal property included with a real property transaction to even out the value of a property exchange is called
   a. cost recovery.
   b. a REIT.
   c. boot.
   d. equity build-up.

3. For a REMIC, the asset test means
   a. funds to buy into the REMIC must come from a previous real estate investment.
   b. investors' interests in the REMIC may consist of only one class of regular interests.
   c. investors are not allowed to hold residual interests in a REMIC.
   d. almost all assets in the REMIC must be qualified mortgages and permitted investments.

4. In terms of real estate investment, another name for depreciation is
   a. leverage.
   b. cost recovery.
   c. liquidity.
   d. intrinsic value.

5. What is an advantage of investing in real estate?
   a. Tax credits for certain types of projects
   b. Not highly liquid in the short term
   c. Investment of large amounts of capital
   d. Need for active management

6. One objective of investing in income property is to generate spendable income, also called
   a. appreciation.
   b. basis.
   c. cash flow.
   d. pyramiding.

7. Which of the following is an advantage of investing in a real estate investment trust (REIT)?
   a. Direct ownership of real estate
   b. At least 90 percent of the income must come from real estate
   c. Access to the same tax benefits as mutual fund investors
   d. Income taxed at corporate rates

8. An increase in the amount of money in circulation is called
   a. stagflation.
   b. intrinsic value.
   c. adjusted cash flow.
   d. inflation.

9. What is straight-line depreciation?
   a. When depreciation is taken periodically in equal amounts over an asset's useful life
   b. When depreciation is taken periodically in equal amounts over a maximum of ten years
   c. When the amount of depreciation increases each year until the asset is sold or devalued
   d. When the amount of depreciation decreases each year until the asset is sold or devalued

10. A man owns an apartment building that generated $60,000 in rental income, $15,000 in expenses, and $35,000 in debt service last year. Also, the property appreciated about $10,000 last year. What was the amount of cash flow on the man's apartment building last year?
   a. $10,000
   b. $15,000
   c. $20,000
   d. $25,000

FILL-IN-THE-BLANK   *Select the word or words that best complete the following statements:*

adjusted basis

basis

boot

capital gain

cash flow

depreciation

equity buildup

intrinsic value

leverage

1. A property that is located in an attractive neighborhood with access to good shopping and business areas has a greater _____ to most buyers than similar property in a more-isolated and less-pleasant location.

2. In terms of income property, another name for spendable income generated by the property is _____.

3. The result of a mortgage loan payment applied to the principal rather than the interest, plus any increase in property value due to appreciation is called _____.

4. To calculate the _____ for a property, add the cost of any physical improvements to the basis and subtract the amount of any depreciation claimed as a tax deduction.

5. Under the Internal Revenue Code, the name for any additional capital or personal property included with a transaction to balance the value of a property exchange is called _____.

6. Cost recovery, or _____, allows investors to recover the cost of an income-producing asset through tax deductions over the asset's useful life.

ACTIVITY: Advantages or Disadvantages of Real Estate Investing

Check the appropriate column to indicate whether each item is an advantage or disadvantage of investing in real estate.

	Advantage	Disadvantage
1. Use leverage of borrowed money to purchase real estate		
2. Greater control over investment		
3. High degree of risk		
4. Must actively manage investment		
5. Generally, above-average rates of return		
6. Investment is high-cost		
7. Tax deductions		
8. Real estate is not highly liquid		

ANSWER KEY

Matching

1. j **2.** g **3.** e **4.** c **5.** f **6.** a **7.** b **8.** i
9. h **10.** d

True or False

1. **False.** The intrinsic value and potential for appreciation are not easy to determine when investing in unimproved land, so these investments are riskier than rental property. p. 431

2. **True.** Real estate investors can defer taxation of capital gains by making property exchanges; the tax is deferred, not eliminated. p. 435

3. **True.** An intrinsic value of real estate is the result of a person's individual choices and preferences for a given geographic area. p. 431

4. **False.** A high degree of leverage means *higher* risk for the investor and lender because of the high ratio of borrowed money to the value of the real estate. Leverage is the use of borrowed money to finance an investment; a high degree of leverage translates into greater risk for the investor and the lender because of the high ratio of borrowed money to the value of the real estate. p. 433

5. **False.** Capital gain is the difference between the *adjusted basis* of the property and its net selling price. The adjusted basis is calculated by making certain additions to, or subtractions from, the *basis*, or initial cost of the property. p. 434

6. **True.** In a real estate mortgage investment conduit (REMIC), the holders of regular interests receive interest or similar payments; holders of residual interests receive distributions (if any), on a pro rata basis. p. 437

7. **False.** Cash flow is the total amount of money remaining after all expenditures have been paid; investors try to keep operating expenses *low* to keep cash flow high. p. 432

8. **True.** Equity buildup is a result of a loan payment directed toward the principal rather than the interest, plus any gain in property value due to appreciation. This accumulated equity is not realized as cash unless the property is sold, refinanced, or exchanged. p. 433

9. **False.** If a taxpayer sells real estate on an installment plan, the seller pays tax only on the *profit* portion of each payment received. Interest received is taxable as ordinary income. p. 436

10. **True.** Pyramiding is the process of using one property to drive the acquisition of additional properties; by holding on to the properties, the investor may delay the capital gains taxes that would result from a sale. p. 434

Multiple Choice

1. **b.** Adjusted basis is the result of adding the cost of any physical improvements to the initial cost of the property and then subtracting the amount of any depreciation claimed as a tax deduction. p. 434

2. **c.** Boot is any additional capital or personal property included with the exchange transaction to balance the value of the exchange. The IRS requires that tax on the boot be paid at the time of the exchange by the party who receives it. p. 436

3. **d.** The RMIC must satisfy the asset test: after a start-up period, almost all assets must be qualified mortgages and permitted investments; investor interest may consist of only one or more classes of regular interests and a single class of residual interests. p. 437

4. **b.** Depreciation, or cost recovery, allows an investor to recover the cost of an income-producing asset through tax deductions over the asset's useful life. p. 435

5. **a.** Tax credits are allowed for renovation of older buildings, low-income housing projects, and historic property. The other choices are disadvantages of real estate investment. p. 436

6. **c.** Cash flow is the total amount of money remaining after all expenditures have been paid. p. 432

7. **c.** Investors in REITs do not have a direct investment in real estate. Generally, shareholders, not the REIT, pays the tax on profits distributed. p. 437

8. **d.** Inflation is the increase in the amount of money in circulation. Intrinsic value of real estate is the result of a person's individual choices and preferences for a given geographic area. Both factors affect appreciation. p. 431

9. **a.** Different depreciation rules apply for property purchased before 1987 that uses the accelerated cost recovery system (ACRS). p. 435

10. **a.** The property generated $10,000 in annual income:

    $60,000 − $15,000 − $35,000 = $10,000

    The amount of appreciation is not considered in cash flow. p. 432

Fill-in-the-Blank

1. A property that is located in an attractive neighborhood with access to good shopping and business areas has a greater *intrinsic value* to most buyers than similar property in a more-isolated and less-pleasant location.

2. In terms of income property, another name for spendable income generated by the property is *cash flow*.

3. The result of a mortgage loan payment applied to the principal rather than the interest, plus any increase in property value due to appreciation, is called *equity buildup*.

4. To calculate the *adjusted basis* for a property, add the cost of any physical improvements to the basis and subtract the amount of any depreciation claimed as a tax deduction.

5. Under the Internal Revenue Code, the name for any additional capital or personal property included with a transaction to balance the value of a property exchange is called *boot*.

6. Cost recovery, or *depreciation*, allows investors to recover the cost of an income-producing asset through tax deductions over the asset's useful life.

Activity: Advantages or Disadvantages of Real Estate Investing

	Advantage	Disadvantage
1. Use leverage of borrowed money to purchase real estate	✓	
2. Greater control over investment	✓	
3. High degree of risk		✓
4. Must actively manage investment		✓
5. Generally, above-average rates of return	✓	
6. Investment is high-cost		✓
7. Tax deductions	✓	
8. Real estate is not highly liquid		✓

Notes

Notes

Notes

Notes